Judaism When Christianity Began

Judaism When Christianity Began

A Survey of Belief and Practice

Jacob Neusner

Westminster John Knox Press
LOUISVILLE • LONDON

Book design by Sharon Adams
Cover design by Lisa Buckley
Cover Art: Stephanie Dalton Cowan / Getty Images

First edition
Published by Westminster John Knox Press
Louisville, Kentucky

This book is printed on acid-free paper that meets the American National Standards Institute Z39.48 standard. ∞

PRINTED IN THE UNITED STATES OF AMERICA

02 03 04 05 06 07 08 09 10 11 — 10 9 8 7 6 5 4 3 2 1

Cataloging-in-Publication Data can be obtained from the Library of Congress.

ISBN 0-664-22527-6

Contents

1 **Introduction**   1
   What Do We Mean by "Judaism"?   1
   Recognizing Diversity in Judaism (among Other Religions)   4
   Judaism When Christianity Began   6
   The World of Judaism: The Human Dimension   10

2 **Revelation and Scripture: The Oral Torah**   15
   How Is God Self-Revealed in the Torah?   15
   Meeting God in Torah-Study   18
   The Role of Reason in Revelation   20
   Torah versus Christ   22

3 **God: "In our image, after our likeness"**   29
   What the Torah Tells about God   29
   The Characterization of God   30
   God as Premise, Presence, Person, and Personality   33
   God as Premise and Presence   35
   God in Person   36
   God's Personality   38
   The Divinity of God: God as Wholly Other   43

4 **The Holy and the Unclean: Sanctification and Pollution**   45
   Defining Sanctification   45
   Holy versus Profane and Unclean   48
   Purity Viewed Whole   50
   The Role of the Human Being in the Process
      of Purity and Uncleanness   53

5 **Exile and Return**   55
   Exile from Eden/The Recovery of Paradise:
      The Paradigm of Judaism   55
   The Invention of the Paradigm of Exile and Return   59
   The Persistence of the Paradigm   63

6 **Return to Eden: The Sabbath and Sacred Time**   67
   Restoring Eden on the Seventh Day: the Sabbath   67
   Sabbath for the Land of Israel: *Shebi'it*, the
      Halakhah of the Seventh Year   68

Sabbath for the People of Israel: *Shabbat-Erubin*, the
      Halakhah of the Israelite Household on the Seventh Day   72
Six Days of Work and the Sabbath of Repose   76

7 **The Story Judaism Tells**   **79**
The Judaic Myth   79
Turning a Story into a Pattern   81
The Presence of the Past, the Pastness of the Present   83
The Story of Israel in Paradigmatic Form   84
Israel's History Taken Over into Israel's Life of Sanctification   88

8 **The Community of Israel**   **91**
What Is an "Israel" in a Judaic Religious System?   91
"Israel" in the Mishnah   93
"Israel" in the Talmud of the Land of Israel   94
The Metaphor of the Family: "Israel's Children"   96
The Importance of "Israel" in Rabbinic Judaism   100

9 **The Chain of Tradition: The Oral Torah**   **103**
The Oral Torah   103
The Contents of the Oral Torah   104
The Priority of the Oral Torah   107
The Disciple of the Sage as a Living Torah   112
The Final Account of the Oral Torah   114
      What did Rabbinic sages mean by the Oral Torah?   114
      What are the components of the myth?   115
      In what contexts did it serve?   115
      What consequences did invoking the myth produce?   116

10 **Miracles in Nature: Illness and Healing**   **119**
Miracles: Rain Making   119
What Compels Divine Favor?   122
Sickness: Its Causes and Its Cure   126
What Accounts for Illness and Suffering?   130
The Resolution of the Matter in the Resurrection of the Dead   132

11 **Sacred Space: The Land and Pilgrimage**   **135**
Why Is the Land of Israel Different from All Other
      Lands? Why Is Jerusalem Different from All Other Cities?   135
Pilgrimage: The Particular Occasion   139
Pilgrims and Their Offerings   141
Entering the State of Cleanness on the Pilgrim Festivals   143
Sharing a Meal with God   144

12   Sacrifice, Repentance, and Atonement   147
    Sacrifice in the Context of Atonement:
       Corporate Israel and the Daily Whole Offering   147
    Sacrifice and the Atonement of Individuals' Inadvertent Sins   151
    Repentance   153
    Atonement   156
    Sacrifice, Repentance, Atonement   160

13   Death and Afterlife   163
    Death   163
    Afterlife: Resurrection   165
    "All Israel Has a Portion in the World to Come"   168
    The Messiah   172

14   The Representation of the Faith:
    Art and Symbol in Judaism   175
    The Art of the Synagogues and Symbolic Discourse in Judaism   175
    Synagogue Iconography: The Distribution over Time   176
    Integrating Symbolic Discourse in Iconic and Verbal Forms   178
    Symbols in Verbal Form   181
    Symbolic Discourse in Iconic and in Verbal Form:
       Convergence or Divergence?   183
    Conclusion: From Scripture to Judaism   185

Notes   189

Index of Ancient Sources   191

Index of Subjects and Names   195

Chapter 1

Introduction

WHAT DO WE MEAN BY "JUDAISM"?

"Judaism" is a religion. A religion, whatever else it is, is a story—"our story" (sometimes: history). A religion is the story that a group tells to explain where it has come from, where it is going, what it is, in accord with God's plan. People who tell themselves that story form the faithful of a religion. Those who tell some other story, or no story at all, do not. The story that embodies a religion may speak of past or future, but it always animates the present and appeals to the here and now: "This tells who we are." When the faithful of Judaism gather at the formal meal, or Seder, to celebrate Passover, "the season of our freedom," when the Israelite slaves, led by Moses, were freed by God from Egyptian slavery, they tell the story. And they say in the narrative of the Passover Seder:

> We were slaves of Pharaoh in Egypt and the Lord our God brought us forth from there with a mighty hand and an outstretched arm. And if the Holy One, blessed be he, had not brought our fathers forth from Egypt, then we and our descendents would still be slaves to Pharaoh in Egypt. And so, even if all of us were full of wisdom, understanding, sages and well informed in the Torah, we should still be obligated to repeat again the story of the exodus from Egypt;

1

> and whoever treats as an important matter the story of the exodus from Egypt
> is praiseworthy. . . . (Passover Haggadah, trans. by Maurice Samuel)

Note that the assembled family speaks of "we," identifying those alive today with the liberation. Telling the story of what happened is critical to the life of the family within the faith. The acutely present-tense timing of the events—they happened; they keep happening—underscores that it is the story that records the religion: God intervenes to save that "us" of which Scripture speaks, the very same "us" that has assembled this very evening. Judaism then is the religion that tells the story of how God saves those that know and worship him:

> This is the promise which has stood by our forefathers and stands by us. For
> neither once, nor twice, nor three times was our destruction planned; in
> every generation they rise against us, and in every generation God delivers
> us from their hands into freedom, out of anguish into joy, out of mourning
> into festivity, out of darkness into light, out of bondage into redemption. . . .

The story then is told and retold because the pattern of events that it portrays happens time and again. That is why, in the present as much as in long-ago times, the faithful retell and relive the story of the liberation from Egyptian bondage.

> For ever after, in every generation, every Israelite must think of himself or
> herself as having gone forth from Egypt. For we read in the Torah: "In that
> day thou shalt teach thy son, saying: All this is because of what God did for
> me when I went forth from Egypt." It was not only our forefathers that the
> Holy One, blessed be He, redeemed; us too, the living, He redeemed
> together with them, as we learn from the verse in the Torah: "And He
> brought us out from thence, so that He might bring us home, and give us
> the land which he pledged to our forefathers. . . ."

The liturgy of the Passover meal now permits us to define Judaism through its story.

Judaism is the religion that tells itself this story of exile and redemption, slavery and deliverance, at God's hands. The community of Judaism, which calls itself "Israel" meaning "supernatural social entity" (not to be confused with the secular and political sense of "Israel," meaning "the state of Israel"), is made up of the people who tell themselves this story and not some other. To practice Judaism is to identify oneself with the story of the Israel redeemed from Egypt, to take for one's personal history and collective destiny the story of Israel, meaning, those that know and worship God, not idols. So much for a definition based on the view of religion as story.

In more analytical terms a religion is made up of an account of (1) a way of life and (2) worldview of (3) a group of people that understands itself to relate to God (however defined) through that way of life and to live by God's will through that worldview.

In this-worldly framework, a religion defines a social system built on supernatural convictions, a system that is comprised of the story the group tells about the life that it leads and about the place of that group within humanity in time and eternity. So the worldview of a religion tells the story of the group and its encounter with God. The way of life embodies that story in concrete activities. The definition of the group explains who that "we" is that talks the talk and walks the walk.

Every religion claims that it possesses truth, or the truth, and religions tend to regard themselves as unique, sui generis. But when we study religion, not just religions, we take as our premise that religions can be compared and contrasted, and through comparative religion we gain perspective on a religion. How should one classify Judaism?

Among religions, Judaism requires a definition as well. Judaism is a monotheist religion, along with Christianity and Islam. A monotheist religion maintains that there is one God alone, who is just and merciful (thus "ethical monotheism") and who created the world and rules. Monotheism is not a matter of arithmetic, counting one God rather than many gods. Its view of God is that God is transcendent, outside the natural world and in charge of it: wholly other. How God, different from humanity, engages with humanity has to be explained by the monotheist religions.

There are three monotheist religions—Judaism, Christianity, and Islam in order—all agreeing that all other religions are false and do not afford knowledge of God. Islam recognizes the revealed character of Christianity and Judaism but deems both insufficient, and Christianity acknowledges Judaism but takes priority for itself as well. Judaism for its part in its classical documents recognizes no other religion at all, regarding all the rest as forms of idolatry. (But some sources acknowledge that Christianity possesses the same Scripture, or Torah, as Judaism.) All three affirm that God rules the world and, within humanity, identifies an abode for God's dwelling on earth. That abode is comprised by the people devoted to doing God's will. These may be classified as a "people," or "nation," as in Judaism, or as "the body of Christ," or "church," as in Christianity, or as "the abode of Islam," as in Islam. In all three instances, the social entity that embodies the religion defines itself in theological, not merely political or sociological or cultural, terms. That entity is those who mean to carry out God's will for all humanity. By definition, in all three cases, that social entity is open to all humanity through an act of adherence, or conversion, to the way of life and worldview that God is held to have set forth: "the kingdom of God" in Christian and Judaic terms.

So much for Judaism in the context of monotheist religions. What marks Judaism apart from the other monotheist religions? Judaism recognizes no other revelation than the Torah, the Teaching, set forth by God to Moses at Mount Sinai, and encompassing the prophets of the Hebrew Scriptures (Joshua, Judges, Samuel, Kings, Isaiah, Jeremiah, Ezekiel, and the twelve minor prophets). The Torah, broadly defined, contains the exhaustive account of God's plan for creation and humanity. Among the books of the Torah, Judaism privileges the Pentateuch (the Five Books of Moses: Genesis, Exodus, Leviticus, Numbers, and

Deuteronomy). So the worldview of Judaism appeals to the Hebrew Scriptures of ancient Israel; the way of life means to embody the laws of those Scriptures, particularly as laid out in Exodus through Deuteronomy. What about the social entity formed by the faithful? Judaism calls the faithful "Israel" and regards them, whether born into the faith or converted to it, as the embodiment of the "Israel" of which Scripture speaks and to which the Torah was revealed.

Christianity and Islam differ from Judaism because each recognizes a prophet and a revelation beyond Moses and the Hebrew Scriptures: the figure of Jesus Christ for Christianity; the Prophet Muhammad for Islam. But the great world religions include Judaism, making it influential beyond its modest numbers, because Christianity and Islam recognize their foundations in the revelation conveyed by the Hebrew Scriptures that define Judaism. The diversity of monotheist religions—Judaism, Christianity, Islam—shows us how a common doctrine will yield variations in detail. But, when it comes to religion, God lives in the details. Monotheism in the abstract is not a religion; it is a theory. But monotheism in nature, as against the laboratory, takes concrete form only in Judaism, Christianity, and Islam, and no "meta-monotheism" has ever succeeded in forming of the three competing monotheist religious systems a single religion.

RECOGNIZING DIVERSITY IN JUDAISM (AMONG OTHER RELIGIONS)

The same conflict between the theory and the everyday reality of monotheism alerts us to the inner diversity of the monotheist religions themselves. Contemporary Christianity is divided into Orthodox, Roman Catholic, and Protestant Christianities; Islam into Sunni and Shiite Islams; and Judaism into Orthodox, Reform, Conservative, and Reconstructionist Judaisms. And these large "divisions" or "movements" within Christianity, Islam, and Judaism exhibit much diversity as well. For example, "Orthodox Judaism" subdivides into groups that wish to segregate themselves from the world and those that opt for integration. The self-segregated Orthodox Judaisms think that Judaism ("the Torah") leaves no space for truth generated outside of the faith, whereas the integrationist one maintains that one can live by the Torah within the framework of modern life.

Though monotheists worship one unique God, the same for all humanity, monotheisms exhibit much diversity. That is because Judaism, Christianity, and Islam come to expression in a wide range of cultural settings and political systems, East and West. All Christians, Muslims, and practitioners of Judaism, respectively, concur on some large, general truths of Christianity, Islam, and Judaism. But these admittedly universal affirmations of the great aggregates of monotheists do not prepare us for their diversity. We understand little of world history and culture if we assume a uniform Christianity or Islam or Judaism—and we miss the causes of much conflict within Christianity, Islam, or Judaism, respectively. If we study religion in the this-worldly framework of actual societies, we are not well-served to focus on generalizations of doctrine that characterize a given religion, viewed whole and autonomous.

In the secular framework of social and cultural reality, on the other hand, we have access to what Christians, Muslims, and Judaists in their everyday, workaday worlds—in the social entities actually constituted by them—do together. So what we can study—describe, analyze, and interpret—are the facts of culture and society (way of life, worldview, theory of the social entity), not merely theological convictions, that is, reports of truth claims people allege in the name of Judaism, Christianity, or Islam. In the framework of a world of facts, not convictions, religion is to be viewed as something people do together: the realization of the story that they tell about their group. And the formation and expression of religion by social groups embody religion as a cultural system. But to accomplish that purpose we have to deal with the enormous diversity characteristic of the social worlds of Judaism, Christianity, and Islam.

Where to begin to sort out the diversity of Judaisms, Christianities, and Islams? People write down their stories, and they preserve them in holy books. If—to concentrate on Judaism—we take all the holy books that Judaic religious systems deem authoritative, we find enormous diversity of opinion. In response, we have three choices. We can, first, try to harmonize the conflict. Or, second, we can select some sayings as authentic and reject others as spurious. Or, third, we can seek a lowest common denominator.

Dealing with the diversity of monotheisms shows the way forward. The Torah, the Bible, and the Quran suffice to make the point. We may speak of "monotheism" in general terms, but as soon as we take up the principal media of revelation—Torah, Bible, Quran—we differentiate or suffocate in confusion. Integrating the three religions into a single monotheism obscures as much as it clarifies. If Muhammad is the seal of prophecy, then the revelation of Moses and of Jesus Christ are insufficient, flawed and incomplete. If God is incarnate in Jesus Christ, then the account of Moses requires considerable revision. And if Moses' Torah is exhaustive and complete, then nothing else is needed. These simple facts of the competing monotheisms underscore what is at stake in recognizing and taking account of difference.

So it is with "Judaism" as against "Judaisms." When may we plausibly speak of "Judaism" as a unitary religion bearing a single theology and define matters in abstract, general terms that stress matters of doctrine (e.g., God, Torah, Israel)? A global definition works only when we characterize matters from a vast distance and ignore all manner of differences. Then, seen from afar, "Judaism" can be defined as a cogent religion different from other, large aggregates, for example, Christianity, Islam, Buddhism, and the like. But when we come closer to the social world that the faithful comprise, we recognize a more complex picture. Close up, "Judaism" divides into "Judaisms," like the "Christianities" and "Islams" of which we spoke a moment ago. That is not to deny the integrity of Judaism, Christianity, and Islam, but only to insist that theological truth, which integrates, not obscure social and historical fact, which differentiates the great

Rabbinic - Hebrew language as used by Rabbis in post-biblical times

MYTH - Religious truth in NARRATIVE form

religions of monotheism. The recognition of the diversity of Judaisms, on the ground, prepares us for the social realities embodied in conflicting holy books. We quickly recognize that, in real life as against theory, there are today, and there have been through time, diverse groups, each with its worldview and way of life, all regarding themselves as "Israel." These groups compete with one another, each telling its own story about itself in the context of the encompassing story that all, in one way or another, tell with variations. So while we may identify certain global doctrines likely to characterize diverse groups of "Israel," once we encounter the real world, we find "Israels."

Mishnah - collection of oRAl laws compiled circa 200 C.E. by Rabbi Judah ha-Nasi & forming the basic part of the Talmud

JUDAISM WHEN CHRISTIANITY BEGAN

Christianity began in the first five centuries C.E. (the Common Era = A.D.). With roots deep in the pre-Christian centuries, Rabbinic Judaism, the particular Judaism that would flourish from the first century to our own times, made its classical statement in that same period of about five to six hundred years. It is that Judaism on which we focus; its sources that we invoke to define the Judaic way of life and the worldview; its religious system and structure that we privilege.

To define Rabbinic Judaism in fundamental terms is not difficult.

Talmud - collection of Jewish law & tradition 1 edition from Palestine circa 400 C.E. 1 edition from Babylonia circa 600 C.E.

Principal Writings

Rabbinic Judaism is portrayed by the writings of the Rabbinic sages of that period. In addition to Scripture, these sages produced a vast library of doctrine, law, and narrative. These writings stretch from the Mishnah, a commentary on the Mishnah, philosophical law code of ca. 200 C.E., to the Talmud of the Land of Israel, through the second of the two Talmuds, the Talmud of Babylonia, of ca. 600 C.E. (just before the advent of Islam). They encompass compilations of interpretations of selected books of the Hebrew Scriptures. These are, particularly, those books that are prominent in synagogue worship—the Pentateuch and scrolls of the Writings, Lamentations, Esther, Ruth, and Song of Songs—and that are read on special occasions as well: the Ninth of Ab (early August), commemorating the destruction of the Temple in Jerusalem in 586 B.C.E. and again in 70 C.E.; Purim, recorded in the book of Esther and Ruth, read for Pentecost; and Song of Songs, read for the celebration of Passover. So if we wish to describe Rabbinic Judaism in its formative centuries, we turn to its authoritative writings.

GemARA - the section of the Talmud, consisting essentially of commentary on the Mishnah

Generative Myth

The story that Rabbinic Judaism tells is captured in a subtle way in the collection of wise sayings of the great Rabbinic sages called *Pirqé Abot*, Sayings of the Fathers. The opening lines embody the story:

1st Temple - (Solomon) built in 957 BCE sole place of Hebrew sacrifice destroyed in 586 BCE by Babylonians
2ND Temple - A reconstruction of the 1st Temple stood from 515 BCE to 70 CE Persians overran Babylonia in 536 BCG

Introduction

Pirqé Abot 1:1

    A. Moses received Torah at Sinai and handed it on to Joshua, Joshua to elders, and elders to prophets.

    B. And prophets handed it on to the men of the great assembly.

    C. They said three things:

        (1) "Be prudent in judgment.

        (2) "Raise up many disciples.

        (3) "Make a fence for the Torah."

Pirqé Abot 1:2

    A. Simeon the Righteous was one of the last survivors of the great assembly.

    B. He would say: "On three things does the world stand:

        (1) "On the Torah,

        (2) "and on the Temple service,

        (3) "and on deeds of loving kindness."

The opening allegation is that Moses received Torah—Instruction—at Sinai. But it is not then claimed that Moses wrote the entire Torah in those very words we now possess in Scripture. Rather, Moses received Torah and handed it on to Joshua and so on in a chain of tradition. That the chain of tradition transcends Scripture's record is clear when we reach "the men of the great assembly," who surely are not part of the biblical record. And it is self-evident when we examine what the men of the great assembly and their successor, Simeon the Righteous, had to say. What they say is not a passage of Scripture. But, in accord with the opening lines, it still is part of the Torah of Sinai. The "three things" fall into the category of "Torah," that is, divine teaching, but not into the framework of Scripture.

We may, then, infer that a doctrine of revelation encompassing another mode besides writing for the formulation and transmission of God's message is in play here. The verbs, *receive* (in Hebrew *qibbel*) and *hand on* (*masar*) as nouns yield *qabbalah* and *masoret*, both of them bearing the sense of tradition. Putting this together, we may say that the generative myth of Rabbinic Judaism tells the story of how Moses received Torah in two media, in writing and in memory, the memorized part of the Torah being received and handed on in a process of oral formulation and oral transmission. Key names on the list of those in the chain of tradition include principals in the Mishnah itself, for example, Hillel and Shammai, founders of great schools of legal and theological doctrine:

   Pirqé Abot 1:12

    A. Hillel and Shammai received [it] from them.

    B. "Be disciples of Aaron, loving peace and pursuing peace, loving people and drawing them near to the Torah."

   Pirqé Abot 1:13

    A. He would say [in Aramaic],

        (1) "A name made great is a name destroyed.

        (2) "And one who does not add subtracts.

        (3) "And who does not learn is liable to death.

        (4) "And the one who uses the crown passes away."

Pirqé Abot 1:14
    A. He would say,
        (1) "If I am not for myself, who is for me?
        (2) "And when I am for myself, what am I?
        (3) "And if not now, when?"
Pirqé Abot 1:15
    A. Shammai says,
        (1) "Make your learning of Torah a fixed obligation.
        (2) "Say little and do much.
        (3) "Greet everybody cheerfully."

What emerges is now clear. The masters of Rabbinic Judaism stand in a chain of tradition from Sinai. Their teachings form part of the Torah God gave to Moses at Sinai. Then the documents that record those teachings participate in the chain of tradition. Since the tradition encompasses both Scripture and this explicitly oral medium, it encompasses Torah—God's Teaching—in two forms, written and oral. Rabbinic Judaism is thus the Judaism that sets forth the whole Teaching of Sinai, written and oral, and that points to its sages, called "rabbis" (a general title of honor, ultimately made particular to the sages of Judaism), who in a process of discipleship acquired ("received") and transmitted ("handed on") that complete Torah, oral and written, that originates with God's instruction to Moses.

That myth is articulated in the following narrative, attributed to late first-century sages or rabbis:

    Babylonian Talmud tractate *Erubin* 54b
        A. *Our rabbis have taught on Tannaite authority:*
        B. What is the order of Mishnah teaching? Moses learned it from the mouth of the All-Powerful. Aaron came in, and Moses repeated his chapter to him and Aaron went forth and sat at the left hand of Moses. His sons came in and Moses repeated their chapter to them, and his sons went forth. Eleazar sat at the right of Moses, and Itamar at the left of Aaron.
        C. R. Judah says, "At all times Aaron was at the right hand of Moses."
        D. Then the elders entered, and Moses repeated for them their Mishnah chapter. The elders went out. Then the whole people came in, and Moses repeated for them their Mishnah chapter. So it came about that Aaron repeated the lesson four times, his sons three times, the elders two times, and all the people once.
        E. Then Moses went out, and Aaron repeated his chapter for them. Aaron went out. His sons repeated their chapter. His sons went out. The elders repeated their chapter. So it turned out that everybody repeated the same chapter four times.
        F. On this basis said R. Eliezer, "A person is liable to repeat the lesson for his disciple four times. And it is an argument a fortiori: If Aaron, who studied from Moses himself, and Moses from the Almighty —so in the case of a common person who is studying with a common person, all the more so!"
        G. R. Aqiba says, "How on the basis of Scripture do we know that a person is obligated to repeat a lesson for his disciple until he

learns it [however many times that takes]? As it is said, 'And you teach it to the children of Israel' (Deut. 31:19). And how do we know that that is until it will be well ordered in their mouth? 'Put it in their mouths' (Deut. 31:19). And how on the basis of Scripture do we know that he is liable to explain the various aspects of the matter? 'Now these are the ordinances which you shall put before them' (Exod. 31:1)."

THE handing down of tradition

What is important here is the story of how Moses learned Mishnah-teaching from God himself, and then repeated what he learned for Aaron, and so on through the disciples.

Christians saw themselves as "Israel" & not early the "church"?

Time when period the church

Other Judaisms

From Second Temple times, down to 70 C.E., when the Temple was destroyed, we possess writings valued by various groups of Jews who saw themselves as the "Israel" of which Scripture speaks. Everyone knows about the Dead Sea Scrolls, the library found in our own times that portrays a Judaic religious system that in some important ways conflicts with the system set forth in the Rabbinic canon. In Alexandria, Egypt, a Jewish philosopher, Philo, wrote a vast corpus in which he set forth a Judaic religious system, built on reading of Scripture in the manner in which Greek writers interpreted philosophy and myth. The apocryphal books of the Hebrew Scriptures encompass writings that emphasize the meaning and end of days. The earliest Christians, Jesus and his family and Paul, all saw themselves as "Israel" and called on Scripture to provide the framework of interpretation of the life and teachings, death and resurrection, of Jesus Christ. All of these groups fall into the category "Judaisms," though each differs in fundamental ways from the others. But from the period after 70, surviving writings derive mainly from Rabbinic Judaism and (of course) from Christianity, the one parting company from the other but both of them valuing Scriptures. The upshot is, while we have data concerning the Jews and some of their religious practices, the way outsiders saw them, and the way they represented themselves in debate with others, we cannot construct in the first five centuries C.E. an account of a Judaic religious system comparable to Rabbinic Judaism. The sources do not permit.

Rabbis — the sages of Rabbinic Judaism

Normative Judaism?

Rabbinic Judaism, claiming to define the norms set by God to Moses at Sinai, cannot be asked to describe the practice of all faithful Israelites. We should not, then, imagine that all Jews are described in the pages of the Mishnah and the Talmuds, any more than that all Christians confessed the Nicaean Creed. If we cannot describe competing Judaic religious systems, we can take for granted that diversity characterized Jews' religious practices and beliefs. First, the pages of the Talmuds attest to conflict between "the rabbis," that is, the sages of Rabbinic Judaism, and ordinary folk. Some of the sages served as part of the Jews'

Exilarch— one in the lineage of hereditary rulers of the Jewish community in Babylonia from circa 200 century CE. to the beginning of the 11th century

10   Introduction

autonomous governments, set up in the Land of Israel/Palestine by the Romans from the second century C.E. forward, and in Babylonia at about the same time, headed by a patriarch, for the former, and an exilarch ("rule of the exilic community of Babylonian Jewry"), for the latter. In that role they were called on to make decisions in accord with the Torah for the government of the Jewish communities. While the sages refer to views contrary to their own, we do not have a systematic account of any Judaism, fully articulated, with which they competed.

As we shall see in chapter 14, we do have evidence produced by archaeology that synagogues were decorated in a manner contrary to, or at least not fully in accord with, the rules prohibiting images of certain kinds (e.g., graven images) of Scripture and Rabbinic reading of Scripture. For example, in the Euphrates city of Dura Europos, discovered in 1929 and excavated from that time, a synagogue was found with wall drawings of a most elaborate character, including portraits of Moses, Aaron, and the like. Biblical figures are represented in the synagogue in forms strikingly congruent with the representation of Greek mythic figures in nearby Temples. Archaeology now concurs with the judgment of Erwin R. Goodenough, in his *Jewish Symbols in the Graeco-Roman Period,* that, at the period between the first and sixth centuries, the manifestations of the Jewish religion were varied and complex, far more varied, indeed, than the extant Talmudic literature would have led us to believe. Besides the groups known from this literature, we have evidence that "there were widespread groups of loyal Jews who built synagogues and buried their dead in a manner strikingly different from that which the men represented by extant literature would have probably approved, and, in a manner motivated by myths older than those held by these men." The content of these myths may never be known with any great precision, but they comprehended a Hellenistic-Jewish mystic mythology far closer to the Qabbalah—the mystical doctrine set forth in medieval Judaic books—than to the Judaism portrayed by Rabbinic literature. In a fairly limited time before the advent of Islam, these groups dissolved.

The upshot is, the Judaism that we study in this presentation represents a group of sages and their disciples who were influential beyond their own circles but by no means in charge of the life of the Jews, on the one side, or of the prevailing Judaic religious system, on the other. What is important is that among the Judaisms of ancient times, both those before 70 that are well documented and whatever systems of the Judaic social order after 70 that have left little or no writing, we have a full account only of the one that, like Christianity, emerged from antiquity and prevailed in medieval and modern times: Judaism pure and simple.

THE WORLD OF JUDAISM: THE HUMAN DIMENSION

From speaking *about* Judaism in its Rabbinic system, we turn to a picture supplied by the Talmud of Babylonia of the human realities of the system: how the sages represented by the Rabbinic writings portrayed their relationship with the world beyond. How, exactly, did the sage interact with the ordinary Jew? To make sense of the story, we have to remember that the sage and his antagonist shared the same worldview, way of life, and picture of that social entity "Israel" to which both belonged. Here, then, is how they got along—the human dimension of Judaism in its formative age:

> Babylonian Talmud to Mishnah tractate *Qiddushin* 4:1–2, V:5/70a–b
> A. There was a man from Nehardea who went into a butcher shop in Pumbedita. He said to them, "Give me meat."
> B. They said to him, "Wait until the servant of R. Judah bar Ezekiel gets his, and then we'll give to you."
> C. He said, "So who is this Judah bar Sheviskel who comes before me to get served before me?"
> D. They went and told R. Judah.
> E. He excommunicated him.

The customer from Nehardea did not pay respect to the local authority of Pumbedita and so was banned from the community. But that did not end the conflict.

> F. They said, "He is in the habit of calling people slaves."
> G. He proclaimed concerning him, "He is a slave."
> H. The other party went and sued him in court before R. Nahman.

Now the conflict shifts to relationships between and among the sages themselves. What we see is how one authority tries to impress the other, to no avail:

> I. When the summons came, R. Judah went to R. Huna, he said to him, "Should I go, or shouldn't I go?"
> J. He said to him, "In point of fact, you really don't have to go, because you are an eminent authority. But on account of the honor owing to the household of the patriarch [of the Babylonian Jews], get up and go."

The activities undertaken by the judge, even the very word choices that he uses, cause the other authority to criticize and to cite traditions in the name of the acknowledged master, as if to say, the judge really is not equipped to make a judgment:

> K. He came. He found him making a parapet.
> L. He said to him, "Doesn't the master concur with what R. Huna bar Idi said Samuel said, 'Once a man is appointed administrator of the community, it is forbidden for him to do servile labor before three persons'?"
> M. He said to him, "I'm just making a little piece of the balustrade."
> N. He said to him, "So what's so bad about the word, 'parapet,' that the Torah uses, or the word 'partition,' that rabbis use?"
> O. He said to him, "Will the master sit down on a seat?"
> P. He said to him, "So what's so bad about 'chair,' which rabbis use, or the word 'stool,' which people generally use?"

Q. He said to him, "Will the master eat a piece of citron-fruit?"

R. He said to him, "This is what Samuel said, 'Whoever uses the word "citron-fruit" is a third puffed up with pride.' It should be called either etrog, as the rabbis do, or 'lemony-thing,' as people do."

S. He said to him, "Would the master like to drink a goblet of wine?"

T. He said to him, "So what's so bad about the word 'wineglass,' as rabbis say, or 'a drink,' as people say?"

U. He said to him, "Let my daughter Dunag bring something to drink?"

V. He said to him, "This is what Samuel said, 'People are not to make use of a woman.'"

W. "But she's only a minor!"

X. "In so many words said Samuel, 'People are not to make use of a woman in any manner, whether adult or minor.'"

Y. "Would the master care to send a greeting to my wife, Yalta?"

Z. He said to him, "This is what Samuel said, 'Even the sound of a woman's voice is [forbidden as] lustful.'"

AA. "Maybe through a messenger?"

BB. He said to him, "This is what Samuel said, 'People are not to inquire after a woman's health.'"

CC. "Through her husband?!"

DD. He said to him, "This is what Samuel said, 'People are not to inquire after a woman's health in any way shape or form.'"

EE. His wife sent word to him, "Settle the man's case for him, so that he not make you like any other fool."

Now comes the complaint:

FF. He said to him, "So what brings you here?"

GG. He said to him, "You sent me a subpoena." He said to him, "Now if even the language of the master I don't know, how in the world could I have sent you a subpoena?!"

HH. He produced the summons from his bosom and showed it to him: "Here is the man, here is the subpoena!"

II. He said to him, "Well, anyhow, since the master has come here, let's discuss the matter, so people should not say that rabbis are showing favoritism to one another."

JJ. He said to him, "How come the master has excommunicated that man?" "He harassed a messenger of the rabbis."

KK. "So why didn't the master flog him, for Rab would flog someone who harassed a messenger of the rabbis?"

LL. "I did worse to him."

MM. "How come the master declared the man that he was a slave?"

NN. "Because he went around calling other people slaves, and there is a Tannaite statement: Whoever alleges that others are genealogically invalid is himself invalid and never says a good thing about other people. And said Samuel, 'By reference to a flaw in himself he invalidates others.'"

OO. "Well, I can concede that Samuel said to suspect such a man of such a genealogy, but did he really say to make a public declaration to that effect?"

PP. In the meanwhile, the litigant from Nehardea came along. Said that litigant to R. Judah, "You called me a slave, I, who descend from the royal house of the Hasmoneans!"

QQ. He said to him, "This is what Samuel said, 'Whoever says that he comes from the house of the Hasmoneans is in fact a slave.'"

RR. [Nahman] said to him, "Doesn't the master concur with what R. Abba said R. Huna said Rab said, 'Any disciple of a sage who teaches a law, if this is prior to the case that he said it, is listened to, but if not, is not listened to'?"

SS. He said to him, "Well, there's R. Mattenah, who concurs with me." Now R. Mattenah had not seen the town of Nehardea for thirteen years, but on that very day, he paid a visit. Said [Judah] to him, "Does the master remember what Samuel said when he was standing with one foot on the bank and one foot on the bridge?"

TT. He said to him, "This is what Samuel said, 'Whoever says that he comes from the house of the Hasmoneans is in fact a slave, for of that family survived only one woman, who climbed up to the roof and shouted in a loud voice, "Whoever says that he comes from the house of the Hasmoneans is in fact a slave." She then fell from the roof and died.'" So they issued a proclamation concerning the litigant that he was a slave.

UU. Now on that day, many marriage contracts were ripped up in Nehardea. So when R. Judah came out, they came out after him to stone him. He said to them, "So if you'll shut up, just shut up, but if not, I'm going to tell concerning you what Samuel said, namely, 'There are two families in Nehardea, the household of the dove and the household of the raven, and the mnemonic is, the unclean is unclean, the clean, clean.'"

VV. So they tossed away their stones, and that made a dam in the royal canal.

I can imagine no more ample judgment of the tension among the sages themselves and between the sage and the ordinary people than this encounter, with its conflicts and curses. Clearly, a vast consensus united them all, a consensus resting on Scripture. And it is that consensus, shaped by the Rabbinic sages represented by the masters of Scripture and tradition before us, that we study when we study Judaism.

Chapter 2

Revelation and Scripture:
The Oral Torah

HOW IS GOD SELF-REVEALED IN THE TORAH?

The Torah contains the record of the encounter with God of those to whom God made himself manifest: the patriarchs and matriarchs, prophets, and sages of holy Israel. Only in the Torah do they learn, with Elijah, "There was a great and strong wind, which split mountains and shattered rocks by the Lord's power, but the Lord was not in the wind." So much for nature. And only in the Torah do they learn their own limits: "You cannot see my face and live." Therein is the record of what they know about God; that is therefore where they meet God; for Israel there is no other place. God revealed himself to Abraham, Isaac, and Jacob—so Genesis records—and then to Moses and the prophets, as indicated in Exodus through Deuteronomy. God also makes himself known in events of nature, such as the bush that burns but is not burnt up (Exodus 3), the sea that splits into two parts so that the Israelites may cross on dry land (Exodus 14), and the like. God is further made manifest through events in history. The prophets represent calamities in ancient Israel's history as statements of God's will, such as the siege of Jerusalem by the Assyrians in 701 B.C.E., and the lifting of that siege, or the capture of Jerusalem by the Babylonians and the destruction of the Temple in 586 B.C.E. God

15

communicates not only with corporate Israel through nature and through history but also with individual Israelites. So revelation takes many forms.

But it is only through Scripture that Judaism takes the measure of events and occasions in God's self-revelation. Scripture, the written part of the Torah or Teaching of Sinai, preserves whatever can be known about how God has revealed himself. It is the writing down of the record of encounter—and the contents of encounter. If, therefore, people wish to know God, they meet God in the Torah. That guides them, to be sure, to know and evaluate and understand God's ongoing revelation of the Torah. Study of the Torah in the chain of tradition formed by the relationship of disciple to master, from the present moment upward to Moses and God at Sinai, then affords that direct encounter with God through his revealed words that Judaism knows as revelation.

Torah-study forms an acutely present-tense encounter with God. It should not be confused with the academic study of the history of Scripture or the history that Scripture may make available, if any. Scripture preserves not the history of God's self-manifestation alone or mainly, but the occasion for humanity's engagement with God in the here and now. Revelation takes place, direct encounter with God becomes possible, whenever and wherever the faithful enter into the disciplines of Torah-study. And those disciplines do not involve historical learning at all.

Why should that be the case? The idea of history, with its rigid distinction between past and present and its careful sifting of connections from the one to the other, came quite late onto the scene of intellectual life. Both Judaism and Christianity for most of their histories have read the Hebrew Scriptures in an other-than-historical framework. They found in Scripture's words paradigms—patterns, models—of an enduring present, by which all things must take their measure; they possessed no conception whatsoever of the pastness of the past. In departing from Scripture's use of history to make a theological point—as the progression from Genesis through Kings means to do—Rabbinic Judaism invented an entirely new way to think about times past and to keep all time, past, present, and future, within a single framework.

For that purpose, a model was constructed, consisting of selected events held to form a pattern that imposes order and meaning on the chaos of what happens, whether past or present or future. Time measured in the paradigmatic manner is time formulated by a freestanding, (incidentally) atemporal model, not appealing to the course of sun and moon, not concerned with the metaphor of human life and its cyclicity either. Moreover, the paradigm obliterates distinctions between past, present, and future, between here and now and then and there. The past participates in the present; the present recapitulates the past; and the future finds itself determined, predetermined really, within the same freestanding structure comprised by God's way of telling time.

This other-than-historical mode of thought, which I call paradigmatic thinking, presents a mode of making connections and drawing conclusions that is captured in its essence by two statements of the Christian church father Augustine, who can have spoken for our sages when he said,

We live only in the present, but this present has several dimensions: the present of past things, the present of present things, and the present of future things. . . .

Your years are like a single day . . . and this today does not give way to a tomorrow, any more than it follows a yesterday. Your today is Eternity. . . .

(*Confessions* 10:13)

TRADITION - TORAH in the medium of MEMORY

I cannot imagine a more accurate précis of sages' conception of time: the past is ever present, and the present takes place on the same plane of existence as the past, the whole forming an eternal paradigm, altogether beyond time. For our sages of blessed memory, the Torah, the written part of the Torah in particular, defined a set of paradigms that served without regard to circumstance, context, or, for that matter, dimension and scale of happening.

It is in that context that we reread the opening chapter of tractate *Abot* and ask what meanings we can impute to such words as "Torah," "receive tradition" and "hand on tradition." The first, and self-evident, claim is that God reveals not "the Torah," a specific set of writings, but simply "Torah," which, lacking the definite article, speaks of instruction in diverse media. It is not Scripture alone that God sets forth but truth that takes shape and reaches us in oral form, that is, Torah in the medium of memory. And that is what we mean, here, by the word "tradition."

If "tradition"—*qabbalah, masoret,* as we saw in chapter 1—stands for "Torah," then what may we say of the players in the process of tradition, on the one side, and of the contents of tradition, on the other? Both point to "tradition" in a different sense from the common meaning we now impute to the word. By "tradition" we ordinarily mean "that which reaches us out of the past, the way things have always been done, the old, the tried, the true, the authentic, the historical." These are common senses that the word "tradition" carries. And every one of them violates the sense of the passage before us. Simeon, Gamaliel, Hillel, and Shammai were not the ancients but nearly contemporary. The sayings assigned to the names on the list were not "historical" in the sense that they belonged to a remote past. They were contemporary, sayings said by figures out of recent times—once more, the opposite of historical. And, it follows, sages understood as "authentic" not that which reaches us out of the distant past at which a once-for-all-time revelation was set forth. Rather, "authentic" in the present context modifies the teachings of sages who stand in the chain of tradition from Sinai. What they say is authentic because they say it, not because what they say they have heard from someone else, who in turn heard the same from someone else, back to Moses at Sinai.

The character of our text argues for a deeply antitraditional definition of Torah and of the word "tradition." Torah is a matter of the standing of the master; authenticity to God's revelation at Sinai finds its criterion not in historical fact but revealed truth, and we know the truth—as we shall see in later chapters—by processes of rational inquiry, reasoning, logical argument, and critical judgment, just as, in our own time, we know the truth in those same ways. To the sages truth comes hard; the past forms a component of the present because all things come to judgment before an eternal, critical logic, which is timeless and which is not changed by circumstances of historical or political moment.

Humanity has every right to engage with God because—in the conception of Judaism—human beings possess powers of reason and rational, critical thought that correspond to those of God. We can understand the Torah that God revealed because God and humanity think in accord with the same rules of reason and logic. When Abraham challenges God, "Will not the Judge of all the earth not do justice?" (Gen. 18:25), and God accepts the premise that he is bound by justice, Scripture underscores the unity of God's and humanity's rationality. The critical spirit of the Rabbinic writings leaves no doubt as to the weight of opinion, which appeals to a well-crafted proposition, properly selected evidence, and correctly framed arguments—to philosophy, not to history; to eternal truth, not to time, circumstance, and mediated authority conferred by status.

MEETING GOD IN TORAH-STUDY

What does it mean to meet God in Torah-study? People may rightly deem exaggerated any such notion, which elevates intellectual exchange to the level of religious encounter. But that is precisely what the Rabbinic sages of ancient times claim:

> *Pirqé Abot* 3:6
> Rabbi Halafta of Kefar Hananiah says, "Among ten who sit and work hard on Torah-study the Presence comes to rest, as it is said, 'God stands in the congregation of God' (Ps. 82:1) [and 'congregation' involves ten persons].
>
> "And how do we know that the same is so even of five? For it is said, 'And he has founded his vault upon the earth' (Amos 9:6).
>
> "And how do we know that this is so even of three? Since it is said, 'And he judges among the judges' [a court being made up of three judges] (Ps. 82:1).
>
> "And how do we know that this is so even of two? Because it is said, 'Then they that feared the Lord spoke with one another, and the Lord hearkened and heard' (Mal. 3:16).
>
> *"And how do we know that this is so even of one? Since it is said, 'In every place where I record my name I will come to you and I will bless you' (Exod. 20:24) [and it is in the Torah that God has recorded His name]."*

Judaism privileges the Torah, giving it the critical place in their public worship and placing special emphasis on its teachings. It is because they receive the Torah as God's revelation (however, within the various theologies of other-than-Orthodox Judaisms, they make sense of the concept of revelation). That view of the Torah comes to concrete expression every time an Israelite is called in public worship to the reading of the Torah and recites the blessing: "Blessed are you,

Lord, their God, ruler of the world, who has chosen us from all peoples by giving us the Torah. Blessed are you, who gives the Torah." And at the end of the reading of the Torah, comes, "Blessed are you, Lord, their God, ruler of the world, who has given us an authentic Torah, planting in our midst life eternal. Blessed are you, who gives the Torah." Here then is the affirmation of Israel at worship: the Torah marks Israel's election as God's first love; the Torah guarantees life eternal. These are the acts of grace that take place when Israel encounters God in the Torah. *God general vs. specifics*

The Torah is not the only place at which humanity and God come together. Some find God in history; others in nature. For philosophers, God serves as a postulate; for mystics, God takes place in an experience of immediate encounter. Some seek God in the depth of the soul; still others in the intersecting paths of human lives, through acts of love and service, where God lives. Many in humanity hear God's voice and find God's presence in the everyday. And within monotheism none errs. But the specificities of the encounter—the who and the what and the why—evade definition. In the Torah, Israel finds the answers that the Torah sets forth to the questions, the who and the what and the why, of human existence. No one can imagine that the Torah contains all truth. True, the Torah itself maintains that in the grandeur of nature—"the heavens declare the Glory of God"—or in the workings of history—"You have seen what I did at the Sea"—they meet God. The encounter takes place in the natural responses of intangible emotion and impalpable sentiment. Furthermore, the personality of the God of mystic encounter or philosophical reflection likewise is difficult to pin down. But in the Torah Israel learns the particulars: "I am the Lord your God who brought you out of the land of Egypt, out of the house of bondage." It is in the Torah that not God, "the divinity in general," but the Lord God who commands and loves and yearns for humanity is made manifest. There they discover what God has to say to them, holy Israel, in particular. In the Torah people find out what God wants them to know about God, and what God wants them to do and to be.

Israel meets God even in Torah-study among small numbers of participants, as Rabbi Halafta says. But its meeting with God in the words of the Torah, with the scroll of the Torah (the Pentateuch) standing for the entirety of the Torah, takes place in public, in community, in an act of sanctity like that of the worship that they carry out together. That meeting always engages not private persons but the totality of Israel, the holy people, all together realized at that time, in that place, by the one or three or five or ten of them that bear the power to embody all Israel. In study as much as in prayer, Israel encounters God. But there is this difference. When people pray, they aim to talk to God. But when they study, they hope that God will speak to them. That is why when they gather together as Israel, the people to whom the Torah is entrusted, in temples and synagogues, they open the Torah to meet God in the here and now. That is what it means to be Israel, the people of God. Here is how the Rabbinic sages make an explicit statement of that view:

Leviticus Rabbah XI:VII.3

   A. "And it came to pass in the days of Ahaz" (Isa. 7:1).

   B. What was the misfortune that took place at that time?

   C. "The Syrians on the east and the Philistines on the west [devour Israel with open mouth]" (Isa. 9:12).

   D. The matter [the position of Israel] may be compared to a king who handed over his son to a tutor, who hated [the son]. The tutor thought, "If I kill him now, I shall turn out to be liable to the death penalty before the king. So what I'll do is take away his wet nurse, and he will die on his own."

   E. So thought Ahaz, "If there are no kids, there will be no he-goats. If there are no he-goats, there will be no flock. If there is no flock, there will be no shepherd. If there is no shepherd, there will be no world."

   F. So did Ahaz plan, "If there are no children, there will be no disciples; if there are no disciples, there will be no sages; if there are no sages, there will be no Torah; if there is no Torah, there will be no synagogues and schools; if there are no synagogues and schools, then the Holy One, blessed be he, will not allow his Presence to come to rest in the world."

   G. What did he do? He went and locked the synagogues and schools.

   H. That is in line with the following verse of Scripture: "Bind up the testimony, seal the Torah [teaching] among my disciples" (Isa. 8:16).

The letters that yield in Hebrew the English "it came to pass" can be rearranged to produce "woe," with the result that, sages maintain, the formula "and it came to pass" introduces a tale of woe. That accounts for the question at hand. Here the point is explicit: children produce disciples; disciples define sages—no one is a teacher without students; no one is a student without teachers. Sages then carry forward Torah-study. Without Torah there are no synagogues and schools, and, when God's presence comes to rest in the world, it is in synagogues and schools. So the conviction that, in Talmud Torah, they undertake the quest for God confirms what the Torah itself says in so many words. Ahaz seeks to destroy Israel, the holy people. He will do so by removing the one reason for their endurance, which is God's presence among them. Ahaz understands that study of the Torah in a spirit of religious quest, aiming at the formation of disciples, who in the passage of time bring about the creation of sages, who in their lives realize the Torah. The Torah calls into being synagogues and schools—and it is in synagogues and schools, where the Torah is declaimed and studied, that God comes to rest in the world. Ahaz sees the stakes as celestial: this is where God is to be found.

THE ROLE OF REASON IN REVELATION

One story powerfully conveys the governing attitude that denies Heaven (that is, God!) the right to intervene when matters of logical inquiry define issues. The Torah belongs, now, to the men and women who have mastered its modes of thought, its rules of argument and evidence, and who have every right therefore to exercise their own judgment, based on well-construed analytical inquiry.

Talmud of Babylonia tractate *Baba Mesia* to Mishnah tractate *Baba Mesia* 4:10.I.15/59a–b

A. There we have learned: If one cut [a clay oven] into parts and put sand between the parts,

B. Rabbi Eliezer declares the oven broken-down and therefore insusceptible to uncleanness.

C. And sages declare it susceptible.

D. [59B] And this is what is meant by the oven of Akhnai [*m. Kelim* 5:10].

E. Why the oven of Akhnai?

F. Said Rabbi Judah said Samuel, "It is because they surrounded it with argument as with a snake and proved it was insusceptible to uncleanness."

G. A Tannaite statement:

H. On that day Rabbi Eliezer produced all of the arguments in the world, but they did not accept them from him. So he said to them, "If the law accords with my position, this carob tree will prove it."

I. The carob was uprooted from its place by a hundred cubits— and some say, four hundred cubits.

J. They said to him, "There is no proof from a carob tree."

K. So he went and said to them, "If the law accords with my position, let the stream of water prove it."

L. The stream of water reversed flow.

M. They said to him, "There is no proof from a stream of water."

N. So he went and said to them, "If the law accords with my position, let the walls of the school house prove it."

O. The walls of the school house tilted toward falling.

P. Rabbi Joshua rebuked them, saying to them, "If disciples of sages are contending with one another in matters of law, what business do you have?"

Q. They did not fall on account of the honor owing to Rabbi Joshua, but they also did not straighten up on account of the honor owing to Rabbi Eliezer, and to this day they are still tilted.

R. So he went and said to them, "If the law accords with my position, let the Heaven prove it!"

S. An echo came forth, saying, "What business have you with Rabbi Eliezer, for the law accords with his position under all circumstances!"

T. Rabbi Joshua stood up on his feet and said, "'It is not in heaven' (Deut. 30:12)."

U. What is the sense of, "'It is not in heaven' (Deut. 30:12)"?

V. Said Rabbi Jeremiah, "[The sense of Joshua's statement is this:] For the Torah has already been given from Mount Sinai, so we do not pay attention to echoes, since you have already written in the Torah at Mount Sinai, 'After the majority you are to incline' (Exod. 23:2)."

W. Rabbi Nathan came upon Elijah and said to him, "What did the Holy One, blessed be he, do at that moment?"

X. He said to him, "He laughed and said, 'My children have overcome me, my children have overcome me!'"

The story conveys that attitude of independent judgment and criticism based on sound reasoning that I have maintained is implicit in the character of tractate *Abot,* chapter 1. That statement—Torah but not quotation, a chain of tradition in which each participant contributes to the tradition—assigns to the contemporaries an active part in the definition of that which is handed over, that which is received. Tradition is not a gift of history but a creation of intelligence. Now, it is equally clear, intelligence requires nurture. Each figure in the chain of tradition has served as a disciple to a predecessor and is going to serve as a master to many disciples to come. So tradition stands for discipline. And what is handed on is two things: the model of how to enter into dialogue with God and also the increment of insight and learning that earlier links in the chain have set forth as eternal truth. What is not handed on is merely a record of how things used to be and used to be done. When we meet God in the Torah, it is not an encounter with a moment out of past time, but an event in an eternal present, shaped by rules of dialogue that pertain through permanent truth.

TORAH VERSUS CHRIST

Is the sage then a kind of prophet, communing with God through learning rather than through self-flagellation or prayer or meditation or other media of encounter? Sages maintain that, in general, prophecy has come to an end, which is why studying the record of prophecy in the Torah takes priority. A different approach to the encounter with God is taken by Jesus, who represents himself as the new Moses, able to recast the Torah altogether. To that view, Rabbinic Judaism responds that prophecy has come to an end. The task now is to master the legacy of prophecy, to learn the rules that, through prophecy, God set forth. That view is spelled out in the following:

Talmud of Babylonia tractate *Sotah* 48B to Mishnah tractate *Sotah* 9:12

O. Rather, said R. Nahman bar Isaac, "What is meant by 'former' prophets? It is used to distinguish Haggai, Zechariah, and Malachi, who are the latter prophets."

P. For our rabbis have taught on Tannaite authority:

Q. When the latter prophets died, that is, Haggai, Zechariah, and Malachi, then the Holy Spirit came to an end in Israel.

R. But even so, they made use of an echo.

S. Sages gathered together in the upper room of the house of Guria in Jericho, and a heavenly echo came forth and said to them, "There is a man among you who is worthy to receive the Holy Spirit, but his generation is unworthy of such an honor." They all set their eyes upon Hillel, the elder.

T. And when he died, they said about him, "Woe for the humble man, woe for the pious man, the disciple of Ezra" [*t. Sotah* 13:3].

U. Then another time they were in session in Yabneh and heard an echo saying, "There is among you a man who is worthy to receive the Holy Spirit, but the generation is unworthy of such an honor."

V. They all set their eyes upon Samuel the younger.

W. At the time of his death what did they say? "Woe for the humble man, woe for the pious man, the disciple of Hillel the Elder!"

X. Also: he said at the time of his death, "Simeon and Ishmael are destined to be put to death, and the rest of the associates will die by the sword, and the remainder of the people will be up for spoil. After this, the great disasters will fall."

The passage clearly affirms that while prophecy in a narrow sense may have ceased, Heavenly communication continued abundantly. To be sure, "the Holy Spirit" and "the echo" clearly are to be differentiated. The former presumably represents direct communication; the latter, indirect; the former an articulated Heavenly message; the latter one given through some indirect means. For example, in the case at hand, the echo announces that the Heavenly Spirit is available. In context, this means that although prophecy remains viable, the generation is unworthy to receive it, even though persons of sufficient standing to serve as prophets, such as Hillel, were available. This is made explicit in the cited prophecy of Samuel, who predicts the coming events.

That fact leaves no doubt that receiving the Holy Spirit and setting forth prophecy are not readily distinguished in the source before us. But it also opens the question of how else, besides prophecy or the Holy Spirit, Heaven conveys its messages. When it came to setting norms of behavior, moreover, Rabbinic Judaism rarely admitted the Holy Spirit or the heavenly echo into the discussion conducted by the sages. Charisma found a cool welcome indeed when the definition of routine demanded rigorous and reasoned debate. Then sages' own rationality took over. The reasons and traditions they could muster decided matters, and a heavenly echo was explicitly dismissed as source of authority over the formation of the law. All the more striking, then, is the presentation of Hillel as the master sage, not as the prophet, and the sage is prepared to say, "All the rest is elaboration—now go study."

The other approach to the Torah—the approach taken by Christianity in assigning to Jesus authority to say, "You have heard it said . . . but I say to you . . . ," is expressed throughout the Gospels. A typical statement is as follows:

Think not that I have come to abolish the Torah and the prophets; I have come not to abolish them but to fulfil them. For truly I say to you, till heaven and earth pass away, not an iota, not a dot, will pass from the Torah until all is accomplished. Whoever then relaxes one of the least of these commandments and teaches men so shall be called least in the kingdom of heaven, but he who does them and teaches them shall be called great in the kingdom of heaven. For I tell you, unless your righteousness exceeds that of the scribes and Pharisees, you will never enter the kingdom of heaven.

(Matt. 5:17–20)

In making these statements, Jesus represents himself not as a sage in a chain of tradition but as an "I," that is, a unique figure, a new Moses, standing on the mount as Moses had stood on Sinai. That view sages never adopted of themselves or granted to anyone else. From the perspective of eternal Israel and its covenant with God, this message surely wins our good will, since the Torah lays out the life of Israel as a kingdom of priests and holy people, under the rule of God through the prophet Moses and through the divinely ordained priesthood founded by Aaron, Moses' brother. When we recite, "Hear O Israel, the Lord our God, the Lord is one," which is called "the Shema" from the opening word "hear" and which refers to Deuteronomy 6:4–9, we tell ourselves that we thereby "accept the yoke of the kingdom of heaven," as the teachers of the Torah say. That is to say, we accept the commandments that God has given to us in the covenant of Sinai. Not only so, but when Jesus proposes to teach Torah to Israel, important parts of his Torah fall well within the range of familiar topics.

We therefore find ourselves at home as a sequence of lessons is set forth, each of them prefaced by the statement that other, prior masters teach a lesser truth, but Jesus, a greater one. These lessons are what is meant by not abolishing but fulfilling the Torah and the prophets, and among them five important ones capture attention:

1. "You have heard that it was said to the men of old, 'You shall not kill . . .' But I say to you that every one who is angry with his brother shall be liable" (Matt. 5:21–22).
2. "You have heard that it was said, 'You shall not commit adultery.' But I say to you that every one who looks at a woman lustfully has already committed adultery with her in his heart" (Matt. 5:27–28).
3. "You have heard that it was said to the men of old, 'You shall not swear falsely, but shall perform to the Lord what you have sworn.' But I say to you, 'Do not swear at all'" (Matt. 5:33–34).
4. "You have heard that it was said, 'An eye for an eye and a tooth for a tooth.' But I say to you, 'Do not resist one who is evil, but if any one strikes you on the right cheek, turn to him the other also'" (Matt. 5:38–39).
5. "You have heard that it was said, 'You shall love your neighbor and hate your enemy.' But I say to you, Love your enemies and pray for those who persecute you. . . . You must be perfect as your heavenly father is perfect" (Matt. 5:43–44, 48).

We have to distinguish the substance of what Jesus is saying from the form that he gives to his statements. Specifically, Jesus sets forth as his demonstration of how not to abolish the Torah and the prophets but to fulfill them a set of teachings that, all together, point to a more profound demand—on the Torah's part—than people have realized. Not only must I not kill; I must not even approach that threshold of anger that in the end leads to murder. Not only must I not commit adultery; I must not even approach the road that leads to adultery. Not only must I not swear falsely by God's name; I should not swear at all. These formulations represent an elaboration of three of the Ten Commandments (later on we shall meet two more of them). In the language of a text of Judaism attributed to authorities long before Jesus' own time, "Make a fence around the Torah." That is to say, conduct yourself in such a way that you will avoid even the things that cause you to sin, not only sin itself.

By seeking reconciliation, I make a fence against wanting to kill; by chastity in thought, against adultery in deed; by not swearing, against not swearing falsely. Here is a message well worth hearing, one that makes plausible the somewhat odd contrast between what I have heard and what I now hear. But that is a good device to win attention. To be sure, rabbis in the great rabbinic documents would in time come to the same conclusion—to avoid anger, to avoid temptation, to avoid vowing and swearing—but that fact is not germane to our argument. What is relevant is that many of the teachings of the wisdom writings and prophecy—Proverbs, for example—will lead to these same laudable conclusions: the Lord hates a false witness; do not desire the beauty of an evil woman in your heart and do not let her capture you with her eyelashes (Prov. 6:25–26), and the like.

But what kind of Torah is it that improves on the teachings of the Torah without acknowledging the source—and it is God who is the Source—of those teachings? So sages would be troubled not so much by the message, though they might take exception to this or that, as by the messenger. The reason is that in form these statements are jarring. On the mountain, Jesus' use of language, "You have heard that it was said . . . but I say to you . . ." contrasts strikingly with Moses' language at Mount Sinai. Sages, we saw, say things in their own names but without claiming to improve on the Torah, to which they aspire to contribute. The prophet, Moses, speaks not in his own name but in God's name, saying what God has told him to say. Jesus speaks not as a sage nor as a prophet. Note, when Moses turns to the people at Mount Sinai, he merely cites what God has said when he always starts with these words: "I am the Lord your God who brought you out of the Land of Egypt, out of the house of bondage." Moses speaks as God's prophet, in God's name, for God's purpose. So how are sages to respond to this "I," who pointedly contrasts what "you" have heard said with what he says.

So for sages, prophecy has ceased, and no new "I" is going to come forth. Rather a we—learning Israel—will take shape around the study of the Torah and the practice of its teachings. And the main point of the Torah, so sages would maintain, emerges in that process of Torah-study, that is, seeking in detail to identify the main point, as Hillel did, or showing how out of a fundamental principle, all else is to be derived—all through the process of learning. That is the view that is expressed in the following passage, which shows the contrast between "You have heard it said but I say to you" and the kind of discourse that sages set forth for holy Israel, a discourse that sustains constant dialogue between revealed Scripture and its statements, on the one side, and sages' own capacities to make their own and recast the revelation of the ages. Here is the way in which the process of setting forth the Torah's main point works itself out. (I have trimmed the original source.)

> Talmud of Babylonia *Makkot* 23b–24a to Mishnah tractate *Makkot*
> 3:16.II.1
>> B. R. Simelai expounded, "Six hundred and thirteen commandments were given to Moses, three hundred and sixty-five negative ones, corresponding to the number of the days of the solar year, and two hundred forty-eight positive commandments, corresponding to the parts of man's body."
>> D. [Simelai continues:] "David came and reduced them to eleven: 'A Psalm of David: Lord, who shall sojourn in thy tabernacle, and who shall dwell in thy holy mountain? (i) He who walks uprightly and (ii) works righteousness and (iii) speaks truth in his heart and (iv) has no slander on his tongue and (v) does no evil to his fellow and (vi) does not take up a reproach against his neighbor, (vii) in whose eyes a vile person is despised but (viii) honors those who fear the Lord. (ix) He swears to his own hurt and changes not. (x) He does not lend on interest. (xi) He does not take a bribe against the innocent' (Ps. 15)."
>> E. "He who walks uprightly": this is Abraham: "Walk before me and be wholehearted" (Gen. 17:1).
>> H. "has no slander on his tongue": this is our father, Jacob: "My father might feel me and I shall seem to him as a deceiver" (Gen. 27:12).
>> I. "does no evil to his fellow": he does not go into competition with his fellow craftsman.
>> J. "does not take up a reproach against his neighbor": this is someone who befriends his relatives.
>> K. "in whose eyes a vile person is despised": this is Hezekiah, king of Judah, who dragged his father's bones on a rope bed.
>> L. "honors those who fear the Lord": this is Jehoshaphat, king of Judah, who, whenever he would see a disciple of a sage, would rise from his throne and embrace and kiss him and call him, "My father, my father, my lord, my lord, my master, my master."
>> Q. "He who does these things shall never be moved":
>> V. [Simelai continues:] "Isaiah came and reduced them to six: '(i) He who walks righteously and (ii) speaks uprightly, (iii) he who despises the gain of oppressions, (iv) shakes his hand from holding bribes, (v) stops his ear from hearing of blood (vi) and shuts his eyes from looking upon evil, he shall dwell on high' (Isa. 33:25–26)."
>> W. *"He who walks righteously:" this is our father, Abraham: "For I have known him so that he may command his children and his household after him"* (Gen. 18:19).
>> X. "speaks uprightly": this is one who does not belittle his fellow in public.
>> AA. "stops his ear from hearing of blood": who will not listen to demeaning talk about a disciple of rabbis and remain silent.
>> FF. [Simelai continues:] "Micah came and reduced them to three: 'It has been told you, man, what is good, and what the Lord demands from you, (i) only to do justly and (ii) to love mercy, and (iii) to walk humbly before God' (Micah 6:8)."

GG. "only to do justly": this refers to justice.

HH. "to love mercy": this refers to doing acts of loving kindness.

II. "to walk humbly before God": this refers to accompanying a corpse to the grave and welcoming the bread.

KK. [Simelai continues:] "Isaiah again came and reduced them to two: 'Thus says the Lord, (i) Keep justice and (ii) do righteousness' (Isa. 56:1).

LL. "Amos came and reduced them to a single one, as it is said, 'For thus says the Lord to the house of Israel. Seek Me and live.'"

NN. Rather, [Simelai continues:] "Habakkuk further came and based them on one, as it is said, 'But the righteous shall live by his faith' (Hab. 2:4)."

If we can reduce "the whole Torah" to a handful of teachings, then clearly the meaning of the word "Torah" has shifted. The word no longer refers to a particular body of writings. Nor does it speak mainly of God's revelation to Moses at Mount Sinai. A variety of meanings now gather around a single word, and it is time systematically to review them.

Chapter 3

God: "In our image, after our likeness"

WHAT THE TORAH TELLS ABOUT GOD

The Torah's single most important teaching about God is that humanity is like God, so Genesis 1:26: "Let us make man in our image, after our likeness." God and the human being are mirror images of one another. Here we find the simple claim that the angels could not discern any physical difference whatever between man—Adam—and God:

> *Genesis Rabbah* VIII:X
>
> A. Said R. Hoshaiah, "When the Holy One, blessed be he, came to create the first man, the ministering angels mistook him [for God, since man was in God's image,] and wanted to say before the latter, 'Holy, [holy, holy is the Lord of hosts].'
>
> B. "To what may the matter be compared? To the case of a king and a governor who were set in a chariot, and the provincials wanted to greet the king, 'Sovereign!' But they did not know which one of them was which. What did the king do? He turned the governor out and put him away from the chariot, so that people would know who was king.

C. "So too when the Holy One, blessed be he, created the first man, the angels mistook him [for God]. What did the Holy One, blessed be he, do? He put him to sleep, so everyone knew that he was a mere man.

D. "That is in line with the following verse of Scripture: 'Cease you from man, in whose nostrils is a breath, for how little is he to be accounted' (Isa. 2:22)."

The task of the Judaic statement of monotheism is to mediate between the paradox that God and humanity correspond by reason of Adam's and Eve's creation in God's image, and that God is creator of the world, giver of the Torah, and redeemer of Israel: omnipotent divinity.

What, precisely, does God reveal about himself in the Torah? Israel the holy people meets God in the Torah at Sinai, when God—not Moses—proclaims, "The Lord, the Lord! a God compassionate and gracious, slow to anger, abounding in kindness and faithfulness, extending kindness to the thousandth generation, forgiving iniquity, transgression, and sin" (Exod. 34:6). The Torah tells the story of God's self-revelation to humanity through Israel, beginning with Abraham. It is because God wants to be known and makes himself known that Israel claims to know God, and the Torah—the written mediated through the oral—contains that knowledge that God wishes to impart to humanity. For those who practice Judaism, the encounter with God takes place in the Torah, hence, in the study of the Torah. The place and time for meeting God is not only at prayer, then, but in the holy circle of sage and disciples, and it is in books that portray God's self-revelation to Moses at the burning bush (Exodus 3) or in the still small voice Elijah heard that Israel finds God through all time.

Does that mean that Judaism's God is the angry and vengeful "God of the Old Testament," as many suppose? The picture of God whom we meet in the Hebrew Scriptures when read without sages' interpretation and the God whom the Judaic faithful worship in synagogue prayer under the tutelage of the sages of the Oral Torah are not the same, for the Hebrew Scriptures that Christianity knows as the Old Testament do not exhaust the Judaic doctrine of God. The Torah of Judaism encompasses not only Scripture—the written part of revelation—but also an oral tradition. Only in the whole Torah, the written as mediated by the oral, do we find the complete doctrine of God that Judaism sets forth. There God appears as infinitely merciful and loving, as passionate as a teenage lover, whom the Judaic community knows above all by the name "the All-Merciful." God is made manifest to Israel in many ways but is always one and the same.

THE CHARACTERIZATION OF GOD

Certainly one of the most memorable characterizations presents God as a warrior (Exod. 15:3), but the following passage shows that presentation as only partial:

Mekhilta Attributed to R. Ishmael Shirata, Chap. 1 = XXIX:2
> "The Lord is a man of war, the Lord is his name" (Exod. 15:3):
> Why is this stated?
> Since when he appeared at the sea, it was in the form of a mighty soldier making war, as it is said, "The Lord is a man of war,"
> and when he appeared to them at Sinai, it was as an elder, full of mercy, as it is said, "And they saw the God of Israel" (Exod. 24:10),
> and when they were redeemed, what does Scripture say? "And the like of the very heaven for clearness" (Exod. 24:10);
> "I beheld until thrones were placed and one that was ancient of days sat" (Dan. 7:9);
> "A fiery stream issued" (Dan. 7:10)—
> [so God took on many forms.] It was, therefore, not to provide the nations of the world with an occasion to claim that there are two dominions in heaven [but that the same God acts in different ways and appears in different forms]
> that Scripture says, "The Lord is a man of war, the Lord is his name."
> [This then bears the message:] The one in Egypt is the one at the sea, the one in the past is the one in the age to come, the one in this age is the one in the world to come: "See now that I, even I, am he" (Deut. 32:39); "Who has wrought and done it? He who called the generations from the beginning. I the Lord who am the first and with the last I am the same" (Isa. 41:4).

The main point then is clear: however we know God, in whatever form or aspect, it is always one and the same God. That is the heart of Judaic monotheism, a point on which Christianity and Islam would concur.

A definitive statement of the proposition that God appears to humanity in diverse forms is in the following, which represents the state of opinion of the fully exposed religious system of Judaism, at the time of the Talmud of the Land of Israel:

Pesiqta deRab Kahana XII:XXV
> A. Another interpretation of "I am the Lord your God [who brought you out of the land of Egypt"](Exod. 20:2):
> B. Said R. Hinena bar Papa, "The Holy One, blessed be he, had made his appearance to them with a stern face, with a neutral face, with a friendly face, with a happy face.
> C. "with a stern face: in Scripture. When a man teaches his son Torah, he has to teach him in a spirit of awe.
> D. "with a neutral face: in Mishnah.
> E. "with a friendly face: in Talmud.
> F. "with a happy face: in lore.
> G. "Said to them the Holy One, blessed be he, 'Even though you may see all of these diverse faces of mine, nonetheless: "I am the Lord your God who brought you out of the land of Egypt"' (Exod. 20:2)."

So far we deal with attitudes. As to the iconic representation of God, the following is explicit:

H. Said R. Levi, "The Holy One, blessed be he, had appeared to them like an icon that has faces in all directions, so that if a thousand people look at it, it appears to look at them as well.

I. "So too when the Holy One, blessed be he, when he was speaking, each Israelite would say, 'With me in particular the Word speaks.'

J. "What is written here is not, 'I am the Lord, your [plural] God, but rather, I am the Lord your [singular] God who brought you out of the land of Egypt' (Exod. 20:2)."

That God may show diverse faces to various people is now established. The reason for God's variety is made explicit. People differ, and God, in the image of whom all mortals are made, must therefore sustain diverse images—all of them formed in the model of human beings:

I. Said R. Yosé bar Hanina, "And it was in accord with the capacity of each one of them to listen and understand what the Word spoke with him.

J. "And do not be surprised at this matter, for when the manna came down to Israel, all would find its taste appropriate to their circumstance, infants in accord with their capacity, young people in accord with their capacity, old people in accord with their capacity.

K. "infants in accord with their capacity: just as an infant sucks from the teat of his mother, so was its flavor, as it is said, 'Its taste was like the taste of rich cream' (Num. 11:8).

L. "young people in accord with their capacity: as it is said, 'My bread also which I gave you, bread and oil and honey' (Ezek. 16:19).

M. "old people in accord with their capacity: as it is said 'the taste of it was like wafers made with honey' (Exod. 16:31).

N. "Now if in the case of manna, each one would find its taste appropriate to his capacity, so in the matter of the Word, each one understood in accord with capacity.

O. "Said David, 'The voice of the Lord is [in accord with one's] strength' (Ps. 29:4).

P. "What is written is not, 'in accord with his strength in particular,' but rather, 'in accord with one's strength,' meaning, accord with the capacity of each one.

Q. "Said to them the Holy One, blessed be He, 'It is not in accord with the fact that you hear a great many voices, but you should know that it is I who [speaks to all of you individually]: I am the Lord your God who brought you out of the land of Egypt' (Exod. 20:2)."

The individuality and particularity of God rest on the diversity of humanity. But, it must follow, the model of humanity—"in our image"—dictates how we are to envisage the face of God. And that is the starting point of our inquiry. The Torah defines what we know about God—but the Torah also tells us that we find God in the face of the other: "in our image," "after our likeness," means that everyone is in God's image, so if we want to know God, we had best look closely into the face of all humanity, one by one. But let us start at the beginning. The supernatural community that calls itself "Israel" knows and loves God as the heart and soul of its life. Three times a day the faithful pray—morning, dusk, and after dark—and throughout the day, responding to blessings that cascade over them, faithful Israelites (that is, Jews who practice the religion Judaism) respond with blessings of thanks for matters as humble as a glass of water or as remarkable as the survival of a car crash. So faithful Israel knows God as intimate friend and companion and never wanders far from God's sight or God's love.

GOD AS PREMISE, PRESENCE, PERSON, AND PERSONALITY

Rabbinic Judaism in its formative sources of the first six centuries C.E. portrays God in four ways: as premise, presence, person, and personality.

1. *God as premise,* occurs in passages in which an authorship reaches a particular decision because that authorship believes God created the world and has revealed the Torah to Israel. We therefore know that God forms the premise of a passage because the particular proposition of that passage appeals to God as premise of all being, for example, as author and authority of the Torah. Things are decided one way rather than some other on that basis. The conviction of the givenness of God who created the world and gave the Torah self-evidently defines the premise of all Judaisms before our own times. There is nothing surprising in it. But a particular indicator in so general a fact derives from the cases in which, for concrete and specific reasons, in quite particular cases, sages invoke God as foundation and premise of the world. When do they decide a case or reach a decision because they appeal to God as premise, and when do they not do so? This conception is much more subtle, since the entire foundation of the Mishnah, the initial statement of the Oral Torah, rests on the conception of the unity of God. The purpose of the Mishnah is to show how, in the here and now of the social and natural world, we see what it means that God is one.

2. *God as presence* stands for yet another consideration. It involves an authorship's referring to God as part of a situation in the here and now. When an authorship—for example, of the Mishnah—speaks of an ox goring another ox, it does not appeal to God to reach a decision for them and does not suggest that God in particular has witnessed the event and plans to intervene. But when an authorship—also in the Mishnah—speaks of a wife's being accused of unfaithfulness to her husband, by contrast that authorship expects that God will intervene in a particular case and in the required ordeal and so declare the decision for the case at hand. In the former instance, God is assuredly a premise of discourse, having revealed in the Torah the rule governing a goring ox. In the latter, God is not only premise but very present in discourse and in decision making. God furthermore constitutes a person in certain settings but not in others.

3. One may readily envisage God as premise without invoking a notion of the particular traits or personality of God. So too, in the case of God as presence, no aspect of the case at hand demands that we specify particular attitudes or traits of character to be imputed to God. But there is a setting in which God is held always to know and pay attention to specific cases, and that involves God as a "you," that is, *as a person.* For example, all discourse concerning liturgy in the Mishnah (obviously not alone in that document) understands that God also hears prayer and is hence not only a presence but a person, a you, responding to what is said, requiring certain attitudes and rejecting others. In a later document, by contrast, God is not only present but also participates, if only implicitly, when the Torah is studied among disciples of sages. Here too we find an interesting indicator of how God is portrayed in one situation as a premise, in a second as a presence, and in a third as a person.

In cases in which God is portrayed as a person, however, there are regulations to which God adheres. These permit us to imagine that God is present, without wondering what particular response God may make to a quite specific situation, for example, within the liturgy. We do not have to wonder because the rules tell us. Accordingly, while God is a liturgical "you," God as person still is not represented in full particularity, reaching a decision on a specific case in accord with traits of mind or heart or soul that yield a concrete decision or feeling or action out of a unique personality, different (by nature) from all other personalities. God as person but not as personality remains within the framework established at the outset when we considered the matters of God as premise and as presence.

corporeal

4. God emerges as a vivid and highly distinctive personality, actor, conversation partner, hero. In references to *God as a personality,* God is given corporeal traits. God looks like God in particular, just as each person exhibits distinctive physical traits. Not only so, but in matters of heart and mind and spirit, well-limned individual traits of personality and action alike endow God with that particularity that identifies every individual human being. When God is given attitudes but no active role in discourse, referred to but not invoked as part of a statement, God serves as person. When God participates as a hero and protagonist in a narrative, God gains traits of personality and emerges as God who is like humanity: God incarnate.

The Hebrew Scriptures portray God in richly personal terms: God feels and thinks in ways analogous to humanity. Thus God wants, cares, demands, regrets, says, and does—just like human beings. In the Written Torah God is not merely a collection of abstract theological attributes and thus rules for governance of reality, nor a mere person to be revered and feared. God is not a mere composite of regularities but a very specific, highly particular personality whom people can know, envision, engage, persuade, impress. Sages painted this portrait of a personality through making up narratives, telling stories in which God figures like other (incarnate) heroes. When therefore the authorships—authors of compositions, compilers of composites—of documents of the canon of the Judaism of the oral half of the dual Torah began to represent God as personality—not merely premise, presence, or person—they reentered that realm of discourse about God that Scripture had originally laid out.

True, that legacy of Scripture's God as actor and personality constituted for the sages who in the first six centuries C.E. created the Judaism of the dual Torah an available treasury of established facts about God—hence, God incarnate. But within the books and verses of Scripture, sages picked and chose, and they did so for God as well. In some points in the unfolding corpus, without regard to the entire range of available facts of Scripture, God was represented only as implicit premise; in others, as presence and source of action; in still others as person. So the repertoire of Scripture tells us solely what might have been. It was only at the end, in the Talmud of Babylonia, that we reach what finally came about—the portrayal, much as in Scripture and on the strength of Scripture's facts, of God as personality, with that same passionate love for Israel that, as Scripture's authorships had portrayed matters, had defined God in the received Written Torah.

GOD AS PREMISE AND PRESENCE

Philosophers work by rational steps, from premises to propositions, sifting evidence, conducting argument, reaching upward to conclusions. For the philosophers of the Mishnah, God is both the unitary premise and also the unitary goal of all being. In the Mishnah—as in all other writings of Judaism—God is present not merely in details, when actually mentioned, but at the foundations. To characterize the encounter with God, whether intellectual or concrete and everyday, we must therefore pay attention not only to passages that speak of God in some explicit way but, even more so, to the fundamental givens on which all particular doctrines or stories of a document depend. What that fact means in the case of the Mishnah is simple. That great philosophical law code demonstrates over and over again that all things are one, that complex things yield uniform and similar components, and that, rightly understood, there is a hierarchy of being, to be discovered through the proper classification of all things.

What this means is that, for the philosophers who wrote the Mishnah, the most important thing they wished to demonstrate about God is that God is one. And this they proposed to prove by showing, in a vast array of everyday circumstances, (1) the fundamental order and unity of all things, all being, and (2) the unity of all things in an ascending hierarchy, ascending upward to God. So all things through their unity and order become one thing, and all being derives from One God.

In the Mishnah many things are placed into sequence and order—"hierarchized"—and the order of all things is shown to have a purpose so that the order, or hierarchization, is purposive, or "teleological." The Mishnah time and again demonstrates these two contrary propositions: (1) many things join together by their nature into one thing, and (2) one thing yields many things. These propositions complement each other because, in forming matched opposites, the two set forth an ontological judgment. It is that all things are not only orderly but, in their deepest traits of being, are so ordered that many things fall into one classification, and one thing may hold together many things of a single classification. For this philosophy then, rationality consists in the hierarchy of the order of things, a rationality tested and proved, time and again, by the possibility always of effecting the hierarchical classification of all things. The proposition that is the Mishnah's is thus a theory of the right ordering of each thing in its classification (or taxon), all the categories (or taxa) in correct sequence, from least to greatest. And showing that all things can be ordered, and that all orders can be set into relationship with one another, we transform the ontological message into its components of proposition, argument, and demonstration.

[margin handwritten note: Purposive]

GOD IN PERSON

In the following passage, God serves as the origin of all great teachings, but as we have seen, that fact bears no consequences for the description of God as a person or personality:

> Talmud of the Land of Israel tractate *Sanhedrin* 10:1.IX
> E. "Given by one shepherd"—
> F. Said the Holy One, blessed be he, "If you hear a teaching from an Israelite minor, and the teaching gave pleasure to you, let it not be in your sight as if you have heard it from a minor, but as if you have heard it from an adult,
> G. "and let it not be as if you have heard it from an adult, but as if one has heard it from a sage,
> H. "and let it not be as if you have heard it from a sage, but as if one has heard it from a prophet,
> I. "and let it not be as if you have heard it from a prophet, but as if one has heard it from the shepherd,
> J. "and there is as a shepherd only Moses, in line with the following passage: 'Then he remembered the days of old, of Moses his servant. Where is he who brought out of the sea the shepherds of his flock? Where is he who put in the midst of them his holy Spirit?' (Isa. 63:11).
> K. "It is not as if one has heard it from the shepherd but as if one has heard it from the Almighty."
> L. "Given by one Shepherd"—and there is only One who is the Holy One, blessed be he, in line with that which you read in Scripture: "Hear, O Israel: the Lord our God is one Lord" (Deut. 6:4).

In studying the Torah, sages and disciples clearly met the living God and recorded a direct encounter with and experience of God through the revealed word of God. But in a statement such as this, alluding to but not clearly describing what it means to hear the word of the Almighty, God at the end of the line simply forms the premise of revelation. There is no further effort at characterization. The exposition of the work of Creation (*y. Hag.* 2:1.II ff.) refers to God's deeds mainly by citing verses of Scripture, for example, "Then he made the snow: 'He casts forth his ice like morsels'" (Ps. 147:17), and so on. So too God has wants and desires, for example, what God wants is for Israel to repent, at which time God will save Israel (*y. Ta'an.* 1:1.X.U), but there is no effort to characterize God.

God is understood to establish a presence in the world. This is accomplished both through intermediaries such as a retinue of angels and also through the hypostatization of divine attributes, such as the Holy Spirit, the Presence or Shekhinah, and the like. The Holy Spirit makes its appearance, for example, "They were delighted that their opinion proved to be the same as that of the Holy Spirit" (*y. Hor.* 3:5.III.PP, *y. 'Abod. Zar.* 3:1.II.AA, etc.). God is understood to enjoy a retinue, a court (*y. San.* 1:1.IV.Q); God's seal is truth. These and similar statements restate the notion that God forms a living presence in the world. God in the very Presence intervened in Israel's history, for example, at the Sea of Reeds:

> Talmud of the Land of Israel tractate *Sanhedrin* 2:1.III.1O
> When the All-Merciful came forth to redeem Israel from Egypt, he did not send a messenger or an angel, but the Holy One, blessed be he, himself came forth, as it is said, "For I will pass through the Land of Egypt that night" (Exod. 12:12)—and not only so, but it was he and his entire retinue.

The familiar idea that God's presence went into exile with Israel recurs (*y. Ta'an.* 1:1.X.E ff.). But not a single passage in the entire Yerushalmi alleges that God's personal presence at a historical event in the time of sages changed the course of events. The notion that God's presence remained in exile leaves God without personality or even ample description.

Where God does take up a presence, it is not uncommonly a literary device, with no important narrative implications. For example, God is assumed to speak through any given verse of Scripture. Therefore the first person will be introduced in connection with citing such a verse, as at *y. San.* 5:1.IV.E, "[God answers,] 'It was an act of love that I did . . . [citing a verse,] for I said, "The world will be built upon merciful love"'" (Ps. 89:2). Here since the cited verse has an "I," God is given a presence in the colloquy. But it is a mere formality.

God was encountered as a very real presence, actively listening to prayers, as in the following:

> Talmud of the Land of Israel tractate *Berakhot* 9:1.VII.E
> See how high the Holy One, blessed be he, is above his world. Yet a person can enter a synagogue, stand behind a pillar, and pray in an

undertone, and the Holy One, blessed be he, hears his prayers, as it says, "Hannah was speaking in her heart; only her lips moved, and her voice was not heard" (1 Sam. 1:13). Yet the Holy One, blessed be he, heard her prayer.

When, however, we distinguish God as person, "you," from God as a well-portrayed active personality, liturgical formulas give a fine instance of the one side of the distinction. In the Yerushalmi's sizable corpus of such prayers, individual and community alike, we never find testimony to a material change in God's decision in a case based on setting aside known rules in favor of an episodic act of intervention, and it follows that thought on God as person remains continuous with what has gone before. Sages, like everyone else in Israel, believed that God hears and answers prayer. But that belief did not require them to preserve stories about specific instances in which the rules of hearing and answering prayer attested to a particular trait of personality or character to be imputed to God. A specific episode or incident never served to highlight the characterization of divinity in one way rather than in some other, in a manner parallel to the use of stories by the authors of Scripture to portray God as a sharply etched personality.

GOD'S PERSONALITY

Telling stories provides the particular means by which theological traits that many generations had affirmed now are portrayed as qualities of the personality of God, who is like a human being. It is one thing to hypostatize a theological abstraction, for example, "The quality of mercy said before the Holy One, blessed be he. . . ." It is quite another to construct a conversation between God and, for example, David, with a complete argument and a rich interchange in which God's merciful character is spelled out as the trait of a specific personality. God then emerges not as an abstract entity with theological traits but as a fully exposed personality. God is portrayed as engaged in conversation with human beings because God and humanity can understand one another within the same rules of discourse. When we speak of the personality of God, we shall see traits of a corporeal, emotional, and social character form the repertoire of appropriate characteristics. To begin with, we consider the particular means by which, in the pages of the Talmud of Babylonia, in particular, these traits are set forth.

The following story shows us the movement from the abstract and theological to the concrete and narrative mode of discourse about God:

> Talmud of Babylonia tractate *Sanhedrin* 111a–b, VI
>> A. "And Moses made haste and bowed his head toward the earth and worshipped" (Exod. 34:8):
>> B. What did Moses see?
>> C. Hanina b. Gamula said, "He saw [God's attribute of] being long-suffering (Exod. 34:7)."

D. Rabbis say, "He saw [the attribute of] truth (Exod. 34:7)." It has been taught on Tannaite authority in accord with him who has said, "He saw God's attribute of being long-suffering."

E. For it has been taught on Tannaite authority:

F. When Moses went up on high, he found the Holy One, blessed be he, sitting and writing, "Long-suffering."

G. He said before him, "Lord of the world, Long-suffering for the righteous?"

H. He said to him, "Also for the wicked."

I. [Moses] said to him, "Let the wicked perish."

J. He said to him, "Now you will see what you want."

K. When the Israelites sinned, he said to him, "Did I not say to you, 'Long-suffering for the righteous'?"

L. [Moses] said to him, "Lord of the world, did I not say to you, 'Also for the wicked'?"

M. That is in line with what is written, "And now I beseech you, let the power of my Lord be great, according as you have spoken, saying" (Num. 14:17). [H. Freedman, *The Babylonian Talmud. Sanhedrin*, (New York, 1948), 764, n. 7: What called forth Moses' worship of God when Israel sinned through the Golden Calf was his vision of the Almighty as long-suffering.]

The statement at the outset is repeated in narrative form at F. Once we are told that God is long-suffering, then it is in particular, narrative form that that trait is given definition. God then emerges as a personality, specifically because Moses engages in argument with God. He reproaches God, questions God's actions and judgments, holds God to a standard of consistency—and receives appropriate responses. God in heaven does not argue with humanity on earth. God in heaven issues decrees, forms the premise of the earthly rules, constitutes a presence, may even take the form of a "you" for hearing and answering prayers.

When God argues, discusses, defends and explains actions, and thus emerges as a personality etched in words, then God attains that personality that imparts to God the status of a being consubstantial with humanity. It is particularly through narrative that that transformation of God from person to personality takes place. Since personality involves physical traits; attitudes of mind, emotion, and intellect consubstantial with those of human beings; and the doing of the deeds people do in the way in which they do them, we shall now see that all three modes of personality come to full expression in the Talmud of Babylonia. This we do in sequence, ending with a clear demonstration that God incarnate takes the particular form of a sage. And that will yield the problem of the final chapter, namely, the difference between God and all (other) sages.

God not only looks like a human being but also does the acts that human beings do. For example, God spends the day much as does a mortal ruler of Israel, at least as sages imagine such a figure. That is, he studies the Torah, makes practical decisions, and sustains the world (i.e., administers public funds for public needs)—just as (in sages' picture of themselves) sages do. What gives us a deeply human God is that for the final part of the day, God plays with his pet, Leviathan, who was like Hydra, the great sea serpent with multiple heads. Some correct that view and hold that God spends the rest of the day teaching youngsters. In passages such as these we therefore see the concrete expression of a process of the personality of God:

> Talmud of Babylonia tractate *Abodah Zarah* 3b
>
> A. Said R. Judah said Rab, "The day is twelve hours long. During the first three, the Holy One, blessed be he, is engaged in the study of the Torah.
> B. "During the next three God sits in judgment on the world and when he sees the world sufficiently guilty to deserve destruction, he moves from the seat of justice to the seat of mercy.
> C. "During the third he feeds the whole world, from the horned buffalo to vermin.
> D. "During the fourth he plays with the leviathan, as it is said, 'There is leviathan, whom you have made to play with' (Ps. 104:26)."
> E. [Another authority denies this final point and says,] What then does God do in the fourth quarter of the day?
> F. "He sits and teaches schoolchildren, as it is said, 'Whom shall one teach knowledge, and whom shall one make to understand the message? Those who are weaned from milk' (Isa. 28:9)."
> G. And what does God do by night?
> H. If you like, I shall propose that he does what he does in daytime.
> I. Or if you prefer: he rides a translucent cherub and floats in eighteen thousand worlds . . .
> J. Or if you prefer: he sits and listens to the song of the heavenly creatures, as it is said, "By the day the Lord will command his loving kindness and in the night his song shall be with me" (Ps. 42:9).

The personality of God encompassed not only physical but also emotional or attitudinal traits. In the final stage of the Judaism of the dual Torah, God emerged as a fully exposed personality. The character of divinity, therefore, encompassed God's virtue, the specific traits of character and personality that God exhibited above and here below. Above all, humility, the virtue sages most often asked of themselves, characterized the divinity. God wanted people to be humble, and God therefore showed humility.

> Talmud of Babylonia tractate *Shabbat* 89a
>
> A. Said R. Joshua b. Levi, "When Moses came down from before the Holy One, blessed be he, Satan came and asked [God], 'Lord of the world, Where is the Torah? [What have you done with it? Do you really intend to give it to mortals?]'
> B. "He said to him, 'I have given it to the earth . . .' [Satan ultimately was told by God to look for the Torah by finding the son of Amram.]
> C. "He went to Moses and asked him, 'Where is the Torah that the Holy One, blessed be he, gave you?'
> D. "He said to him, 'Who am I that the Holy One, blessed be he, should give me the Torah?'
> E. "Said the Holy One, blessed be he, to Moses, 'Moses, you are a liar!'

F. "He said to him, 'Lord of the world, you have a treasure in store which you have enjoyed everyday. Shall I keep it to myself?'

G. "He said to him, 'Moses, since you have acted with humility, it will bear your name: "Remember the Torah of Moses, my servant" (Mal. 3:22).'"

God is represented here as favoring humility and rewarding the humble with honor. What is important is that God does not cite Scripture or merely paraphrase it; the conversation is an exchange between two vivid personalities. True enough, Moses, not God, is the hero. But the personality of God emerges in vivid ways. The following passage shows how traits imputed to God also define proper conduct for sages, not to mention other human beings.

Just as Israel glorifies God, so God responds and celebrates Israel. In the passages at hand, the complete personality of God—in physical, emotional, and social traits—comes to expression. God wears phylacteries, an indication of a corporeal sort. God further forms the correct attitude toward Israel, which is one of love, an indication of an attitude on the part of divinity corresponding to right attitudes on the part of human beings. Finally, to close the circle, just as there is a "you" to whom humanity prays, so God, too, says prayers—to God—and the point of these prayers is that God should elicit from himself forgiveness for Israel:

Talmud of Babylonia tractate *Berakhot* 6
6A–B.XXXIX

A. Said R. Nahman bar Isaac to R. Hiyya bar Abin, "As to the phylacteries of the Lord of the world, what is written in them?"

B. He said to him, "'And who is like your people Israel, a singular nation on earth' (1 Chron. 17:21)."

C. "And does the Holy One, blessed be he, sing praises for Israel?"

D. "Yes, for it is written, 'You have avouched the Lord this day . . . and the Lord has avouched you this day' (Deut. 26:17, 18).

E. "Said the Holy One, blessed be he, to Israel, 'You have made me a singular entity in the world, and I shall make you a singular entity in the world.

F. "'You have made me a singular entity in the world,' as it is said, 'Hear O Israel, the Lord, our God, the Lord is one' (Deut. 6:4a–b).

G. "'And I shall make you a singular entity in the world,' as it is said, 'And who is like your people, Israel, a singular nation in the earth' (1 Chron. 17:21)."

H. Said R. Aha, son of Raba to R. Ashi, "That takes care of one of the four subdivisions of the phylactery. What is written in the others?"

I. He said to him, "'For what great nation is there. . . . And who is like you, O Israel . . .' (Deut. 33:29), 'Or has God tried . . . ,' (Deut. 4:34). And 'To make you high above all nations' (Deut. 26:19)."

J. "If so, there are too many boxes!"

K. "But the verses, 'For what great nation is there' and 'And what great nation is there,' which are equivalent, are in one box, and

'Happy are you, O Israel' and 'Who is like your people Israel' are in one box, and 'Or has God tried . . . ,' in one box, and 'To make you high' in one box.

L. "And all of them are written in the phylactery that is on the arm."

7A. XLIX

A. Said R. Yohanan in the name of R. Yosé, "How do we know that the Holy One, blessed be he, says prayers?

B. "Since it is said, 'Even them will I bring to my holy mountain and make them joyful in my house of prayer' (Isa. 56:7).

C. "'Their house of prayer' is not stated, but rather, 'my house of prayer.'

D. "On the basis of that usage we see that the Holy One, blessed be he, says prayers."

E. What prayers does he say?

F. Said R. Zutra bar Tobiah said Rab, "'May it be my will that my mercy overcome my anger, and that my mercy prevail over my attributes, so that I may treat my children in accord with the trait of mercy and in their regard go beyond the strict measure of the law.'"

7A

A. It has been taught on Tannaite authority:

B. Said R. Ishmael b. Elisha [who is supposed to have been a priest in Temple times], "One time I went in to offer up incense on the innermost altar, and I saw the crown of the Lord, enthroned on the highest throne, and he said to me, 'Ishmael, my son, bless me.'

C. "I said to him, 'May it be your will that your mercy overcome your anger, and that your mercy prevail over your attributes, so that you treat your children in accord with the trait of mercy and in their regard go beyond the strict measure of the law.'

D. "And he nodded his head to me."

E. And from that story we learn that the blessing of a common person should not be negligible in your view.

The corporeal side to the personality of God is clear at the outset: God's wearing phylacteries. The consubstantial traits of attitude and feeling are made explicit—just as humanity feels joy, so does God; just as humanity celebrates God, so does God celebrate Israel. The social transactions of personality are specified as well. Just as Israel declares God to be unique, so God declares Israel to be unique. And just as Israel prays to God, so God says prayers. What God asks of God is that God transcend God—which is what, in prayer, humanity asks for as well. In the end, therefore, to be "in our image, after our likeness"—the power of the powerless, the riches of the disinherited, the valuation and valorization of the will of those who have no right to will—is to be not the mirror image of God but to be very much like God. That is how, once more, the dimension of *zekhut* enters in. And with *zekhut*, we come to the category that defines the proper relationship of a human being to God: one in which what a person does does not coerce God but invokes in God an attitude of concern and love for the person. We now turn to the single most characteristic and important theological idea in Rabbinic

Judaism—and one that is most difficult to grasp and most profound in its theological implications.

THE DIVINITY OF GOD: GOD AS WHOLLY OTHER

What we know about God and ourselves, Judaism maintains, we know because God's grace has permitted us to know—that alone. So the proposition is that the facts provided by the Torah themselves comprise an act of grace. This is demonstrated syllogistically on the basis of three givens that were listed in the opening sentences of the following syllogism. These three fundamental truths govern throughout: humanity is made in the image of God; Israel are children of God; Israel possesses the most precious of gifts. These are givens. Wherein lies the gift? The act of grace is that we are told that they are God's gifts to us. We are not only in God's image—something we cannot have known on our own—but God has told us so. The people of Israel are not only God's children—it would have been arrogance to have supposed so on their own—but God has so stated in so many words. Israel possesses the greatest gift of all. They know it: God has said so. So the syllogism draws on three facts to make one point that is not stated but that lies at the goal of the argument.

> Mishnah tractate *Abot* 3:13–14
> R. Aqiba says, "Precious is the human being, who was created in the image [of God].
> "It was an act of still greater love that it was made known to him that he was created in the image [of God], as it is said, 'For in the image of God he made man' (Gen. 9:6).
> "Precious are Israelites, who are called children to the Omnipresent.
> "It was an act of still greater love that they were called children to the Omnipresent, as it is said, 'You are the children of the Lord your God' (Deut. 14:1).
> "Precious are Israelites, to whom was given the precious thing.
> "It was an act of still greater love that it was made known to them that to them was given that precious thing with which the world was made, as it is said, 'For I give you a good doctrine. Do not forsake my Torah' (Prov. 4:2)."

These six statements form the paradigm of Judaic theology: not truth alone, but truth enhanced because of the Torah's verification and validation. That is what it means to say that Israel knows God through the Torah. God is known because God makes himself known.

Chapter 4

The Holy and the Unclean: Sanctification and Pollution

DEFINING SANCTIFICATION

To be "holy" in Judaism means "to be like God," who is called "the Holy One, blessed be he," and to be unclean means to belong to the realm of death. God is called "the Holy One, blessed be he," and to be "holy" is to be like God. "Holy" means "set apart for God" and stands for life. "Unclean" refers to that which is to be kept from contaminating the sacred and stands for death. In concrete terms, the holy Temple in Jerusalem; the holy people, Israel; the holy days, Sabbaths and Festivals, are to be kept separate and distinct from the ordinary, the profane, and the unclean.

The Torah, written and oral, defines the matter with precision. At Leviticus 19:2, God calls on Israel to be holy like God: "You shall be holy, for I the Lord your God am holy," and the requirements of sanctification or holiness (the two words are equivalent in this setting) are spelled out. The exposition of the meaning of sanctification at Leviticus 19 is deemed to spell out most of the principles of the Torah. In line with the fundamental character of Judaism as a religion of ethical monotheism, "holiness" bears profound implications for ethical conduct. One cannot be both holy and unethical. In concrete terms, one cannot utilize

stolen property in the performance of a religious duty or sanctify to the Temple—
set apart as holy for God's use—what is stolen and not one's own property. The
Rabbinic exposition of Leviticus 19 underscores that to be like God, that is, to
be holy, means to act in accord with the rules of morality and compassion. One
cannot overemphasize that fact, since people do not always correlate "holiness"
with morality and ethical conduct in the way in which the Torah insists they are
to match.

The sages' reading of the Holiness Code of Leviticus begins with the statement that the chapter at hand contains most of the principles of the Torah and
that the starting point of holiness is separateness:

> *Sifra* CXCV:I.1-CC:III.6
> CXCV:I
>> 1. A. "And the Lord said to Moses, 'Say to all the congregation of the
>> people of Israel, You shall be holy, [for I the Lord your God am
>> holy. Every one of you shall revere his mother and his father,
>> and you shall keep my Sabbaths; I am the Lord your God. Do
>> not turn to idols or make for yourselves molten gods; I am the
>> Lord your God]'" (Lev. 19:1–4):
>> B. This teaches that this chapter was stated in the assembly of all
>> Israel.
>> C. And why was it stated in the assembly of all Israel?
>> D. It is because most of the principles of the Torah depend upon
>> its contents.
>> 2. A. "You shall be holy":
>> B. "You shall be separate."

The correspondence of holiness to keeping the Ten Commandments is spelled
out in the following amplification of Leviticus 19 in line with Exodus 20:

> CXCIX:I
>> 6. A. "And you shall not swear by my name falsely [and so profane
>> the name of your God]:"
>> B. What is the point of Scripture?
>> C. Since it is said [in the Ten Commandments], "You shall not
>> take the name of the Lord your God in vain" (Exod. 20:7),
>> I might have supposed that one incurs liability only if he takes
>> in vain the ineffable name of God. How do I know that all
>> of the euphemisms for God's name also are involved in a false
>> oath?
>> D. Scripture says, "[And you shall not swear] by my name [falsely]
>> [and so profane the name of your God],"
>> E. encompassing all names that I have.
>> 7. A. " . . . and so profane the name of your God":
>> B. This teaches that a false oath is a profanation of God's name.

The upshot is, to be holy means to be upright in oath taking, not to take God's
name in vain. But there is more. Being "holy, like God" means to treat people
fairly and justly:

CC:I

1. A. "You shall do no injustice in judgment; [you shall not be partial
      to the poor or defer to the great, but in righteousness shall you
      judge your neighbor. You shall not go up and down as a slanderer
      among your people, and you shall not stand forth against the life
      of your neighbor: I am the Lord]" (Lev. 19:15–16):
   B. This teaches that a judge who misjudges a case is called
      "unjust," "hated," "an abomination," "beyond all use," "an
      abhorrent."
   C. And he causes five things to happen: he imparts uncleanness to
      the land, he desecrates the divine name, he makes the Presence
      of God depart, he impales Israel on the sword, and makes Israel
      go into exile from its land.

Above all, to be holy like God means not to bear a grudge but to love one's neighbor as oneself. That comes at the climax of Leviticus 19 and forms the Golden
Rule of Judaism:

CC:III

1. A. "You shall not hate your brother in your heart, [but reasoning,
      you shall reason with your neighbor, lest you bear sin because
      of him. You shall not take vengeance or bear any grudge against
      the sons of your own people, but you shall love your neighbor
      as yourself: I am the Lord]" (Lev. 19:17–18).
   B. Might one suppose that one should not curse him, set him
      straight, or contradict him?
   C. Scripture says, "in your heart."
   D. I spoke only concerning hatred that is in the heart.
2. A. And how do we know that if one has rebuked him four or five
      times, he should still go and rebuke him again?
   B. Scripture says, "reasoning, you shall reason with your neighbor."
   C. Might one suppose that that is the case even if one rebukes him
      and his countenance blanches?
   D. Scripture says, "lest you bear sin."
4. A. "You shall not take vengeance [or bear any grudge]":
   B. To what extent is the force of vengeance?
   C. If one says to him, "Lend me your sickle," and the other did
      not do so.
   D. On the next day, the other says to him, "Lend me your spade."
   E. The one then replies, "I am not going to lend it to you, because
      you didn't lend me your sickle."
   F. In that context, it is said, "You shall not take vengeance."
5. A. ". . . or bear any grudge":
   B. To what extent is the force of a grudge?
   C. If one says to him, "Lend me your spade," but he did not do so.
   D. The next day the other one says to him, "Lend me your sickle,"
   E. and the other replies, "I am not like you, for you didn't lend
      me your spade [but here, take the sickle]!"
   F. In that context, it is said, "or bear any grudge."
6. A. "You shall not take vengeance or bear any grudge against the
      sons of your own people":
   B. "You may take vengeance and bear a grudge against others."

7. A. ". . . but you shall love your neighbor as yourself: [I am the
Lord]":
   B. R. Aqiba says, "This is the encompassing principle of the Torah."
   C. Ben Azzai says, "'This is the book of the generations of Adam'
   (Gen. 5:1) is a still more encompassing principle."

When we use the language "ethical monotheism," we now see the full meaning
of that characterization of Judaism, Christianity, and Islam: these are the religions
that identify holiness with moral behavior, modeled on God's account of his own
conduct and expectations of humanity.

HOLY VERSUS PROFANE AND UNCLEAN

Profane

If one antonym for "holy" is "immoral," another, more familiar one is "profane,
ordinary": that is, as in "holy" versus "profane," or "common," or that which is
available in everyday terms and that which is kept separate for special purposes
and occasions. Genesis 2:3 frames matters in just this way: "So God blessed the
seventh day and sanctified it, because on it God rested from all his work which
he had done in creation." Here, "sanctify" means set aside from the everyday. And
that brings us to the meaning of "holy" when it is attached to the life of service
to God that is conducted in the Temple and its sacrifices. In that context, "sanctification" means that which is set aside in a hierarchical structure for God's purposes. So "holy" means not only "like God" but designated for the service and
use of God. And "profane" means available for humanity's ordinary use. In this
context, the Sabbath is a holy day; the six days of creation are profane or common. The Sabbath is observed through acts of sanctification; ordinary days are
not.

Unclean

Scripture and the Oral Torah know a third antonym for "holy," and that is the
most important: "unclean." What is "unclean" is not to be permitted to contaminate what is "holy." In this context Scripture and the Mishnah define matters
clearly. The corpse is the most virulent source of uncleanness, so in this sense,
"unclean" stands for death; and "holy," for life. The Temple is to be protected
from death and preserved as holy for life. So too, the holy people, Israel, is to be
protected from what endangers its life, which is gossip. And a kind of uncleanness analogous to death is the uncleanness of the skin ailment (Leviticus 13–14),
which, sages hold, signifies that the victim has gossiped or been arrogant.

   That is made explicit in the discussion of sources of uncleanness deemed comparable to the person afflicted with the skin ailment described in Leviticus 13–14.
When Miriam and Aaron questioned Moses' supreme leadership ("Has the Lord

indeed spoken only through Moses? Has he not spoken through us also?" [Num. 12:2]), Miriam was punished with an attack of the skin ailment: "Miriam was afflicted with the skin ailment, as white as snow." Aaron then turns to Moses and says, "Let her not be as one dead, of whom the flesh is half consumed when he comes out of his mother's womb" (Num. 12:12). The explicit comparison of the skin ailment to death—the skin is like that of a corpse—shows what is at stake. That conception that the skin ailment contaminates like a corpse is embodied in the details of the law. The advent of the skin uncleanness signifies that the victim gossiped or behaved arrogantly. The upshot is, in cause and effect, the skin uncleanness is a social disease:

> *Sifra* CLV:I.8
> A. ". . . saying" (Lev. 14:35)—
> B. The priest will say to him words of reproach: "My son, the marks of the skin ailment come only because of gossip [*t. Nega'im* 6:7], as it is said, 'Take heed of the skin ailment to keep very much and to do, remember what the Lord God did to Miriam' (Deut. 24:80).
> C. "And what has one thing to do with the other?
> D. "But this teaches that she was punished only because of gossip.
> E. "And is it not an argument a fortiori?
> F. "If Miriam, who did not speak before Moses' presence, suffered so, one who speaks ill of his fellow in his very presence, how much the more so?"
> G. R. Simeon b. Eleazar says, "Also because of arrogance do marks of the skin ailment come, for so do we find concerning Uzziah,
> H. "as it is said, 'And he rebelled against the Lord his God and he came to the Temple of the Lord to offer on the altar incense and Azariah the Priest came after him and with him priests of the Lord, eighty strong men, and they stood against Uzziah and said to him, It is not for you to do, Uzziah, to offer to the Lord, for only the priests the sons of Aaron who are sanctified do so. Go forth from the sanctuary. And Uzziah was angry,' etc. (2 Chron. 26:16)" [*t. Nega'im* 6:7h].

The Halakhic texts then state explicitly that the aberrant individual has deliberately violated the integrity of corporate Israel. Gossip endangers the health of the household of Israel. All forms of wicked speech fall within that same category. In the principle of measure for measure, gossip, which disrupts community harmony, finds its penalty in ostracism, inflicted on the person who gossips through the medium of the skin ailment that is treated by excluding the afflicted from the common life.

In the Pentateuch, uncleanness affects the conduct of three activities: eating, procreation, and attendance at the Temple. When the priests ate their priestly rations, they were to do so in a condition of cultic cleanness. Furthermore, all Israelites are to abstain from unclean foods and from sexual relations during a woman's menstrual period or when affected by the uncleanness of the sexual organs to which Leviticus 15 makes allusion. All Israelites also must become clean to participate in the Temple cult, which would affect many at the time of the pilgrim festivals, Passover, Pentecost, and Tabernacles. In addition, among the Judaisms that flourished in Second Temple times, before 70 C.E. when the Temple was destroyed, some groups, such as the Pharisees, the Essenes, and some represented by law codes found in the Dead Sea Scrolls, kept the rules of cultic purity in eating food at home, not in the Temple, a practice that did not characterize the bulk of the communities of Judaism. After 70, when attaining cleanness to participate in the cult no longer pertained, uncleanness rules governing food and sexual relations continued to apply, as they do in Judaism to the present day. But in matters of public worship it was primarily the Temple, not the synagogue, to which considerations of cleanness applied, and no one would refrain from attending synagogue worship by reason of having contracted uncleanness, for example, by having attended a funeral and so contracting corpse uncleanness.

In Judaism, therefore, what is unclean is abnormal and disruptive of the economy of nature, and what is clean is normal and constitutive of the economy and the wholeness of nature. What is unclean is restored to a condition of cleanness through the activity of nature—unimpeded by human intervention—in removing the uncleanness through the natural force of water collected in its original state. Accordingly, if to be clean is normal, then it is that state of normality restored by natural processes themselves. So to be unclean is abnormal and is the result of unnatural processes: death, menstrual blood, flux of blood outside of the menstrual cycle, and a flow from the penis outside of the normal reproductive process. Procreation and sustenance of life define what is at stake in the condition of cleanness en route to the state of sanctification, as in the hierarchical statement by Pinhas b. Yair:

> Mishnah tractate *Sotah* 9:15
> R. Pinhas b. Yair says, "Heedfulness leads to cleanliness, cleanliness leads to cultic cleanness, cleanness leads to abstinence [*perishut*, a.k.a., Pharisaism], abstinence leads to holiness, holiness leads to modesty, modesty leads to the fear of sin, the fear of sin leads to piety, piety leads to the Holy Spirit, the Holy Spirit leads to the resurrection of the dead, and the resurrection of the dead comes through Elijah, blessed be his memory, Amen."

Uncleanness and sanctification form opposites because the one stands for death; the other, the predisposition, the preparation, for eternal life.

PURITY VIEWED WHOLE

Viewed as a whole, the law of purities set forth in the Mishnah and the Tosefta treats the interplay of persons, food, and liquids. Dry inanimate objects or food are not susceptible to uncleanness, explicitly stated at Leviticus 11:34, 37. What is wet is susceptible. So liquids activate the system. What is unclean, moreover, emerges from uncleanness through the operation of liquids, specifically, through immersion in fit water of requisite volume and in natural condition. Liquids thus deactivate the system. Thus, water in its natural condition is what concludes the process by removing uncleanness. Water in its unnatural condition, that is, deliberately affected by human agency, is what imparts susceptibility to uncleanness to begin with.

The uncleanness of persons, furthermore, is signified by body liquids or flux in the case of the menstruating woman (*Niddah*, Leviticus 15) and the *Zab*, a woman who suffers vaginal flow not during her regular menstrual period, or a man who suffers a flux of semen from a flaccid penis (*Zabim*, Leviticus 15). Corpse uncleanness is conceived to be a kind of effluent, a viscous gas, which flows like a liquid (Numbers 19). Utensils, for their part, receive uncleanness when they form receptacles able to contain liquid. In sum, we have a system in which the invisible flow of fluid-like substances or powers serves to put food, drink, and receptacles into the status of uncleanness and to remove those things from that status. Whether or not we call the system "metaphysical," it certainly has no material base but is conditioned on highly abstract notions. Thus, in material terms the effect of liquid is on food, drink, utensils, and man. The consequence has to do with who may eat and drink what food and liquid, and what food and drink may be consumed in which pots and pans. These loci are specified by tractates on utensils (tractate *Kelim*) and on food and drink (tractates *Tohorot* and *Uqsin*).

Human beings fall in the middle, between sources and loci of uncleanness. They are both: they serve as sources of uncleanness; they also become unclean. The *Zab*, the menstruating woman, the woman after childbirth, the person who has immersed and waits for sunset to complete the purification process, and the person afflicted with the skin ailment— all are sources of uncleanness. But being unclean, they fall within the system's loci, its program of consequences. So they make other things unclean and are subject to penalties because they *are* unclean. Unambiguous sources of uncleanness never also constitute loci affected by uncleanness. They always are unclean and never can become clean: the corpse, the dead creeping thing, and things like them. Inanimate sources of uncleanness and inanimate objects are affected by uncleanness. Systemically unique man and liquids have the capacity to inaugurate the processes of uncleanness (as sources) and also are subject to those same processes (as objects of uncleanness).

What is unclean, analogous to death, is abnormal and disruptive of the economy of nature, and what is clean is normal and constitutive of the economy and the wholeness of nature. That becomes clear in the way in which what is unclean is restored to a condition of cleanness. By immersion in a pool of water that has gathered naturally, without human intervention in collecting the water, a utensil or a person rises from the status of uncleanness to that of cleanness. So it is through the activity of nature, unimpeded by human activity, in removing the uncleanness through the natural force of water collected in its original state. Accordingly, if to be clean is normal, then it is that state of normality that is restored by natural processes themselves. It follows that to be unclean is abnormal and is the result of unnatural processes. The first of these—as we should anticipate—is death, which disturbs the house of life by releasing, in quest of a new house, corpse uncleanness, to be defined as that which is released by death. Corpse uncleanness may be contained in a tent, which is a small enclosed space, or in a broken utensil, as the sages read Numbers 19. Once corpse uncleanness finds that new home, its capacity for contamination ends. The second is menstrual blood, flux of blood outside of the menstrual cycle, and a flow from the penis outside of the normal reproductive process. Here too the source of uncleanness, in the case of the *Zabah* and the *Zab*, most certainly is constituted by that which functions contrary to nature or which disrupts what is deemed to be the normal course of nature.

The system of purities forms its meanings on a two-dimensional grid. One is laid out so that the Temple stands in the middle, the world roundabout, with the sanctity of the Temple definitive of the potential sanctification of table and bed, the profane and unclean world outside. The other, superimposed on the former, places man at one pole, nature at the other, each reciprocally complementing and completing the place and role of the other. Nature produces uncleanness and removes uncleanness. Man subjects food and utensils to uncleanness and, through his action, also imparts significance to the system as a whole. For in the end the question is, What can a man do? And the answer is, Man stands at the center of this world's complementary loci of sanctification and uncleanness. The sustenance of his life and his reproductive activity form the focus of intense concentration.

The life of man which is central—the rhythm of his eating, drinking, and sexual activity—defines the working of the system, and the intention and will of man provide the key to the system. Without human will the system is inert. Utensils that are not useful are not susceptible. Vegetable matter and liquid not subject to human use are not going to be made unclean. Things that are dry are permanently clean. Only produce that is wet down deliberately and purposefully to serve his needs is susceptible to uncleanness. What man does not do is equally decisive in the process of forming the principal means of purification. He does not intervene in nature's processes at the end of the system, just as he must determine to inaugurate the forces of uncleanness by deciding to use a utensil or to eat an apple. He cannot stimulate the bodily sources of uncleanness, for example, in the case of the *Zab*, all the more so in the case of the *nega'* or, under normal circumstances, in the case of the corpse. But he must impart purpose and significance to the things affected by those bodily sources of uncleanness.

When we describe the formation of the system of purity and uncleanness, we discover at its very foundations the definitive place of man. What the system proposes is to locate a place of critical importance in the unseen world of uncleanness and holiness, in the processes of the sanctification of this profane world in the model of the holy Temple's sanctity, for the activity and purpose of man. He is not helpless in the works of sanctification but, on the contrary, he is the responsible, decisive figure, both in what he does deliberately and in what he sedulously refrains from doing. He is not a passive object of an independent process of material sanctification, begun and elected by Heaven working solely through nature, but the principal subject in the contingent process of relative and circumstantial sanctification. And the arena for his activity is his own basic life processes: eating food and so sustaining life, engaging in sexual relations and so maintaining life's continuity. Since the bodily function on which emphasis is laid is nourishment, we must attempt to understand the principle of selection. Here the scriptural heritage of the Priestly Code seems decisive: God is served meals of meat and meal, wine and oil, not holocausts of jewelry, not logs of wood, not perpetual fires, not mounds of ore, not fish or insects, and not ejaculations of semen. What sustains man nourishes God. What sustains God nourishes man. God is perceived to be congruent with man. In God's image is man made, and all of the circles of creation are concentric with the inner circle formed of man's creation.

THE ROLE OF THE HUMAN BEING
IN THE PROCESS OF PURITY AND UNCLEANNESS

In the process of purity and uncleanness, what can a human being do? By an act of will, a human being possesses the power of sanctification. He or she declares something holy, for example, an animal for the altar. He or she imparts susceptibility to uncleanness to what is neutral.

What sustains man then is what the system proposes to sanctify. The purpose is that man, renewing life as God perpetually lives in the cult, may be formed and nourished by sustenance that is like God's, and so, in nature, become like supernature. To state the self-evidently valid answer to the urgent question in a simple way: by eating like God man becomes like God. And this "eating-like-God" is done naturally and routinely, in the context and course of ordinary life, with utensils available for any purpose, with food and drink, bed and chair, commonly used in the workaday world. Man at his most domestic and in his most natural context is susceptible to uncleanness and therefore potentially capable also of sanctification. What is unclean can be holy. What is most susceptible to uncleanness also is most available for sanctification. For what does man do within the system? In a profound sense, he does perfectly routine, ordinary actions in a commonplace way. The system is remarkably lacking in specific cultic rituals or rites. The food is not subjected to blessing in order to become susceptible. The utensil is not made to pass through a rite but is susceptible without prayer. The corpus of law lacks mythic expression. The laws are wholly descriptive of how things are, speaking of the natural course of events, not onetime actions. Eating takes place all the time. Utensils are always available for use. All things are neutral, except for human intervention.

What the man does is merely use things, not muttering incantations, blessings, prayers, or other sacred formulas or doing gestures analogous to those of the priests in the cult. He immerses in any suitable, natural pond without a word or deed of ritual concerning the pond or immersion therein. When the cow is burned and the ashes are collected and mixed with suitable water (as required by Numbers 19) not a word (excluding the confirmatory formulas or unnecessary action) is prescribed. When the hands are rinsed two times, the name of Heaven is not invoked, so far as *Yadayim*—the uncleanness of hands—is concerned. *Kelim*—utensils susceptible to uncleanness—speaks of the creation of ordinary objects for domestic use; *Tohorot* (food susceptible to uncleanness) of ordinary olives and grapes, oil and wine for the workaday table. *Ohalot*—on the uncleanness of the corpse in the tent of Numbers 19—which proposes to describe how the economy of nature is restored when the body dies that has contained that which is emitted by the body at death—is remarkably reticent on the subject of funeral rites, of which it knows nothing.

The several sources of uncleanness represent the perfectly natural workings of the body in life or in death. Nothing man does brings uncleanness on himself. Constraint, intention, accident are explicitly excluded from effective causes of the bodily flows that contaminate. The natural character of the sources of uncleanness and the modes of its removal, on the one side, and the highly deliberate and conscious action of man required to subject food and drink, domestic utensils and objects, to the affect of the system, on the other, are complementary. The structure is formed of these two opposite elements: the availability of inert nature and the deliberation of man who forms intention and acts to effect it. So the Pentateuch's and the Mishnah's purity laws are not discrete and unrelated rules but rules that work together. They function as, and form, a whole and complete system: "a regularly interacting and interdependent group of rules forming a unified whole, an organized set of doctrines, ideas, and principles intended to explain the arrangement and working of a systematic whole."[1] And, as we shall see, they participate in making the statement of an encompassing system: Judaism or (as it calls itself) "the Torah."

Chapter 5

Exile and Return

EXILE FROM EDEN/THE RECOVERY
OF PARADISE: THE PARADIGM OF JUDAISM

In monotheism as framed by Judaism, "evil" has no objective existence; all things are relative to God. Sin, in Judaism, stands for rebellion against God, and people sin by exercising their freedom of will in ways contrary to God's will. But that theory of matters does not capture the full narrative power that conveys the story of humanity in exile from God and humanity's task of returning to God. The stories told by Judaisms through the ages rework the theme of exile from God and return to God and to the condition God had in mind in creation, which is to say, paradise.

Rabbinic Judaism, in particular, focuses on the comparison of Israel, viewed as a corporate body, a moral entity, and Adam and Eve. The stories of Adam and Eve and Israel are compared, and that yields the task of Israel, which is, to return to Eden by regaining the Land of Israel. Here is a classic statement of the paradigm, or pattern, that governs:

Genesis Rabbah XIX:IX.1–2

2. A. R. Abbahu in the name of R. Yosé bar Haninah: "It is written, 'But they are like a man [Adam], they have transgressed the covenant' (Hos. 6:7).

  B. "'They are like a man,' specifically, like the first man. [We shall now compare the story of the first man in Eden with the story of Israel in its land.]"

Now the composer identifies an action in regard to Adam with a counterpart action in regard to Israel, in each case matching verse for verse, beginning with Eden and Adam:

  C. "'In the case of the first man, I brought him into the garden of Eden, I commanded him, he violated my commandment, I judged him to be sent away and driven out, but I mourned for him, saying "How . . ."'[which begins the book of Lamentations, hence stands for a lament, but which, as we just saw, also is written with the consonants that also yield, 'Where are you'].

  D. "'I brought him into the garden of Eden,' as it is written, 'And the Lord God took the man and put him into the garden of Eden' (Gen. 2:15).

  E. "'I commanded him,' as it is written, 'And the Lord God commanded . . .' (Gen. 2:16).

  F. "'And he violated my commandment,' as it is written, 'Did you eat from the tree concerning which I commanded you' (Gen. 3:11).

  G. "'I judged him to be sent away,' as it is written, 'And the Lord God sent him from the garden of Eden' (Gen. 3:23).

  H. "'And I judged him to be driven out.' 'And he drove out the man' (Gen. 3:24).

  I. "'But I mourned for him, saying, "How. . ."' 'And he said to him, "Where are you"' (Gen. 3:9), and the word for 'where are you' is written, 'How. . . .'"

Now comes the systematic comparison of Adam and Eden with Israel and the Land of Israel:

  J. "'So too in the case of his descendants, [God continues to speak,] I brought them into the Land of Israel, I commanded them, they violated my commandment, I judged them to be sent out and driven away but I mourned for them, saying, "How. . . ."'

  K. "'I brought them into the Land of Israel.' 'And I brought you into the land of Carmel' (Jer. 2:7).

  L. "'I commanded them.' 'And you, command the children of Israel' (Exod. 27:20). 'Command the children of Israel' (Lev. 24:2).

  M. "'They violated my commandment.' 'And all Israel have violated your Torah' (Dan. 9:11).

  N. "'I judged them to be sent out.' 'Send them away, out of my sight and let them go forth' (Jer. 15:1).

  O. "'. . . and driven away.' 'From my house I shall drive them' (Hos. 9:15).

  P. "'But I mourned for them, saying, "How. . . ."' 'How has the city sat solitary, that was full of people' (Lam. 1:1)."

Israel is like Adam, but Israel is the other, the last Adam, comparable to but ultimately the opposite of the first Adam: God's final solution to the Adam problem. Students of Christianity will find familiar this comparison, for Jesus Christ is represented as the Last Adam. For Judaism, what is important is how sages explicitly compare Adam and Israel, the first man and the last, and show how the story of Adam matches the story of Israel—but with a difference not to be missed.

We recall that, through time, there have been many Judaisms, that is, many Judaic systems that have defined for Jews the way they should live and understand life and their world. These Judaisms do not unfold in a linear pattern, one begetting the next, nor do they stand in a continuous and incremental relationship to one another, one on the ruins of the last. Each Judaism takes shape on its own, identifying a critical question that urgently demands an answer, and presenting a self-evidently valid answer to that question. For justification, all then refer back to a remote and continuous past. None may as a matter of fact trace itself in a unitary and linear path to "Sinai," that is, the moment of God's revelation. But all as a matter of fact recapitulate a single experience, the experience of exile and return, captured in the story that compares Adam and Israel.

This represents a variation on, a reading of, what happened to some Jews between 586 and 450 B.C. It is the actual, historical experience of exile and return, and a very specific set of historical events is interpreted by those two categories.

Exile

In 586 B.C., Judaeans of the land of Israel suffered the destruction of their capital Jerusalem, their government, and their Temple. Some of them—the political classes mainly—were removed from Jerusalem and brought by the victors to their own country, Babylonia, the area around present-day Baghdad in Iraq. For what they called "three generations," these Jews lived in Babylonia.

Return

Their captors, the Babylonians, lost a war with the Iranians under the emperor Cyrus, who came from Persia, in the southwestern corner of Iran. In the process of inheriting the Babylonians, Cyrus and his successor reversed the policy of the former empire and gave permission to go back where they came from ("return home") to diverse groups taken away from their places of origins ("exiled") by the Babylonians. Not much happened in Judea—the rebuilt Temple added up to little, so the prophets of the time complained—until, around 450 B.C., a Jewish viceroy for Jerusalem appointed by the Iranian government took up his duties and rebuilt the Temple of that city. A small number of the Jews who had settled in Babylonia ("the exiles") went with Ezra and participated in the project of resettling the land. Most did not. Whether or not they saw themselves as "exiles," they did not then "return." That, sum and substance, is the experience of exile and return. Exile and return formed the basic experience that defined the basic structure of every Judaism that would come into being. How and why the exile and return became the pattern for Judaic systems to which the actual experience of exile and return was alien tells us much about the power of religion not merely to respond to but to define the world.

The Pentateuchal Construction of Exile and Return

The "exiles" at that time—in the generation of return to the Land of Israel—then drew together whatever stories, laws, prophecies, and other writings that they had inherited out of their past in the land of Israel and produced the Pentateuch, the Five Books of Moses: Genesis, Exodus, Leviticus, Numbers, and Deuteronomy. The Torah (together with the prophetic writings) that reached closure between the destruction of 586 and the reconstruction concluded in 450 preserved the judgment of the generation that first—and for all time—experienced what became the paradigm and pattern, the definitive paradigm that would impart its outline on every Judaic system that appealed to those original scriptures, and, to date, that has encompassed them all.

In particular the Five Books of Moses, promulgated by Ezra in 450 at the climax of the process of restoration of Israel to its Temple and its Land, made the first and authoritative statement of the paradigm that Israel could never take its very existence as permanent and unconditional. That statement, based on the experience that began in 586 and ended in 450, came to expression in such diverse propositions of the Mosaic narrative as these: the land is not a given, but promised; the promise to Israel is conditional; the land is there to be lost and the people there to lose it and to cease to be—all because of what they do or do not do. That document then captured, for perpetual restatement, the original point of resentment. As repeated by diverse Israels in various circumstances, the document would recapitulate for all Israels the original experience, transformed into pattern and paradigm, of alienation and reconciliation. To state the matter in one sentence: the life of an "Israel" was never to be taken for granted but always to be received as a gift.

The Mosaic Torah's interpretation of the diverse experiences of the Israelites after the destruction of the Temple in 586 invoked the categories of exile and return, so constructing as paradigmatic the experience of only a minority of the families of the Jews (most in Babylonia stayed there; many in the Land of Israel never left). Through the formation of the Pentateuch, the Five Books of Moses, the events from 586 to 450 B.C. thus became for all time to come the generative and definitive pattern of meaning. Consequently, whether or not the paradigm fit in with their actual circumstances, groups of Jews in diverse settings have constructed their worlds, that is, shaped their identification, in accord with that one, generative model. They therefore have perpetually rehearsed that human experience imagined by the original authorship of the Torah in the time of Ezra. That pattern accordingly was not merely preserved and perpetuated. It also precipitated and provoked its own replication in age succeeding age.

A Judaism therefore would for time to come represent a reworking of the theme of exile and return, alienation and reconciliation, by an Israel, a group troubled by the resentment of that uncertain past and of that future subject to stipulation. Each Judaism therefore recapitulates the original experience. All Judaisms that have come into being have conformed to that paradigm, and, so long as framers of Judaic systems—ways of life, worldviews, addressed to an Israel subject to particular definition—refer to that same holy Scripture, the Five Books of Moses in particular, all Judaisms that will emerge will focus, in one way or another, on that same generative pattern.

Many maintain that religion originates in or expresses extrinsic considerations. Religions talk about God but mean class interest, for instance. So motives of a psychological or economic or political character are asked to explain religion, but religion is not asked to explain anything. In the language of social science, religion is represented as a dependent variable that is explained by other considerations, not an independent variable that explains other factors. That theory overstates the impact on religion of the society and politics that sustain religion. I argue that in the case of Judaism, religion exercises the power to impart *its* pattern on its social world, the polity of Jews. A particular experience, transformed by a religious system into a paradigm of the life of the social group, became normative—and therefore generative. The Pentateuch then would be read not as a one-time history but as an eternal paradigm that would shape what people saw and anticipated seeing.

Under other circumstances, in other times and places, that experience preserved in Scripture consequently imparted its form and substance on Jewish polities. But these, in point of fact, faced the task of explaining a social world quite different from the one that had generated that original and paradigmatic experience. That is why one may maintain that the social world recapitulates the mythic experience made available by religion, not that religion recapitulates that social and political datum. Religion in the form of Judaism shapes the world, not the world, religion. In our setting and language, religion creates social worlds of meaning and explanation. Specifically, it is the Jews' religion, Judaism, that has formed their world and framed their realities, and not the world of politics, culture, and society that has made their religion.

THE INVENTION OF THE
PARADIGM OF EXILE AND RETURN

Having a Land and losing it but then recovering it created permanent uncertainty. Nothing was any longer a given; all things were a gift, like life itself. Since the formative pattern imposed that perpetual, self-conscious uncertainty, treating the life of the group as conditional and discontinuous, Jews have asked themselves who they are and invented Judaisms to answer that question. Accordingly, on account of the definitive paradigm affecting their group life in various contexts, no circumstances have permitted Jews to take for granted their existence as a group. Looking back on Scripture and its message, Jews have ordinarily treated as special—subject to conditions and therefore uncertain—what (in their view) other groups enjoyed as unconditional and simply given. Why the paradigm renewed itself is clear: this particular view of matters generated expectations that could not be met and hence created resentment—and then provided comfort and hope that made possible coping with that resentment. Promising what could not be delivered, then providing solace for the consequent disappointment, the system at hand precipitated in age succeeding age the very conditions necessary for its own replication.

The original reading of the Jews' existence as exile and return is an experience that is invented, for no one person or group went into "exile" in 586 and also "returned home" "three generations later." An infant in 586 would have reached a very ripe old age to participate in the return to Zion. Surely some did, but most of those who went into exile died in Babylonia, and most of those who returned to Zion were born in Babylonia. Diverse experiences have been sorted out, various persons have been chosen, and the whole has been worked into a system by those who selected history out of happenings and models out of masses of persons. That is why I say "selected." Few Jews after 586 actually experienced what in the aggregate Scripture says happened as the norm of Israel's experience. So, to begin with, Scripture does not record a particular person's experience.

More to the point, if it is not autobiographical writing, giving society at large the personal insight of a singular figure, Scripture also is not an account of a whole nation's story. The reason is that the original exile encompassed mainly the political classes of Jerusalem and some useful populations alongside. Many Jews in the Judea of 586 never left. Those who returned to Zion precipitated acute tension with those who never went into exile. And, as is well known, a great many of those who ended up in Babylonia stayed there. Only a minority of the "exiles" of Babylonia actually went back to Jerusalem, a matter on which the postexilic writings concur. Consequently, the story of exile and return to Zion encompasses what happened to only a few families. These then identified themselves as the family of Abraham, Isaac, and Jacob, who went into exile in Egypt but returned to the Land with the Torah, and their genealogy as the history of Israel. Those families that stayed and those that never came back, had they written the Torah, would have told as normative and paradigmatic a different tale altogether.

The experience of the few that formed the paradigm for Israel beyond the restoration taught lessons of alienation as normative. Let me state with emphasis the lessons people claimed to learn out of the events they had chosen for their history: the life of the group is uncertain, subject to conditions and stipulations. Nothing is set and given; all things are a gift: land and life itself. But what actually did happen in that uncertain world—exile but then restoration—marked the group as special, different, select.

There were other ways of seeing things. Those Jews who did not go into exile, as well as those who did not "come home," had no reason to take the view of matters that characterized the authorship of Scripture. The life of the group need not have appeared more uncertain, more subject to contingency and stipulation, than the life of any other group. The land did not require the vision that imparted to it the enchantment, the personality, that, in Scripture, it received: "The land will vomit you out as it did those who were here before you." And the adventitious circumstance of Iranian imperial policy—a political happenstance—did not have to be recast into return. So nothing in the system of Scripture followed necessarily and logically. Everything was invented: interpreted.

That experience of the uncertainty of the life of the group in the century or so from the destruction of the First Temple of Jerusalem by the Babylonians in 586 to the building of the Second Temple of Jerusalem by the Jews, with Persian permission and sponsorship returned from exile, formed the paradigm. With the promulgation of the "Torah of Moses" under the sponsorship of Ezra, the Persians' viceroy, at ca. 450 B.C., all future Israels would then refer to that formative experience as it had been set down and preserved as the norm for Israel in the mythic terms of that "original" Israel. This was the Israel not of Genesis and Sinai or the Israel at the moment of entry into the promised land, but the "Israel" of the families that recorded the story of exile and the return as the rule and the norm. We find in that minority genealogy—that story of exile and return, alienation and remission, imposed on the received stories of preexilic Israel and adumbrated time and again in the Five Books of Moses and addressed by the framers of that document in their work over all—the paradigmatic statement in which every Judaism, from then to now, found its structure and deep syntax of social existence, the grammar of its intelligible message.

That experience (in theological terms) rehearsed the conditional moral existence of sin and punishment, suffering and atonement and reconciliation, and (in social terms) the uncertain and always conditional national destiny of disintegration and renewal of the group. That moment captured within the Five Books of Moses—that is to say, the judgment of the generation of the return to Zion, led by Ezra, about its extraordinary experience of exile and return—would inform the attitude and viewpoint of all the Israels beyond. In its original statement, the system of the Torah after 586 did not merely describe things that had actually happened, normal events so to speak, but rendered them normative and mythic and turned an experience into a paradigm of experience.

So the paradigm *began* as a paradigm, not as a set of actual events transformed into a normative pattern. And the conclusions generated by the paradigm, it must follow, derived not from reflection on things that happened but from the inner logic of the paradigm—there alone. Moreover, that same paradigm would create expectations that could not be met and would thus renew the resentment captured by the myth of exile while at the same time setting the conditions for remission of resentment, thus resolving the crisis of exile with the promise of return. This self-generating, self-renewing paradigm formed that self-fulfilling prophecy that all Judaisms have offered as the generative tension and critical symbolic structure of their systems.

The paradigm that imparted its imprint on the history of the day did not emerge from, thus was not generated by, the events of the age. First came the system, its worldview and way of life formed whole we know not where or by whom. Then came the selection, by the system, of consequential events and their patterning into systemic propositions. Finally, at a third stage (of indeterminate length of time) came the formation and composition of the canon that would express the logic of the system and state those "events" that the system would select or invent for its own expression.

Since the notion of the election of Israel effected in the covenant is chief among the propositions of the system as the Torah of Moses defined it, we may say that, systemically speaking, Israel—the Israel of the Torah and historical-prophetic books of the sixth and fifth centuries—selected itself. The system created the paradigm of the society that had gone into exile and come back home, and, by the way, the system also cut its own orders, that contract or covenant that certified not election but self-selection.

At the very foundations of the original and generative Judaic paradigm, we find history systemically selected, therefore by definition invented, and not described. That would make slight difference—everyone understands the myth-making power of belief—except for one thing. A particular experience, transformed by a religious system into a paradigm of the life of the social group, has become normative and therefore generative. That particular experience *itself* happened, to begin with, in the minds and imaginations of the authorships of Scripture, not in the concrete life or in the politics and society of Israel in its land and in exile. No one of course imagined that the Temple lay in ruins. But as to its restoration and reconstruction, people clearly differed, as the incessant complaints of the postexilic prophets about the neglected condition of the altar attest. No one denied that some of Israel had stayed home and some had gone into exile. But as to the exclusion of those who had stayed home and not undergone the normative experience of alienation and return, opinion surely differed, since it was only by force that the dissolution of families was effected.

While making ample use of ancient tales, the framers of the Pentateuch as we now have it flourished in Babylonia after 586 and conceived as their systemic teleology the return to Zion and the rebuilding of the Temple—hence the centrality in the wilderness narratives of the tabernacle and its cult. So the setting of the Judaism of the priests imparts to the Scripture of that first setting its ultimate meaning: response to historical disaster followed by (to the Jews' mind) unprecedented triumph. Their vision is characterized as follows:

> In the priests' narrative the chosen people are last seen as pilgrims moving through alien land toward a goal to be fulfilled in another time and place, and this is the vision, drawn from the ancient story of their past, that the priests now hold out to the scattered sons and daughters of old Israel. They too are exiles encamped for a time in an alien land, and they too must focus their hopes on the promise ahead. Like the Israelites in the Sinai wilderness, they must avoid setting roots in the land through which they pass, for Dias-

pora is not to become their permanent condition, and regulations must be adopted to facilitate this. They must resist assimilation into the world into which they are now dispersed, because hope and heart and fundamental identity lay in the future. Thus, the priestly document not only affirms Yahweh's continuing authority and action in the lives of his people but offers them a pattern for life that will ensure them a distinct identity.[2]

The net effect of the Pentateuchal vision of Israel, that is, its worldview seen in the aggregate, lays stress on the separateness and the holiness of Israel, all the while pointing to dangers of pollution by the other, the outsider. The way of life, with its stress on distinguishing traits of an Israel distinct from and threatened by the outsider, corresponds. The fate of the nation, moreover, depends on the loyalty of the people in their everyday lives, to the requirements of the covenant with God, so history forms the barometer of the health of the nation. In these ways the several segments of the earlier traditions of Israel were so drawn together as to make the point peculiarly pertinent to Israel in exile. It follows that the original Judaic system, the one set forth by the Pentateuch, answered the urgent issue of exile with the self-evident response of return. The question was not to be avoided; the answer not to be doubted. The center of the system, then, lay in the covenant, the contract that told Israel the rules that would govern: Keep these rules and you will not again suffer as you have suffered. Violate them and you will. At the heart of the covenant was the call for Israel to form a kingdom of priests and a holy people.

THE PERSISTENCE OF THE PARADIGM

Now, we wonder why the system of exile and return persisted as paradigmatic and why its structure proved definitive long after the political facts had shifted dramatically; indeed, had ceased to pertain at all. The original Judaism captured by the Pentateuch answered the question of exile and restoration. With the continuing authority of the Torah in Israel, the experience to which it originally constituted a profound and systematic response was recapitulated, age after age, through the reading and authoritative exegesis of the original Scripture that preserved and portrayed it: "Your descendants will be aliens living in a land that is not theirs . . . but I will punish that nation whose slaves they are, and after that they shall come out with great possessions" (Gen. 15:13–14). The long-term reason for the persistence of the priests' Judaism as the self-evidently valid explanation of Israel's life derives from two facts.

First, the Scriptures themselves retained their authority. But that begs the question. For the reason does not account for the continuing assent to and acknowledgment as authoritative of those Scriptures.

Second, the Judaic system devised in the Pentateuch by the Temple priests retained its power of self-evidence because that system in its basic structure addressed *but also created* a continuing and chronic social fact of Israel's life. It represents a self-sustaining system, which solves the very problem that to begin with it precipitates: a self-fulfilling prophecy.

To explain: So long as the people perceived the world in such a way as to make urgent the question that Scripture framed and compellingly answered, Scripture enjoyed that power of persuasion beyond all need for argument that imparted to it the self-evident status of God's revealed will to Israel. And that interval lasted for a very long time. But Scripture gained its own authority, independent of the circumstance of society. The priests' paradigm therefore imposed itself even in situations in which its fundamental premises hardly pertained. Accordingly, when the world imposed on Jewry questions of a different order, then Jews would go in search of more answers—an additional Torah (hence the formation of the Judaism of the dual Torah)—and even different answers (hence the formation, in modern times, of Judaic systems of a different character altogether). But even then a great many Jews continued to envision the world through that original perspective created in the aftermath of destruction and restoration, that is, to see the world as a gift instead of a given, themselves as chosen for a life of special suffering but also special reward.

Two reasons account for the perennial power of the priests' system and perspective. One is that the generative tension, precipitated by the interpretation of the Jews' life as exile and return, that had formed the critical center of the Torah of Moses persisted. Therefore the urgent question answered by the Torah retained its original character and definition, and the self-evidently valid answer—read in the synagogue every Sabbath morning, as well as on Monday and on Thursday—retained its relevance. With the persistent problem renewing that same resentment generation after generation, the product of a memory of loss and restoration—joined to the recognition in the here and now of the danger of a further loss—the priests' authoritative answer would not lose its power to persist and to persuade. But the other is that people saw what was not always there, because through the Torah of Moses they were taught to.

That is why the second of the two reasons—the one explaining the long-term power of the Judaic system of the priests to shape the worldview and way of life of the Israel addressed by that Judaism—is the more important: the question answered by the Five Books of Moses persisted at the center of the national life and remained, if chronic, also urgent. The answer provided by the Pentateuch therefore retained its self-evident importance. The question persisted, to be sure, because Scripture kept reminding people to ask that question, to see the world as the world was described in Scripture's mythic terms, out of the perception of the experience of exile and return. Thus to those troubled by the question of exile and return—that is, the chronic allegation that Israel's group life did not constitute a given but formed a gift accorded on conditions and stipulations—the answer enjoyed the status of (mere) fact.

The human condition takes on heightened intensity when God cares about what you eat for lunch, on the one side, but will reward you for having a boiled egg, on the other. For a small, uncertain people, captured by a vision of distant horizons behind and before, who were a mere speck on the crowded plain of humanity, such a message became a powerful and immediate map of meaning. Israel's death and resurrection—as the Torah portrayed matters—therefore left nothing as it had been and changed everything for all time. But the matter—central to the history of Judaism—demands yet another angle of analysis. We have to ask what was at stake and so penetrate into the deepest layers of the structure to state the issues at their most abstract and general. For the sacred persistence in the end rested on judgments found self-evidently valid in circumstances remote from the original world subject to those judgments.

The problems addressed and solved by the Judaism of the Five Books of Moses remained chronic long after the period of its formation, from the seventh century onward down to its closure in the time of Ezra and Nehemiah. The Priestly Code states a powerful answer to a pressing and urgent question. Since that question would remain a perplexity continuing to trouble Israelites for a long time, it is not surprising that the categorical structure of the priestly answer to it, so profound and fundamental in its character, should for its part have continued to define systems that would attract and impress people.

We have once more to locate ourselves in the time of closure of the Mosaic Scriptures, that is, in the late sixth and fifth centuries B.C., and to specify the critical tensions of that period. Once we have seen the character of these tensions, without needing much exposition we shall realize that the same tensions persisted and confronted the thinkers whose reflection led to the conclusion, in resolution of those ongoing points of dissonance, that the Temple's holiness enveloped and surrounded Israel's Land and demarcated its people too. What marks ancient Israel as distinctive is its preoccupation with defining itself.

The reason for that obsession—that is to say, the persistence of the exegesis of the everyday as a sequence of acts of sanctification—was the Torah's encapsulation, as normative and recurrent, of the experience of the loss and recovery of the land and of political sovereignty. Israel, because of its (in its mind) amazing experience, had attained a self-consciousness that continuous existence in a single place under a long-term government denied. There was nothing given, nothing to be merely celebrated or at least taken for granted, in the life of a nation that had ceased to be a nation on its own land and then once more had regained that (once-normal, now abnormal) condition. Judaism took shape as the system that accounted for the death and resurrection of Israel, the Jewish people, and pointed for the source of renewed life toward sanctification now and salvation at the end of time.

The Torah of Moses created the world that it revealed, which in no way corresponded with the world either out of which it emerged or to which, for the following centuries, it spoke. The paradigm persisted because the condition for the continuing power of the Judaic system of the Torah not only required the recapitulation of resentment but also produced what was required. That requirement was the constant renewal of the resentment precipitated and provoked by the discrepancy to begin with, present in the Torah's own system. The Torah of Moses therefore did more than recapitulate resentment. In age succeeding age, the Torah generated the resentment that powered the system.

That is why I argued earlier that religion imparts its pattern on the social world and polity of Jews. What the record of 586 *says* happened and what that same record shows happened do not correspond. What really happened, the biblical narrative makes explicit, is that the Babylonians destroyed Jerusalem and exiled its political classes as well as its skilled workers. The scriptural record is equally explicit that large numbers of Jews remained in the land and continued to live out their lives there. The system of the Torah then not only presented the paradigm of Israel as the covenanted people, whose heightened social reality derived from the experience of exile and return. The system of the Torah also invented that paradigm, treating the experience of those for whom it spoke—those who had gone into exile and who had come back to the land—as normative, when, descriptively speaking, it was not even normal. The reason is that since sizable numbers of Jews did not go into exile, the experience of exile and restoration—presented as normative and paradigmatic in the Torah and in the historical-prophetic literature redacted in the sixth and fifth centuries—simply did not describe what happened to them. And, it goes without saying, it also had no bearing on those other Jews who did not leave Babylonia and return to the land. Consequently, events—mere facts of history as such, let alone facts of history as interpreted—scarcely can be said to have generated the paradigm at hand.

The system selected happenings, treated them as consequential events, ranked the selected events in order of priority, then interpreted those important events as a pattern that embodied a larger system: a worldview, a way of life, addressed to its particular Israel. So the order of the systemic process is (1) system, then (2) selection of things that have happened as events, and finally (3) the formation of a pattern that is called variously either "history" or "theology." There is no material difference.

Chapter 6

Return to Eden: The Sabbath and Sacred Time

Thus the heavens and the earth were finished and all the host of them. And on the seventh day God finished his work that he had done, and he rested on the seventh day from all his work that he had done. So God blessed the seventh day and sanctified it, because on it God rested from all his work that he had done in Creation.

Genesis 2:1–3

RESTORING EDEN ON THE SEVENTH DAY: THE SABBATH

The Sabbath embodies Judaism's model of sacred time—the restoration of that perfect moment of repose that God sanctified in creating Eden. God's act of sanctification of the seventh day defines for Judaism the meaning of sacred time. Eden then stands for not only a location but especially an occasion, a condition that matches a moment. That is the account of matters in the Ten Commandments: "Remember the Sabbath day to keep it holy . . . for in six days the Lord made heaven and earth, the sea and all that is in them, and rested on the seventh day; therefore the Lord blessed the Sabbath day and sanctified it" (Exod. 20:8, 11). Keeping the Sabbath day holy means replicating the condition of Eden: repose in God's image, after God's likeness, on the seventh day of Creation.

Sacred time in Judaism marks the restoration of the condition of paradise, or Eden. By "Eden" Scripture means that place whole and at rest that God sanctified; "Eden" stands for Creation in perfect repose. In Judaism, realized by its normative law or Halakhah, Eden stands mainly for not a particular place but nature in a defined condition, at a particular moment. That is Creation in Sabbath repose, sanctified. Thus a place in repose at the climax of Creation, at sunset at the start of

67

the seventh day, whole and at rest, embodies, realizes Eden. The Halakhah means to systematize the condition of Eden, to define Eden in its normative traits, and also to localize Eden within the holy people, Israel. So, on the one hand, that place is or ought to be the Land of Israel. Scripture provides an ample basis for identifying with the Land of Israel that place perfected on the Sabbath. It is the Land of Israel, enchanted as it is, that, in the Written Torah's explicit account of matters, claims the right to repose on the seventh day and in the seventh year of the septennial cycle. But, as we shall see, it is on the other hand the location of Israel wherever that may be at the advent of sunset on the eve of the seventh day of the week of Creation. We begin with enlandised Israel, that is, Israel the Land of Israel, at the moment at which, then and there, Eden was made real: when Israel entered into the Land at the moment of perfection. That moment recovered, Eden is restored—the correct starting point, therefore, for a theology of the Halakhah that claims the whole holds together as a systematically restorationist theology.

SABBATH FOR THE LAND OF ISRAEL: *SHEBI'IT*, THE HALAKHAH OF THE SEVENTH YEAR

The position just described is the explicit position of the Halakhah of *Shebi'it*, which elaborates the Written Torah's commandment, at Leviticus 25:2–7:

> When you enter the land that I am giving you, the land shall observe a Sabbath of the Lord. Six years you may sow your field and six years you may prune your vineyard and gather in the yield. But in the seventh year the land shall have a Sabbath of complete rest, a Sabbath of the Lord; you shall not sow your field or prune your vineyard. You shall not reap the aftergrowth of your harvest or gather the grapes of your untrimmed vines; it shall be a year of complete rest for the land. But you may eat whatever the land during its Sabbath will produce—you, your male and female slaves, the hired-hand and bound laborers who live with you, and your cattle and the beasts in your land may eat all its yield.

Sages thus find in Scripture the explicit correlation of the advent of the Sabbath and the condition of the Land, meaning, "the land that I am giving you," which is to say, the Land of Israel. After six years of Creation, the Land is owed a Sabbath, as much as is Man. So the Holy Land is accorded a Sabbath, a restoration of the condition of Eden. A second, correlative commandment, at Deuteronomy 15:1–3, is treated as well: "Every seventh year you shall practice remission of debts. This shall be the nature of the remission: every creditor shall remit the due that he claims from his neighbor; he shall not dun his neighbor or kinsman, for the remission proclaimed is of the Lord. You may dun the foreigner, but you must remit whatever is due you from your kinsmen." This is another way of relinquishing private domain and sharing ownership for the sacred time.

What links the Sabbatical Year to Eden's restoration? The reason is clear: the Sabbatical Year recovers that perfect time of Eden when the world was at rest, all things in place. Before the rebellion, man did not have to labor on the land; he picked and ate his meals freely. And, in the nature of things, everything belonged to everybody; private ownership in response to individual labor did not exist, because man did not have to work anyhow. These then represent the Halakhah's provisions for the Seventh Year. Reverting to that perfect time, the Torah maintains that the land will provide adequate food for everyone, including the flocks and herds, even—or especially—if people do not work the land. But that is on condition that all claim of ownership lapses; the food is left in the fields, to be picked by anyone who wishes, but it may not be hoarded by the landowner in particular. Alan J. Avery-Peck states this matter as follows:

> Scripture thus understands the Sabbatical year to represent a return to a perfected order of reality, in which all share equally in the bounty of a holy land that yields its food without human labor. The Sabbatical year provides a model through which, once every seven years, Israelites living in the here-and-now may enjoy the perfected order in which God always intended the world to exist and toward which, in the Israelite world view, history indeed is moving. . . . The release of debts accomplishes for Israelites' economic relationships just what the agricultural Sabbatical accomplishes for the relationship between the people and the land. Eradicating debt allows the Israelite economy to return to the state of equilibrium that existed at the time of Creation, when all shared equally in the bounty of the Land.
> (*Yerushalmi Shebi'it* [Chicago: University of Chicago Press, 1986], 3)

The Priestly Code expresses that same concept when it arranges for the return of inherited property at the Jubilee Year to the original family ownership:

> You shall count off seven weeks of years, so that the period of seven weeks of years gives you a total of forty-nine years. . . . You shall proclaim release throughout the land for all its inhabitants. It shall be a jubilee for you; each of you shall return to his holding and each of you shall return to his family.
> (Lev. 25:8–10)

The Jubilee Year is observed as is the Sabbatical Year, meaning that for two successive years the land is not to be worked. The Halakhah we shall examine in due course will establish that when land is sold, it is for the span of time remaining to the next Jubilee Year. That then marks the reordering of landholding to its original pattern, when Israel inherited the land to begin with and commenced to enjoy its produce.

Just as the Sabbath commemorates the completion of Creation, the perfection of world order, so does the Sabbatical Year. So too, the Jubilee Year brings about the restoration of real property to the original division. In both instances, Israelites so act as to indicate they are not absolute owners of the Land, which belongs to God and which is divided in the manner that God arranged in perpetuity. Avery-Peck states the matter in the following way:

On the Sabbath of Creation, during the Sabbatical year, and in the Jubilee year, diverse aspects of Israelite life are to return to the way that they were at the time of Creation. Israelites thus acknowledge that, in the beginning, God created a perfect world, and they assure that the world of the here-and-now does not overly shift from its perfect character. By providing opportunities for Israelites to model their contemporary existence upon a perfected order of things, these commemorations further prepare the people for messianic times, when, under God's rule, the world will permanently revert to the ideal character of the time of Creation.

(*Yerushalmi Shebi'it*, 4)

Here we find the Halakhic counterpart to the restorationist theology that the Oral Torah sets forth in the Aggadah. Israel matches Adam, the Land of Israel, and Eden, and, we now see, the Sabbatical Year commemorates the perfection of Creation and replicates it. (Later in this chapter we shall see that the same conception of relinquishing ownership of one's real property operates to facilitate everyday activities on the Sabbath.)

The comparison of Eden and the Land, as well as Adam's entry into Eden and Israel's entry into the Land, is made explicit. The Sabbatical Year takes effect at the moment of Israel's entry into the Land, counterpart to Adam's and Eve's entering Eden on the sixth day of Creation. That repeated point of insistence then treats the moment of the entry into the Land as the counterpart to the moment of repose, of perfection at rest, of Creation. Observing the commandments of the Sabbatical Year marks Israel's effort at keeping the Land like Eden: six days of Creation, one day of rest. And so too here:

> *Sifra* CCXLV:I.2
>   A. "When you come [into the land which I give you, the land shall keep a Sabbath to the Lord]":
>   B. Might one suppose that the sabbatical year was to take effect once they had reached Transjordan?
>   C. Scripture says, "into the land."
>   D. It is that particular land.

Now comes the key point: the Sabbatical Year takes effect only when Israel enters the Land, which is to say, Israel's entry into the Land marks the counterpart to the beginning of the Creation of Eden. But a further point will register in a moment. It is when Eden/the Land enters into stasis, the families receiving each its share in the Land, that the process of the formation of the new Eden comes to its climax; then each Israelite bears responsibility for his share of the Land. That is when the Land has reached that state of order and permanence that corresponds to Eden at sunset on the sixth day:

>   E. Might one suppose that the sabbatical year was to take effect once they had reached Ammon and Moab?
>   F. Scripture says, "which I give you,"
>   G. and not to Ammon and Moab.
>   H. And on what basis do you maintain that when they had con-

quered the land but not divided it, divided it among familiars
but not among fathers' houses so that each individual does not
yet recognize his share—

I. might one suppose that they should be responsible to observe
the sabbatical year?

J. Scripture says, "[Six years you shall sow] your field,"

K. meaning, each one should recognize his own field.

L. " . . . your vineyard":

M. meaning, each one should recognize his own vineyard.

N. You turn out to rule:

O. Once the Israelites had crossed the Jordan, they incurred liability to separate dough-offering and to observe the prohibition
against eating the fruit of fruit trees for the first three years after
planting and the prohibition against eating produce of the new
growing season prior to the waving of the sheaf of new grain
[that is, on the fifteenth of Nisan].

P. When the sixteenth of Nisan came, they incurred liability to
wave the sheaf of new grain.

Q. With the passage of fifty days from then they incurred the liability to the offering of the Two Loaves.

R. At the fourteenth year they became liable for the separation of
tithes.

The Sabbatical takes over only when the Israelite farmers have asserted their ownership of the land and its crops. Then the process of counting the years begins.

S. They began to count the years of the sabbatical cycle, and in the
twenty-first year after entry into the land, they observed the sabbatical year.

T. In the sixty-fourth year they observed the first Jubilee [*t. Menahot* 6:20].

So much for the systematic exploration of the enlandisement of Eden in the Land
of Israel—the formulation of Israel's relationship with God through Israel's use
of the Land of Israel and its produce, in a way analogous to Adam's use of Eden—
and abuse thereof.

The counterpart in the matter of the remission of debts works out the conception that all Israelites by right share in the Land and its gifts, and if they have
fallen into debt, they have been denied their share; that imbalance is righted every
seven years. God therefore relates to Israel through the Land and the arrangements that he imposes on the Land. In that context God relates to the Land in
response to Israel's residence thereon. But God relates to the Land in a direct way,
providing for the Land, as he provides for Israel, the sanctifying moment of the
Sabbath. So a web of relationships, direct and indirect, hold together God, Land,
and Israel. That is for the here and now, all the more so for the world to come.
And if that is how God relates to Israel, Israel relates to God in one way above
all: by exercising ways that show love for God and acceptance of God's dominion the power of free will that God has given man.

SABBATH FOR THE PEOPLE OF ISRAEL:
SHABBAT-ERUBIN, THE HALAKHAH OF THE
ISRAELITE HOUSEHOLD ON THE SEVENTH DAY

The Land in the seventh year compares with the Israelite household on the seventh day. The Israelite household at rest on the Sabbath day recapitulates the celebration of God at the moment of the conclusion and perfection of Creation. Then the Israelite household is sanctified: separated from the profane world and distinguished as God's domain. With all things in place and in order, at the sunset that marks the advent of the seventh day, the rest that marks the perfection of Creation descends. Like God at the celebration of Creation, now man achieves perfect, appropriate rest. That takes place when time, circumstance, but—as we shall see—demarcated space too, come together. The advent of the Sabbath marks the time; the household, the space; and the conduct of home and family life, the circumstance.

Why the stress on location in private domain for Sabbath sanctification? The reason is found at Exodus 16:29–30, verses that link the act of eating with the locus of residence for the Sabbath: "See! The Lord has given you the Sabbath, therefore on the sixth day he gives you bread for two days; remain every man of you in his place; let no man go out of his place on the seventh day. So the people rested on the seventh day." The juxtaposition of a double supply of bread for Friday and Saturday and remaining in place leaves no doubt that (1) one stays home, on the one side, and (2) home is where one eats, on the other. The issue of residence therefore becomes critical to an account of how Israel meets God within the walls of the Israelite household, because on the Sabbath one is to remain in place, that is, within the limits of private domain. But the transformation of private domain—what is private, what is shared—on the Sabbath forms the generative problematic of the Halakhah—that, and the meaning of "eating in his place." Private domain defines the critical focus of the Halakhah. To effect that shift in concern, bringing people within the walls of the courtyards and alleyways in which they are imagined to reside, realizes the intent of the Written Torah when it says, "Remain every man of you in his place." Consequently, activities in public domain are severely circumscribed by the prohibition against carrying therein, as well as by the one that prohibits unlimited travel.

At the heart of matters, profound reflection on the meaning of what is private and what is shared takes place. The tractate in detail therefore addresses the problem of how Israelites on the Sabbath move about from one private domain to another, so arranging matters that shared and common ownership of private domain secures for all parties the right to carry in the space held in common. One answer is that since one resides where one eats, people may prepare a symbolic, or fictive, meal, the right to which is shared by all. All householders thereby commingle their property rights so that they will then form of various private domains a single common estate. Another answer is to establish a boundary around the entire set of private domains, one that, like a wall, forms of them all a single property. The medium by which the one or the other procedure is carried out is called an *'erub*, a medium of commingling, thus referring to either the symbolic, shared meal or the equally fictive demarcation line, as the case requires: a meal of commingling, or a boundary marker for commingling ownership of private property. In play throughout the exposition of the Halakhah of *Erubin* are these propositions that have already come to full exposition in the Halakhah of *Shabbat*: (1) one may not transport objects from private to public domain, but (2) there are types of domain that are neither the one nor the other, specifically, the courtyard linking a number of private properties and the alleyway onto which a number of courtyards open up.

Sages' thinking about the Sabbath invokes in the formation of the normative law defining the matter the model of the first Sabbath, the one of Eden. The two paramount points of concern—(1) the systematic definition of private domain, where ordinary activity is permitted, and (2) the rather particular definition of what constitutes a prohibited act of labor on the Sabbath—both precipitate deep thought. They animate the handful of principles brought to concrete realization in the two tractates. So we ask two questions: (1) What does it mean to remain "in his place," and (2) what constitutes the theory of forbidden activity, the principles that shape the innumerable rules and facts of the prohibition? Accordingly, we must ask a basic question: What is it about the Sabbath of Creation that captures sages' attention?

The Sabbatical Year, *Shebi'it*, supplies the key. *Erubin*, with its sustained exercise of thought on the commingling of ownership of private property for the purpose of Sabbath observance and on the commingling of meals to signify shared ownership, accomplishes for Israel's Sabbath what *Shebi'it* achieves for the Land's. On the Sabbath inaugurated by the Sabbatical Year, the Land, so far as it is otherwise private property, no longer is possessed exclusively by the householder. So too, the produce of the Land consequently belongs to everybody. It follows that the Halakhah of *Erubin* realizes for the ordinary Sabbath of Israel the very same principles that are embodied in the Halakhah of *Shebi'it*. That Halakhah defines the Sabbath of the Land in exactly the same terms: the Land is now no longer private, and the Land's produce belongs to everybody. The Sabbath that the Land enjoys marks the advent of shared ownership of the Land and its fruit. Sharing is so total that hoarding is explicitly forbidden, and what has been hoarded has now to be removed from the household and moved to public domain, where anyone may come and take it.

Here we find the Sabbath of Creation overspreading the Sabbath of the Land, as the Priestly Code at Genesis 1 and at Leviticus 25:2–7, cited earlier, define matters. The Sabbatical Year bears the message that, on the Sabbath, established arrangements as to ownership and possession are set aside and a different conception of private property takes over. What on ordinary days is deemed to belong to the householder and to be subject to his exclusive will on the Sabbath falls into a more complex web of possession. The householder continues to use his property but not as a sole proprietor does. The sole proprietor exercises his will without restraint; he alone dictates what is to be done with what he owns. But that is not the situation of the Israelite householder on the Sabbath. He gives up exclusive access thereto and gains in exchange rights of access to other peoples' property. Private property is commingled; everybody shares in everybody's. The result is that private property takes on a new meaning, different from the secular one. So far as the householder proposes to use his private property, he must share it with others, who do the same for him. To own then is to abridge ownership in favor of commingling rights thereto; to possess is to share. And that explains why the produce of the Land belongs to everyone as well, a corollary to the fundamental postulate of the Sabbath of the Land.

What qualities of Eden then impress sages? With the Halakhah as the vast corpus of facts, we focus on two matters: (1) time and space, (2) time and activity. How is space demarcated at the specified time; how is activity classified at that same time? The former works itself out in a discussion of where people may move on the Sabbath and how they may conduct themselves (carry things as they move). The latter finds its definition in the model of labor that is prohibited. With Eden as the model and the metaphor, we take a simple sighting on the matter. First, Adam and Eve are free to move in Eden where they wish, possessing all they contemplate. God has given it to them to enjoy. If Eden then belongs to God, he freely shares ownership with Adam and Eve. And—all the more so—the produce of Eden is ownerless. With the well-known exception, all the fruit is theirs for the taking. The Sabbatical Year recovers that perfect time of Eden when the world was at rest, all things in place. Before the rebellion, man did not have to labor on the land; he picked and ate his meals freely. And, in the nature of things, everything belonged to everybody; private ownership in response to individual labor did not exist, because man did not have to work anyhow. Reverting to that perfect time, the Torah maintains that the land will provide adequate food for everyone, including the flocks and herds, even if people do not work the land. But that is on condition that all claim of ownership lapses; the food is left in the fields, to be picked by anyone who wishes, but it may not be hoarded by the landowner in particular.

It is in this context that we read the Halakhah of *Shabbat-Erubin*, with special reference to the division of the world into private and public domain, the former the realm of permitted activity on the Sabbath, the latter not. If we may deal with an *'erub* fence or an *'erub* meal, how are we to interpret what is at stake in these matters? It in both instances is to render private domain public through the sharing of ownership. The *'erub* fence for its part renders public domain private, but only in the same sense that private domain owned by diverse owners is shared, ownership being commingled. The *'erub* fence signals the formation for purposes of the sanctification of time of private domain—but with the ownership commingled. So what is "private" about "private domain" is different on the Sabbath from what it is in secular time. By definition, for property to be private in the setting of the Sabbath, it must be shared among householders. On the Sabbath, domain that is totally private, its ownership not commingled for the occasion, becomes a prison, the householder being unable to conduct himself in the normal manner in the courtyard beyond his door, let alone in other courtyards in the same alleyway, or in other alleyways that debauch onto the same street. And the Halakhah, as we have seen, makes provision for those—whether Israelite or gentile—who do not offer their proprietorship of their households for commingling for the Sabbath.

What happens, therefore, through the 'erub fence or 'erub meal is the redefinition of proprietorship: what is private is no longer personal, and no one totally owns what is his, but then everyone (who wishes to participate, himself and his household together) owns a share everywhere. So much for the "in his place" part of "each man in his place." His place constitutes an area where ordinary life goes on, but it is no longer "his" in the way in which the land is subject to his will and activity in ordinary time. If constructing a fence serves to signify joint ownership of the village, now turned into private domain, or constructing the gateway, of the alleyway and its courtyards, what about the meal? The 'erub meal signifies the shared character of what is eaten. It is food that belongs to all who wish to share it. But it is the provision of a personal meal, also, that allows an individual to designate for himself a place of Sabbath residence other than the household to which he belongs.

So the Sabbath loosens bonds, those of the householder to his property, those of the individual to the household. It forms communities, the householders of a courtyard into a community of shared ownership of the entire courtyard, the individual into a community other than that formed by the household to which he belongs—now the community of disciples of a given sage, the community of a family other than that in residence in the household, to use two of the examples common in the Halakhah. Just as the Sabbath redefines ownership of the Land and its produce, turning all Israelites into a single social entity, "all Israel," which, all together, possesses the Land in common ownership, so the Sabbath redefines the social relationships of the household, allowing persons to separate themselves from the residence of the household and designate some other, some personal, point of residence instead.

The main point of the law of private domain in *Shabbat* and *Erubin* seen in the model of *Shebi'it* then is to redefine the meaning of "private domain," where each man is to remain in "his" place. The law aims to define the meaning of "his," and to remove the ownership of the land and its produce from the domain of a householder, rendering ownership public and collective. Taking as our model *Shebi'it*, we note that in the year that is a Sabbath, the land is held to be owned by nobody and everybody, and the produce of the Land belongs to everyone and no one, so that one may take and eat but thank only God. It is no one's, so all may take; it is everyone's, so everyone may eat, and God alone is to be acknowledged. Since, on the Sabbath, people are supposed to remain within their own domain, the counterpart to *Shebi'it* will provide for the sharing of ownership, thus for extending the meaning of "private domain" to encompass all the partners in a shared locus. "Private domain," his place, now bears a quite different meaning from the one that pertains in profane time. The Sabbath recapitulates the condition of Eden, when Adam and Eve could go where they wished and eat what they wanted, masters of all they contemplated, along with God. Israel on the Sabbath in the Land, like Adam on the Sabbath of Eden that celebrates Creation, shares private domain and its produce.

SIX DAYS OF WORK AND THE SABBATH OF REPOSE

Israel on the Sabbath in the Land, like God on the Sabbath of Eden rests from the labor of Creation. And that brings us to the question, What about that other principle of the Sabbath, the one set forth by the Halakhah of tractate *Shabbat*? The richly detailed Halakhah of *Shabbat* defines the matter in a prolix, yet simple way. It is to be stated with emphasis: on the Sabbath it is prohibited deliberately to carry out in a normal way a completed act of constructive labor, one that produces enduring results, one that carries out one's entire intention: the whole of what one planned, one has accomplished, in exactly the proper manner. That definition takes into account the shank of the Halakhah of *Shabbat* as set forth in the Mishnah tractate, and the amplification and extension of matters in the Tosefta and the two Talmuds in no way revise the basic principles. Here there is a curious, if obvious, fact: it is not an act of labor that itself is prohibited (as the Ten Commandments in Exodus and Deuteronomy would have it), but an act of labor of a very particular definition.

What is striking is that no prohibition impedes performing an act of labor in an other-than-normal way. In theory, one may go out into the fields and plow, if he does so in some odd manner. He may build an entire house, so long as it collapses promptly. The issue of activity on the Sabbath therefore is removed from the obvious context of work, conventionally defined. Now the activity that is forbidden is of a very particular sort, modeled in its indicative traits after a quite specific paradigm. A person is not forbidden to carry out an act of destruction, or an act of labor that produces no lasting consequences. He may start an act of labor if he does not complete it. He may accomplish an act of labor in some extraordinary manner. None of these acts of labor are forbidden, even though, done properly and with consequence, they represent massive violations of the Halakhah. Nor is part of an act of labor that is not brought to conclusion prohibited. Nor is it forbidden to perform part of an act of labor in partnership with another person who carries out the other requisite part. Nor does one incur culpability for performing an act of labor in several distinct parts, for example, over a protracted, differentiated period of time. A person may not willingly carry out the entirety of an act of constructive labor, start to finish. The issue is not why not, since we know the answer: God has said not to do so. The question is, Whence the particular definition at hand?

Clearly, a definition of the act of labor that is prohibited on the Sabbath has taken over and recast the commonsense meaning of the commandment not to labor on the Sabbath. For considerations enter that recast matters from an absolute to a relative definition. One may tie a knot—but not one that stands.

One may carry a package, but not in the usual manner. One may build a wall, only if it falls down. And, as I have stressed, one may do pretty much anything without penalty—if he did not intend matters as they actually happened. The metaphor of God in Eden, as sages have reflected on the story of Creation, yields the governing principles that define forbidden labor. What God did in the six days of Creation provides the model.

Let us review the main principles item by item. They involve the three preconditions. The act must fully carry out the intention of the actor, as Creation carried out God's intention. The act of labor must be carried out by a single actor, as God acted alone in creating the world. An act of labor is the like of one that is required in the building and maintenance of God's residence in this world, the tabernacle. The act of labor prohibited on the Sabbath involves two considerations. The act must be done in the ordinary way, just as Scripture's account leaves no doubt that God accomplished Creation in the manner in which he accomplished his goals from Creation onward, by an act of speech. And, weightier still, the forbidden act of labor is one that produces enduring consequences. God did not create only to destroy, but he created the enduring world. And it goes without saying, Creation yielded the obvious consequences that the act was completely done in all ways, as God himself declared. The act was one of consequence, involving what was not negligible but what man and God alike deemed to make a difference. Sages would claim, therefore, that the activity that must cease on the Sabbath finds its definition in the model of those actions that God carried out in making the world.

That such a mode of thought is more than a mere surmise, based on the congruence of the principles by which labor forbidden on the Sabbath spin themselves out of the Creation story, emerges when we recall a striking statement. It is the one that finds the definition of forbidden labor in those activities required for the construction and maintenance of the tabernacle, which is to say, God's residence on earth. The best statement, predictably, is the Talmud of Babylonia *Shabbat* 39a:

> People are liable only for classifications of labor the like of which was done in the tabernacle. They sowed, so you are not to sow. They harvested, so you are not to harvest. They lifted up the boards from the ground to the wagon, so you are not to lift them in from public to private domain. They lowered boards from the wagon to the ground, so you must not carry anything from private to public domain. They transported boards from wagon to wagon, so you must not carry from one private domain to another.

Sages found in the classifications of labor that pertain the analogy of how, in theory, the tabernacle was maintained. In the tabernacle these activities are permitted, even on the Sabbath. In God's house, the priests and Levites must do for God what they cannot do for themselves—and the identification of acts of labor forbidden on the Sabbath follows.

The details of the Halakhah then emerge out of a process in which two distinct sources contribute. One is the model of the tabernacle. What man may do for God's house he may not do for his own—God is always God; the Israelite aspires only to be "like God," to imitate God, and that is a different thing. The other is the model of the Creation of the world and of Eden. Hence to act like God on the Sabbath, the Israelite rests; he does not do what God did in Creation. The former source supplies generative metaphors, the like of which may not be done; thus acts like sowing, like harvesting, like lifting boards from public to private domain, and the like, are forbidden. The latter source supplies the generative principles, the abstract definitions involving the qualities of perfection and causation: intentionality, completion, the normality of the conduct of the action, and the like. The mode of analogical thinking governs, but, as we see, a double metaphor pertains, the metaphor of God's activity in Creation, the metaphor of the priests' and Levites' activity in the tabernacle. Creation yields those large principles that we have identified: the traits of an act of labor for God in Creation define the prohibited conditions of an act of labor on the Sabbath. By appeal to those two metaphors, we can account for every detail of the Halakhah.

What then takes place inside the walls of the Israelite household when time takes over space and revises the conduct of ordinary affairs? Israel goes home to Eden. How best to make the statement that the Land is Israel's Eden, that Israel imitates God by keeping the Sabbath—meaning, not doing the things that God did in creating the world but the things God ceased to do on the Sabbath—and that to restore its Eden, Israel must sustain its life—nourish itself—where it belongs? To set forth those most basic convictions about God in relationship to man and about Israel in relationship to God, I can imagine no more eloquent, no more compelling and appropriate, medium of expression than the densely detailed Halakhah of *Shebi'it, Shabbat,* and *Erubin.* Indeed, outside of the setting of the household, its ownership, use, and maintenance, I cannot think of any other way of fully making that statement stick. In theory implausible for its very simplicity (as much as for its dense instantiation!) and in Halakhic fact, compelling, the Oral Torah's statement accounts for the human condition. Israel's Eden takes place in the household open to others, on the Sabbath, in acts that maintain life, share wealth, and desist from Creation.

Chapter 7

The Story Judaism Tells

THE JUDAIC MYTH

By "myth," people mean religious truth in narrative form. The Hebrew Scriptures appeal to narrative, specifically, history, from Creation through the destruction of the First Temple. Whether that narrative records exactly what actually happened is much debated, and certainly the character of the biblical story, with its divine interventions and wonder-workers, prophets, and anointed kings and generals, hardly corresponds to secular, this-worldly history in any sense. But the narrative forms the medium for expressing the religious system. The story Judaism tells then conveys the main lines of the worldview of Judaism, fully responsive to Scripture's account. In this context, then, "story," "myth," and "history" speak interchangeably of the same fact: Judaism conveys its theology through its narrative. The great biblical scholar Brevard Childs explains the collaboration of history, memory, and tradition in ancient Israel's Scriptures:

> Actualization is the process by which a past event is contemporized for a generation removed in time and space from the original event. When later Israel responded to the continuing imperative of her tradition through her memory, that moment in historical time likewise became an Exodus experience.

79

Not in the sense that later Israel again crossed the Red Sea. This was an irreversible, once-for-all event. Rather, Israel entered the same redemptive reality of the Exodus generation. Later Israel, removed in time and space from the original event, yet still in time and space, found in her tradition a means of transforming her history into redemptive history. Because the quality of time was the same, the barrier of chronological separation was overcome.[3]

It would be difficult to imagine a more concise statement of the religious experience of the historical mode of organizing matters than Childs's, since he touches on every element critical to the description of history—the pastness of the past, the singularity and irreversibility of events, but also the power of events in times past to affect the present moment and to effect change therein.

The scriptural version of that story, which we considered in chapter 5, is reworked by Judaism. Scripture tells the twin stories of Adam gaining, then losing Eden and Israel entering, then losing, the Land. What the sages of the Oral Torah added was that story defines a pattern that accounts for the condition of holy Israel even in their own day. Scripture told about the loss and recovery of the Temple and the Land, and, the sages knew, the Temple and Land once more had been lost. Then, they insisted, what happened before would happen once more. The following story captures the Judaic myth: the notion that events form patterns, and patterns govern what is going to happen in the future.

> *Sifré* to Deuteronomy to *Eqeb* XLIII:III.7
> A. Rabban Gamaliel, R. Joshua, R. Eleazar b. Azariah, and R. Aqiba were going toward Rome. They heard the sound of the city's traffic from as far away as Puteoli, a hundred and twenty *mil* away. They began to cry, while R. Aqiba laughed.
> B. They said to him, "Aqiba, why are we crying while you are laughing?"
> C. He said to them, "Why are you crying?"
> D. They said to him, "Should we not cry, since gentiles, idolaters, sacrifice to their idols and bow down to icons, but dwell securely in prosperity, serenely, while the house of the footstool of our God has been put to the torch and left [Hammer:] a lair for beasts of the field?"
> E. He said to them, "That is precisely why I was laughing. If this is how he has rewarded those who anger; him, all the more so [will he reward] those who do his will."
> 8. A. Another time they went up to Jerusalem and go to Mount Scopus. They tore their garments.
> B. They came to the mountain of the house [of the temple] and saw a fox go forth from the house of the holy of holies. They began to cry, while R. Aqiba laughed.
> C. They said to him, "You are always giving surprises. We are crying when you laugh!"
> D. He said to them, "But why are you crying?"
> E. They said to him, "Should we not cry over the place concerning which it is written, 'And the common person who draws near shall be put to death' (Num. 1:51)? Now lo, a fox comes out of it.

F. "In our connection the following verse of Scripture has been carried out: 'For this our heart is faint, for these things our eyes are
dim, for the mountain of Zion which is desolate, the foxes walk
upon it' (Lam. 5:17–18)."

G. He said to them, "That is the very reason I have laughed. For lo,
it is written, 'And I will take for me faithful witnesses to record,
Uriah the priest and Zechariah the son of Jeberechiah' (Isa.
8:2).

H. "And what has Uriah got to do with Zechariah? What is it that
Uriah said? 'Zion shall be plowed as a field and Jerusalem shall
become heaps and the mountain of the Lord's house as the high
places of a forest' (Jer. 26:18).

I. "What is it that Zechariah said? 'Thus says the Lord of hosts,
"Old men and women shall yet sit in the broad places of
Jerusalem"' (Zech. 8:4).

J. "Said the Omnipresent, 'Lo, I have these two witnesses. If the
words of Uriah have been carried out, then the words of
Zechariah will be carried out. If the words of Uriah are nullified,
then the words of Zechariah will be nullified.

K. "'Therefore I was happy that the words of Uriah have been carried out, so that in the end the words of Zechariah will come
about.'"

L. In this language they replied to him: "Aqiba, you have given us
comfort."

Here the paradigm that Aqiba finds in Scripture tells him what data require attention and what do not. The prosperity of the idolaters matters only because the
paradigm explains why, to begin with, we may take account of their situation.
The destruction of the Temple matters also because it conforms to an intelligible
paradigm. In both cases, we both select and also understand events by appeal to
the pattern defined by the working of God's will. The data at hand then yield
inferences of a particular order—the prosperity of idolaters, the disgrace of Israel
in its very cult. We notice both facts because they both complement one another
and also illustrate the workings of the model: validating prophecy, interpreting
experience in light of its message.

TURNING A STORY INTO A PATTERN

What the sages have done with Scripture then becomes clear. They have taken
its narrative and discerned a pattern within it, and this pattern then has guided
them in thinking about the present. Whatever happens finds its place within the
paradigm, or the model, that they have formed of Scripture's narrative. The paradigm forms a medium for the description, analysis, and interpretation of
selected data: the facts of everyday existence, rightly construed. Paradigmatic
thinking thus forms a counterpart to that of the mathematics that produces
models. Specifically, mathematicians compose models that, in the language and
symbols of mathematics, set forth a structure of knowledge that forms a "surro-

gate for reality."[4] These models state in quantitative terms the results of controlled observations of data. Among them, the one that generates plausible analytical generalizations will serve. Seeking not so much the regularities of the data as a medium for taking account of a variety of variables among a vast corpus of data, the framer of a model needs not simply observations of fact but also regularities or patterns. What is essential is a structure of thought, which mathematicians call "a philosophy":

> As a philosophy it has a center from which everything flows, and the center is a definition. . . .[5]

What is needed for a model is not data alone, however voluminous, but some idea of what you are trying to compose—a model of the model:

> Unless you have some good idea of what you are looking for and how to find it, you can approach infinity with nothing more than a mishmash of little things you know about a lot of little things.[6]

So, in order to frame a model of explanation, we start with a model in the computer, and then test data to assess the facility of the model. We may test several models and have the same outcome: the formation of a philosophy in the mathematical sense. To understand the relevance of this brief glimpse at model making in mathematics, let me cite the context in which the matter comes to me: the use of mathematics to give guidance on how to fight forest fires:

> If mathematics can be used to predict the intensity and rate of spread of wildfires of the future (either hypothetical fires or fires actually burning but whose outcome is not yet known), why can't the direction of the analysis be reversed in order to reconstruct the characteristics of important fires of the past? Or why can't the direction be reversed from prophecy to history? [7]

Here the reversibility of events, their paradigmatic character, their capacity to yield a model unlimited by context or considerations of scale—the principal traits of paradigmatic thinking—turn out to enjoy a compelling rationality of their own. Reading those words, we can immediately grasp the service that models or patterns or paradigms served for the Rabbinic sages, even though the framing of mathematical models began long after the birth of this writer, and even though our sages lived many centuries before the creation of contemporary mathematics that would yield models to which sages' paradigms correspond in kind and function. Before us is a mode of thought that is entirely rational and the very opposite of "insubstantial."

To understand the kind of storytelling that animates Judaism, then, we have to compare the reaction of Aqiba to the destruction of the Second Temple in 70 with the reaction of the framers of Scripture, particularly Genesis through Kings, to the destruction of the First Temple in 586. The latter produced the authorized history from creation to destruction that is told from Genesis through Kings, history as an explanation of what has happened. The former—Aqiba and his colleagues—identified in place of historical narrative a pattern, a model, a "philosophy, in the mathematical sense," which would guide them in interpreting the meaning of the crisis in their own time. We have then to ask, Why did paradigmatic rather than historical thinking predominate in Judaism? The reason is clear from the story of Aqiba, who shows (to state matters simply) how an event is turned into a series, how what happens once is changed into something that happens. How has the pattern replaced the one-time historical events of the familiar narrative? The reason is that, in their day, in 70 C.E., and again in the defeat of Bar Kokhba in 135 C.E., they witnessed the transformation of the singular event, the destruction of the First Temple in 586 B.C.E., into a pattern of destruction. And having lived through events that they could plausibly discover in Scripture—Lamentations for one example; Jeremiah another—they also found entirely natural the notion that the past took place in the present as well.

THE PRESENCE OF THE PAST,
THE PASTNESS OF THE PRESENT

For them the past is a presence, and they form part of the past as well. When we speak of the presence of the past, therefore, we speak of the concrete experience that generations actively mourning the Temple endured. When we speak of the pastness of the present, we describe the consciousness of people who could open Scripture and find themselves right there, in its record—but not only in Lamentations, but also in prophecy, and, especially, in the books of the Torah. Here we deal not with the spiritualization of Scripture but with the acutely contemporary and immediate realization of Scripture: once again, as then; Scripture in the present day, the present day in Scripture. That is why it was possible for sages to formulate out of Scripture a paradigm that imposed structure and order on the world that they themselves encountered.

Sages who assembled the documents of Rabbinic Judaism, from the Mishnah forward, recognized the crisis precipitated by the destruction of the Second Temple, and all took for granted that that event was to be understood by reference to the model of the destruction of the First. That is the meaning of the colloquy between Aqiba and sages about the comfort to be derived from the ephemeral glory of Rome and the temporary ruin of Jerusalem. It follows that for the Rabbinic sages, the destruction of the Temple in 70 did not mark a break with the past, such as it had for their predecessors some five hundred years earlier, but rather a recapitulation of the past. Paradigmatic thinking then began in that very event that precipitated thought about history to begin with: the end of the old order.

But paradigm replaced history because what had taken place the first time as unique and unprecedented took place the second time in precisely the same pattern and therefore formed of an episode a series. Paradigmatic thinking replaced historical thinking when history as an account of one-time, irreversible, unique events, arranged in linear sequence and pointing toward a teleological conclusion, lost all plausibility. If the first time around, history—with the past marked off from the present, events arranged in linear sequence and narrative of a sustained character serving as the medium of thought—provided the medium for making sense of matters, then the second time around, history lost all currency.

How, precisely, does the story of Rabbinic Judaism work? Paradigmatic thinking by definition treats events of the past as exemplary. History is subordinated to the model or pattern, and the paradigm takes into itself data in no way historical in category alongside events of a world-historical order. No better example of paradigmatic thinking and its outcome in Rabbinic Judaism can be presented than the one that follows. Here, the history of Israel among the nations is foreseen by prophecy and conveyed by apocalyptic. The nations at hand are Babylonia, Media, Greece, and Rome, time and again differentiated from the first three. These represent the four great monarchies that subdued Israel. The matter unfolds rather majestically, introducing first one theme—the nations' role in the history of Israel, their hostile treatment of Israel—and then the next, the food taboos, finally bringing the two themes together.

THE STORY OF ISRAEL IN PARADIGMATIC FORM

How, in concrete terms, does this mode of storytelling through models or patterns or paradigms actually work? In the exposition that follows, the story of Israel is contained within the symbolism of the animals that Israelites are not to eat. We can identify each of the successive kingdoms with the four explicitly tabooed animals of Leviticus 11:1–8: camel, rock badger, hare, and pig. Then, as we see, the reasons for the taboo assigned to each of them are worked out in a triple sequence of plays on words, with special reference to the secondary possibilities presented by the words for "chew the cud," "bring up GRH." So while the first impression is that a diverse set of materials has been strung together, on closer glance we see quite the opposite: a purposive and careful arrangement of distinct propositions, each leading to and intensifying the force of the next. That is why at the climax comes the messianic reference to Israel's ultimate inheritance of the power and dominion of Rome. The following statement best represents paradigmatic thinking: encompassing; balanced; proportionate; pertinent to all the dimensions of human existence; taking account of time past, present, and future within a single, homogenizing structure. Once more, I abbreviate and give only a few of the systematic demonstrations of the same proposition:

> *Leviticus Rabbah* XIII:V
>> 1. A. Said R. Ishmael b. R. Nehemiah, "All the prophets foresaw what
>> the pagan kingdoms would do [to Israel]. . . .
>> 7. A. "Abraham foresaw what the evil kingdoms would do [to Israel].

B. "[As the sun was going down,] a deep sleep fell on Abraham; [and lo, a dread and great darkness fell upon him]" (Gen. 15:12).

C. "Dread" (YMH) refers to Babylonia, on account of the statement, "Then Nebuchadnezzar was full of fury (HMH)" (Dan. 3:19).

D. "Darkness" refers to Media, which brought darkness to Israel through its decrees: "to destroy, to slay, and to wipe out all the Jews" (Esth. 7:4).

E. "Great" refers to Greece.

J. "Fell on him" (Gen. 15:12).

K. This refers to Edom, on account of the following verse: "The earth quakes at the noise of their [Edom's] fall" (Jer. 49:21).

9. A. Moses foresaw what the evil kingdoms would do [to Israel].

B. "The camel, rock badger, and hare" (Deut. 14:7). [Compare: "Nevertheless, among those that chew the cud or part the hoof, you shall not eat these: the camel, because it chews the cud but does not part the hoof, is unclean to you. The rock badger, because it chews the cud but does not part the hoof, is unclean to you. And the hare, because it chews the cud but does not part the hoof, is unclean to you, and the pig, because it parts the hoof and is cloven-footed, but does not chew the cud, is unclean to you" (Lev. 11:4–8).]

C. The camel (GML) refers to Babylonia, [in line with the following verse of Scripture: "O daughter of Babylonia, you who are to be devastated!] Happy will be he who requites (GML) you, with what you have done to us" (Ps. 147:8).

D. "The rock badger" (Deut. 14:7)—this refers to Media.

E. Rabbis and R. Judah b. R. Simon.

F. Rabbis say, "Just as the rock badger exhibits traits of uncleanness and traits of cleanness, so the kingdom of Media produced both a righteous man and a wicked one."

G. Said R. Judah b. R. Simon, "The last Darius was Esther's son. He was clean on his mother's side and unclean on his father's side."

H. "The hare" (Deut. 14:7)—this refers to Greece. The mother of King Ptolemy was named "Hare" [in Greek: *lagos*].

I. "The pig" (Deut. 14:7)—this refers to Edom [Rome].

It would not be possible to identify a more ample statement of paradigmatic thinking about matters also dealt with by history. Here we transform events into patterns and patterns into encompassing structures, capable of accommodating all of the experience of humanity that the community addressed by the paradigm chooses to take into account. The basic outline set forth here governs in numerous other passages in the documents of the present group and the next set as well. Given this rather substantial abstract, we need not review the broad range of ways in which the same ideas are laid out. One of the traits of paradigmatic thinking—by definition—is its repetitious character. Just as in historical thinking events are set forth because they are singular and proceed one to the next, so in paradigmatic thinking events are set forth because they are exemplary and conform to no single linear pattern at all.

The purpose of paradigmatic narrative, as much as of historical, is to foresee the future. History is important to explain the present and also to help peer into the future; paradigms serve precisely the same purpose. The choice between the one model and the other, then, rests on which appeals to the more authentic data. In that competition, Scripture, treated as paradigm, met no competition in linear history, and it was paradigmatic, not historical, thinking that proved compelling for a thousand years or more. The future history of Israel is written in Scripture, and what happened in the beginning is what is going to happen at the end of time. That sense of order and balance prevailed. It comes to expression in a variety of passages, of which a severely truncated selection will have to suffice:

> *Genesis Rabbah* XLII:II
> 2. A. Said R. Abin, "Just as [Israel's history] began with the encounter with four kingdoms, so [Israel's history] will conclude with the encounter with the four kingdoms.
>   B. "'Chedorlaomer, king of Elam, Tidal, king of Goiim, Amraphel, king of Shinar, and Arioch, king of Ellasar, four kings against five' (Gen. 14:9).
>   C. "So [Israel's history] will conclude with the encounter with the four kingdoms: the kingdom of Babylonia, the kingdom of Medea, the kingdom of Greece, and the kingdom of Edom."

Another pattern serves as well, resting as it does on the foundations of the former. It is the familiar one that appeals to the deeds of the founders. The lives of the patriarchs stand for the history of Israel; the deeds of the patriarchs cover the future historical periods in Israel's destiny. A single formulation of matters suffices to show how the entire history of Israel was foreseen at the outset:

> *Pesiqta deRab Kahana* XXI:V
> 1. A. R. Hiyya taught on Tannaite authority, "At the beginning of the creation of the world the Holy One, blessed be He, foresaw that the Temple would be built, destroyed, and rebuilt.
>   B. "'In the beginning God created the heaven and the earth' (Gen. 1:1) [refers to the Temple] when it was built, in line with the following verse: 'That I may plant the heavens and lay the foundations of the earth and say to Zion, You are my people' (Isa. 51:16).
>   C. "'And the earth was unformed'—lo, this refers to the destruction, in line with this verse: 'I saw the earth, and lo, it was unformed' (Jer. 4:23).
>   D. "'And God said, Let there be light'—lo, it was built and well constructed in the age to come."

A single specific example of the foregoing proposition suffices. It is drawn from that same mode of paradigmatic thinking that imposes the model of the beginning on the end. In the present case the yield is consequential: we know what God is going to do to Rome. What God did to the Egyptians foreshadows what God will do to the Romans at the end of time. What we have here is the opposite of cyclical history; here history conforms to a pattern, the end time recapitulating creation's events and complementing them. Here we see a good example of how paradigmatic thinking addresses the possibility of cyclicality and insists instead on closure:

Pesiqta deRab Kahana VII:XI.3

    A. R. Levi in the name of R. Hama bar Hanina: "He who exacted vengeance from the former [oppressor] will exact vengeance from the latter.

    B. "Just as, in Egypt, it was with blood, so with Edom it will be the same: 'I will show wonders in the heavens and in the earth, blood, and fire, and pillars of smoke' (Job 3:3).

    C. "Just as, in Egypt, it was with frogs, so with Edom it will be the same: 'The sound of an uproar from the city, an uproar because of the palace, an uproar of the Lord who renders recompense to his enemies' (Isa. 66:6).

    D. "Just as, in Egypt, it was with lice, so with Edom it will be the same: 'The streams of Bosrah will be turned into pitch, and the dust thereof into brimstone, and the land thereof shall become burning pitch' (Isa. 34:9). 'Smite the dust of the earth that it may become lice' (Exod. 8:12).

    E. "Just as, in Egypt, it was with swarms of wild beasts, so with Edom it will be the same: 'The pelican and the bittern shall possess it' (Isa. 34:11).

    F. "Just as, in Egypt, it was with pestilence, so with Edom it will be the same: 'I will plead against Gog with pestilence and with blood' (Ezek. 38:22).

    G. "Just as, in Egypt, it was with boils, so with Edom it will be the same: 'This shall be the plague wherewith the Lord will smite all the peoples that have warred against Jerusalem: their flesh shall consume away while they stand upon their feet' (Zech. 14:12).

    H. "Just as, in Egypt, it was with great stones, so with Edom it will be the same: 'I will cause to rain upon Gog . . . an overflowing shower and great hailstones' (Ezek. 38:22).

    I. "Just as, in Egypt, it was with locusts, so with Edom it will be the same: 'And you, son of man, thus says the Lord God: Speak to birds of every sort . . . the flesh of the mighty shall you eat . . . blood shall you drink . . . you shall eat fat until you are full and drink blood until you are drunk' (Ezek. 39:17–19).

    J. "Just as, in Egypt, it was with darkness, so with Edom it will be the same: 'He shall stretch over Edom the line of chaos and the plummet of emptiness' (Isa. 34:11).

    K. "Just as, in Egypt, he took out their greatest figure and killed him, so with Edom it will be the same: 'A great slaughter in the land of Edom, among them to come down shall be the wild oxen' (Isa. 34:6–7)."

The exposition of matters through the small sample given here leaves no doubt on precisely how paradigmatic thinking recast Israel's recorded experience ("history") into a set of models that pertained everywhere and all the time.

For Judaism, then, the myth takes the form of a paradigm set forth in narrative language or in a narrative context. A model or pattern or paradigm will set forth an account of the life of the social entity (village, kingdom, people, territory) in terms of differentiated events—wars, reigns, for one example; building a given building and destroying it, for another—yet entirely out of phase with sequences of time. A paradigm imposed on time does not call on the day or month or year to accomplish its task. It will simply set aside nature's time altogether, regarding years and months as bearing a significance other than the temporal one (sequence, span of time, aggregates of time) that history, inclusive of cyclical time's history, posits. Paradigmatic thinking presents a mode of making connections and drawing conclusions and is captured in its essence by two statements of Augustine:

> We live only in the present, but this present has several dimensions: the present of past things, the present of present things, and the present of future things. . . .
>   Your years are like a single day . . . and this today does not give way to a tomorrow, any more than it follows a yesterday. Your today is Eternity. . . .
>   (*Confessions* 10:13)

For the Rabbinic sages, the Torah defined a set of paradigms that served without regard to circumstance, context, or, for that matter, dimension and scale of happening. A very small number of models emerged from Scripture, captured in the sets (1) Eden and Adam, (2) Sinai and the Torah, (3) the land and Israel, and (4) the Temple and its building, destruction, and rebuilding.

These paradigms served severally and jointly, for example, Eden and Adam on its own but also superimposed on the Land and Israel; Sinai and the Torah on its own but also superimposed on the Land and Israel. Of course, the Temple, embodying natural creation and its intersection with national and social history, could stand entirely on its own or be superimposed on any and all of the other paradigms. In many ways, then, we have the symbolic equivalent of a set of two- and three- or even four-dimensional grids. A given pattern forms a grid on its own, one set of lines being set forth in terms of, for example, Eden or timeless perfection, in contrast against the other set of lines, Adam or temporal disobedience. But on that grid a comparable grid can be superimposed, the Land and Israel being an obvious one; and on the two, yet a third and fourth: Sinai and Torah, Temple and the confluence of nature and history.

ISRAEL'S HISTORY TAKEN OVER
INTO ISRAEL'S LIFE OF SANCTIFICATION

In the following passage, as the single best formulation of paradigmatic thinking in the Rabbinic canon, Israel's history is taken over into the structure of Israel's life of sanctification, and all that happens to Israel forms part of the structure of holiness built around cult, Torah, synagogue, sages, Zion, and the like. Here I give only a small part, for we meet the same passage again in chapter 14:

> *Genesis Rabbah* LXX:VIII
>   2. A. "As he looked, he saw a well in the field":
>   B. R. Hama bar Hanina interpreted the verse in six ways [that is, he divides the verse into six clauses and systematically reads each of the clauses in light of the others and in line with an overriding theme]:

C. "'As he looked, he saw a well in the field': this refers to the well [of water in the wilderness (Num. 21:17)].

D. "'. . . and lo, three flocks of sheep lying beside it': specifically, Moses, Aaron, and Miriam.

E. "'. . . for out of that well the flocks were watered': from there each one drew water for his standard, tribe, and family."

F. "And the stone upon the well's mouth was great":

G. Said R. Hanina, "It was only the size of a little sieve."

H. [Reverting to Hama's statement:] "'. . . and put the stone back in its place upon the mouth of the well': for the coming journeys. [Thus the first interpretation applies the passage at hand to the life of Israel in the wilderness.]

3. A. "'As he looked, he saw a well in the field': refers to Zion.

B. "'. . . and lo, three flocks of sheep lying beside it': refers to the three festivals.

C. "'. . . for out of that well the flocks were watered': from there they drank of the holy spirit.

D. "'. . . The stone on the well's mouth was large': this refers to the rejoicing of the house of the water-drawing."

E. Said R. Hoshaiah, "Why is it called 'the house of the water drawing'? Because from there they drink of the Holy Spirit."

F. [Resuming Hama b. Hanina's discourse:] "'. . . and when all the flocks were gathered there': coming from 'the entrance of Hamath to the brook of Egypt' (1 Kgs. 8:66).

G. "'. . . the shepherds would roll the stone from the mouth of the well and water the sheep': for from there they would drink of the Holy Spirit.

H. "'. . . and put the stone back in its place upon the mouth of the well': leaving it in place until the coming festival. [Thus the second interpretation reads the verse in light of the Temple celebration of the Festival of Tabernacles.]

5. A. "'As he looked, he saw a well in the field': this refers to Zion.

B. "'. . . and lo, three flocks of sheep lying beside it': this refers to the first three kingdoms [Babylonia, Media, Greece].

C. "'. . . for out of that well the flocks were watered': for they enriched the treasures that were laid upon up in the chambers of the Temple.

D. "'. . . The stone on the well's mouth was large': this refers to the merit attained by the patriarchs.

E. "'. . . and when all the flocks were gathered there': this refers to the wicked kingdom, which collects troops through levies over all the nations of the world.

F. "'. . . the shepherds would roll the stone from the mouth of the well and water the sheep': for they enriched the treasures that were laid upon up in the chambers of the Temple.

G. "'. . . and put the stone back in its place upon the mouth of the well': in the age to come the merit attained by the patriarchs will stand [in defense of Israel]." [So the fourth interpretation interweaves the themes of the Temple cult and the domination of the four monarchies.]

7. A. "'As he looked, he saw a well in the field': this refers to the synagogue.

B. "'. . . and lo, three flocks of sheep lying beside it': this refers to the three who are called to the reading of the Torah on weekdays.

C. "'... for out of that well the flocks were watered': for from there they hear the reading of the Torah.

D. "'... The stone on the well's mouth was large': this refers to the impulse to do evil.

E. "'... and when all the flocks were gathered there': this refers to the congregation.

F. "'... the shepherds would roll the stone from the mouth of the well and water the sheep': for from there they hear the reading of the Torah.

G. "'... and put the stone back in its place upon the mouth of the well': for once they go forth [from the hearing of the reading of the Torah] the impulse to do evil reverts to its place." [The sixth and last interpretation turns to the twin themes of the reading of the Torah in the synagogue and the evil impulse, temporarily driven off through the hearing of the Torah.]

In the passage just reviewed, paradigms take over the organization of events. Time is no longer sequential and linear. What endures are the structures of cosmos and society: prophets, Zion, Sanhedrin, holy seasons, and on and on. Clearly, the one thing that plays no role whatsoever in this tableau and frieze is Israel's linear history; past and future take place in an eternal present. That forms the concrete statement of the story Judaism tells.

The sages did not believe the Temple would be rebuilt and destroyed again, rebuilt and destroyed, and so on into endless time. They stated the very opposite: the Temple would be rebuilt but never again destroyed. And that represented a view of the second destruction that rejected cyclicity altogether. Sages instead opted for patterns of history and against cycles because they retained that notion for the specific and concrete meaning of events that characterized Scripture's history. They did that even while rejecting the historical approach of Scripture, which viewed events as one-time and unique and the past as separate from the present. What they maintained, as we have seen, is that a pattern governed, and the pattern was not a cyclical one. Here, Scripture itself imposed its structures, its order, its system—its paradigm. And the history from Genesis through Kings left no room for the conception of cyclicality.

If matters do not repeat themselves but conform to a pattern, then the pattern itself must be identified. Scripture laid matters out, and the Rabbinic sages then drew conclusions from that layout that conformed to their experience. So the second destruction precipitated thinking about paradigms of Israel's life, such as came to full exposure in the thinking behind the Midrash compilations we have surveyed. With the episode made into a series, sages' paradigmatic thinking asked of Scripture different questions from the historical ones of 586 because the Rabbinic sages brought to Scripture different premises and drew from Scripture different conclusions. But in point of fact, not a single paradigm set forth by sages can be distinguished in any important component from the counterpart in Scripture—not Eden and Adam in comparison to the land of Israel and Israel, and not the tale of Israel's experience in the spinning out of the tension between the word of God and the will of Israel.

Chapter 8

The Community of Israel

WHAT IS AN "ISRAEL" IN A JUDAIC RELIGIOUS SYSTEM?

To whom is the story told, and who finds the story self-evident as an explanation of the social world? It is the group that calls itself "Israel," whatever it means by that word. In the religion Judaism, "Israel" stands for the social entity formed by the faithful. In the Rabbinic system of the early centuries C.E., "Israel" refers to the holy people, whom God has called into being through Abraham and Sarah and their descendants, to whom the prophetic promises were made, and with whom the covenants were entered. In every Judaic religious system, "Israel" defines a theological category, shaped within the larger systemic logic of that system. "Israel" in that context does not represent a fact of sociology or ethnic culture or secular politics but a principal part of a Judaism. The "Israel" of Judaism—of every Judaism of ancient times—within its setting forms a supernatural social entity, "chosen," "holy," subject to God's special love and concern. "Israel" should not, then, be confused with the ethnic group "the Jews," nor should references to "Israel" in the supernatural framework of humanity's salvation be understood as ethnocentric. As we shall see, "Israel" refers to those who know God, and "not-Israel" ("gentiles") refers to idolaters, pure and simple. In

Rabbinic Judaism there are no other categories of the social order formed by all humanity.

In the context of the study of Judaism the religion, that category, "Israel," is therefore not to be confused with "the Jewish people," which may refer to an ethnic group, to the community of fate formed by the people, Israel, in a this-worldly framework, or to the state of Israel, a modern nation-state, and "Israelites"— meaning the faithful of Judaism—are not to be confused with "Israelis," citizens of the state of Israel. "Israel" in Judaism compares to "the Torah" in that as the latter is not just another book, so the former is not just another social entity. Just as the story of the Torah speaks of transcendent matters, so the tale of Israel, in Judaism, tells of God's relationship with humanity through the instrument God has chosen for self-manifestation: "You alone have I singled out of all the families of the earth—that is why I will call you to account for all your iniquities," as the prophet Amos put it (Amos 3:2, NJPS).

All Judaisms deem their "Israel" to form a continuity with the Israel of whom the Hebrew Scriptures speak. In modern times some deem the connection to be genealogical and fundamentally ethnic, putting forth a secular definition. But Rabbinic Judaism defines its Israel in supernatural terms, deeming the social entity to form a transcendental community, by faith. In the documents of Judaism from the Mishnah through the Talmud of Babylonia, Rabbinic Judaism's "Israel" does not speak of a merely ethnic, this-worldly people. It is, rather, a social entity defined by supernatural genealogy, on the one side, or religious conversion, on the other. The child of a Jewish mother automatically belongs to the Israel of Rabbinic Judaism; circumcision on the eighth day admits the male child to the covenant of God with Israel into which he was born.

But "Israel" is no more a narrow ethnic category than is "church" or "abode of Islam." That is shown by the simple fact that a gentile of any origin or status, slave or free, Greek or barbarian, may enter its "Israel" on equal terms with those born into the community, becoming children of Abraham and Sarah. The children of converts are accepted as Israelite without qualification. No distinction is made between the child of a convert and the child of a native-born Israelite. Since that fact bears concrete and material consequences, for example, in the right to marry any other Israelite without distinction by reason of familial origin, it follows that the Israel of Rabbinic Judaism must be understood in a wholly theological framework. This Judaism knows no distinction between children of the flesh and children of the promise and therefore cannot address a merely ethnic "Israel." That is because for Rabbinic Judaism, "Israel" is always and only defined by the Torah, received and represented by "our sages of blessed memory" as the word of God, never by the happenstance of secular history.

To explain what is at stake in the category "Israel," we have to recognize that the raw materials of definition are not how things are in practical terms but in the constructive imagination of the system builders. In any Judaic system, an "Israel"—that is, a theory of what Israel is and who is counted as part of Israel or as himself or herself Israel—finds its shape and structure within that system. That

"Israel" takes shape out of materials selected by the systemic framers from a miscellaneous, received or invented repertoire of possibilities. It goes without saying that, in the context of the description of the structure of a Judaism, its "Israel" is the sole Israel (whether social group, caste, family, class, or "population," or any of the many social entities admirably identified by sociology) defined by that "Judaism." The best systemic indicator is a system's definition of its Israel. And Judaisms, or Judaic systems, from the priests' Pentateuchal system onward, made their statement principally through their response to the question framed in contemporary Judaic and Jewish-ethnic discourse as "Who is a Jew?"

But the systemic component, Israel, finds its definition within the systemic imagination, not out of the raw materials of the social world beyond the system. For a system never accommodates the givens of politics and a sheltering society. The notion that society gives birth to religion is systemically beside the point. Systems do not recapitulate a given social order, they define one. Then their framers, if they can, go about realizing their fantasy. An "Israel" within a given Judaic system forms the invention of the system's builders and presents traits that they deem self-evidently true. That is quite without regard to realities beyond the range of systemic control. All that the context presents is a repertoire of possibilities. The framers of the contents then make their choices among those possibilities, and, outside of the framework of the system, there is no predicting the shape and structure of those choices. The system unfolds within its own inner logic, making things up as it goes along—because it knows precisely how to do so.

"ISRAEL" IN THE MISHNAH

In first-century Christianity, the apostle Paul framed the theory of a merely ethnic Israel, "Israel after the flesh," as distinct from a spiritual Israel, "Israel after the spirit," which embodied the promises of prophecy and the covenant of Scripture. Christians claimed to form "the Israel after the spirit," while Jews who did not adopt Christianity were merely "Israel after the flesh." While Christianity would deny to the Jewish people the status of the "Israel" of whom Scriptures spoke and to whom the prophets prophesied, these views did not play a role in the thinking of the earlier Rabbinic writings about "Israel." The Mishnah took shape at a time at which Christianity formed a minor irritant, perhaps in some few places a competing Judaism, but not a formative component of the social order and certainly not the political power that it was to become. Hence the Mishnah's framers' thinking about "Israel," representing Rabbinic Judaism in the first and second centuries C.E., in no way took account of the competing claim to form the true Israel put forth by Christianity. "Israel" remained intransitive, bearing no relationships to any other distinct social entity.

We know that is so when we ask about the antonym for "Israel." The opposite of "Israel" in the Mishnah is "the nations," on the one side, or "Levite, priest," on the other: always taxonomical, never defined out of relationship to others within the same theoretical structure. As the Mishnah defines "Israel," the category bears two identical meanings: the "Israel" of (all) the Jews now and here, but also the "Israel" of which Scripture—the Torah—spoke. And that encompassed both the individual and the group, without linguistic differentiation of any kind. Thus in the Mishnah "Israel" may refer to an individual Jew (always male) or to "all Jews," that is, the collectivity of Jews. The individual woman is nearly always called *bat yisra'el*, daughter of (an) Israel(ite). The sages in the Mishnah did not merely assemble facts and define the social entity as a matter of mere description of the given. Rather, they portrayed it as they wished. They imputed to the social group, Jews, the status of a systemic entity, "Israel." To others within Jewry it was not at all self-evident that "all Jews" constituted one "Israel," and that that one "Israel" formed the direct and immediate continuation, in the here and now, of the "Israel" of holy writ and revelation.

The Mishnaic identification of Jewry in the here and now with the "Israel" of Scripture therefore constituted an act of metaphor, comparison, contrast, identification, and analogy. It is that Judaism's most daring social metaphor. Implicitly, moreover, the metaphor excluded a broad range of candidates from the status of (an) "Israel," the Samaritans for one example, the scheduled castes of Mishnah tractate *Qiddushin* chapter 4, for another. Calling (some) Jews "Israel" established the comprehensive and generative metaphor that gives the Mishnaic system its energy. From that metaphor all else derived momentum.

The Mishnah defines "Israel" in antonymic relationships of two sorts: first, "Israel" as against "not-Israel," or gentile; and second, "Israel" as against "priest," or "Levite." "Israel" serves as a taxonomic indicator, specifically part of a more encompassing system of hierarchization; Israel defined the frontiers, on the outer side of society, and the social boundaries within, on the other. To understand the meaning of "Israel" as the Mishnah and its associated documents of the second and third centuries sort matters out, we consider the sense of "gentile." The authorship of the Mishnah does not differentiate among gentiles, who represent an undifferentiated mass. To the system of the Mishnah, whether or not a gentile is a Roman or an Aramaean or a Syrian or a Briton does not matter. That is to say, differentiation among gentiles rarely, if ever, makes a difference in systemic decision making. The upshot is that just as "gentile" is an abstract category, so is "Israel." "Kohen [priest]" is a category, and so is "Israel." For the purposes for which Israel/priest are defined, no further differentiation is undertaken. That is where for the Mishnaic system matters end. But to the Judaic system represented by the Yerushalmi and its associated writings, "gentile" (in the collective) may be Rome or other-than-Rome, for instance, Babylonia, Media, or Greece. That act of further differentiation—we may call it "speciation"—makes a considerable difference in the identification of gentile. In the Israel of the Mishnah's authorship, therefore, we confront an abstraction in a system of philosophy.

"ISRAEL" IN THE TALMUD OF THE LAND OF ISRAEL

Rabbinic Judaism began to pay attention to Christianity in the documents that reached closure at the end of the fourth century and thereafter. That is the time at which Christianity had become the licit, then the established, religion of the Roman state, following the conversion of Constantine. Two metaphors, rarely present and scarcely explored in the writings of Mishnah and related documents (ca. 200–300 C.E.) in the formation of the Judaism of the dual Torah came to prominence in the Talmud of the Land of Israel (ca. 400 C.E.) and Midrash compilations put together at the same period. These were, first, the view of "Israel" as a family, the children and heirs of the man Israel; second, the conception of Israel as sui generis. While "Israel" in the first phase of the formation of Judaism perpetually finds definition in relationship to its opposite, "Israel" in the second phase constituted an intransitive entity, defined in its own terms and not solely or mainly in relationship to other, comparable entities. The enormous investment in the conception of "Israel" as sui generis makes that point blatantly. But "Israel" as family bears that same trait of autonomy and self-evident definition.

The "Israel": in the second stratum of the canon of the Judaism of the dual Torah bears a socially vivid sense. Now "Israel" forms a family, and an encompassing theory of society built on that conception of "Israel," permits us to describe the proportions and balances of the social entity at hand, showing how each component both is an "Israel" and contributes to the larger composite as well. "Israel" as sui generis carried in its wake a substantial doctrine of definition, a weighty collection of general laws of social history governing the particular traits and events of the social group. In comparing transitive to intransitive "Israel," we move from "Israel" as not-gentile and "Israel" as not-priest to powerful statements of what "Israel" is. Now to specify in concrete terms the reasons adduced to explain the rather striking shift before us. Two important changes account for the metaphorical revolution at hand, one out at the borders, the other within, the Jews' group.

By claiming that "Israel" constituted "Israel after the flesh"—the actual, living, present family of Abraham and Sarah, Isaac and Rebecca, Jacob and Leah and Rachel—the sages met head-on the Christian claim that there was—or could ever be—some other "Israel," of a lineage not defined by the family connection at all, and that the existing Jews no longer constituted "Israel." By representing "Israel" as sui generis, the sages moreover focused on the systemic teleology, with its definition of salvation, in response to the Christian claim that salvation is not of Israel but of the church, now enthroned in this world as in heaven. The sage, model for Israel in the model of Moses, our rabbi, represented on earth the Torah that had come from heaven. Like Christ, in earth as in heaven, and like the church, the body of Christ, ruler of earth (through the emperor) as of heaven, the sage embodied what Israel was and was to be. So Israel as family in the model of the sage, like Moses our rabbi, corresponded in its social definition to the church of Jesus Christ, the New Israel, the salvation of humanity. The metaphors given prominence in the late fourth- and fifth-century writings of "our sages of blessed memory" then formed a remarkable counterpoint to the social metaphors important in the mind of significant Christian theologians, as both parties reflected on the political revolution that had taken place.

In response to the challenge of Christianity, the sages' thought about "Israel" centered on the issues of history and salvation, issues made not merely chronic but acute by the political triumph. That accounts for the unprecedented reading of the outsider as differentiated, a reading contained in the two propositions concerning Rome: first, as Esau or Edom or Ishmael, that is, as part of the family; second, of Rome as the pig. Differentiating Rome from other gentiles represented a striking concession indeed, without counterpart in the Mishnah. Rome is represented as only Christian Rome can have been represented: it looks kosher, but it is unkosher. Pagan Rome cannot ever have looked kosher, but Christian Rome, with its appeal to ancient Israel, could and did and moreover claimed to. It bore some traits that validated but lacked others.

The metaphor of the family proved equally pointed. The sages framed their political ideas within the metaphor of genealogy, because to begin with they appealed to the fleshly connection, the family, as the rationale for Israel's social existence. A family beginning with Abraham, Isaac, and Jacob, Israel could best sort out its relationships by drawing into the family other social entities with which it found it had to relate. So Rome became the brother. That affinity came to light only when Rome had turned Christian, and that point marked the need for the extension of the genealogical net. But the conversion to Christianity also justified the sages' extending membership in the family to Rome, for Christian Rome shared with Israel the common patrimony of Scripture—and said so. The character of the sages' thought on Israel therefore proved remarkably congruent to the conditions of public discourse that confronted them.

THE METAPHOR OF THE FAMILY: "ISRAEL'S CHILDREN"

When the sages wished to know what (an) "Israel" was, in the fourth century they reread the scriptural story of "Israel's" origins for the answer. To begin with, as Scripture told them the story, "Israel" was a man, Jacob, and his children are "the children of Jacob." That man's name was also "Israel," and, it followed, "the children of Israel" comprised the extended family of that man. By extension, "Israel" formed the family of Abraham and Sarah, Isaac and Rebecca, Jacob and Leah and Rachel. "Israel" therefore invoked the metaphor of genealogy to explain the bonds that linked persons unseen into a single social entity; the shared traits were imputed, not empirical. That social metaphor of "Israel"—a simple one and easily grasped—bore consequences in two ways.

First, children in general are admonished to follow the good example of their parents. The deeds of the patriarchs and matriarchs therefore taught lessons on how the children were to act. Of greater interest in an account of "Israel" as a social metaphor, "Israel" lived twice, once in the patriarchs and matriarchs, a second time in the life of the heirs as the descendants relived those earlier lives. The stories of the family were carefully reread to provide a picture of the meaning of the latter-day events of the descendants of that same family. Accordingly, the lives of the patriarchs signaled the history of Israel.

The polemical purpose of the claim that the abstraction "Israel" was to be compared to the family of the mythic ancestor lies right at the surface. With another "Israel," the Christian church, now claiming to constitute the true one, the sages found it possible to confront that claim and to turn it against the other side. "You claim to form 'Israel after the spirit.' Fine, and we are Israel after the flesh—and genealogy forms the link, that alone." (Converts did not present an anomaly since they were held to be children of Abraham and Sarah, who had "made souls," that is, converts, in Haran, a point repeated in the documents of the period.) That fleshly continuity formed of all of "us" a single family, rendering spurious the notion that "Israel" could be other than genealogically defined. But that polemic seems to me adventitious and not primary for the metaphor provided a quite separate component to the sages' larger system.

The metaphor of Israel as family supplied an encompassing theory of society. It not only explained who "Israel" as a whole was but also set forth the responsibilities of Israel's social entity, its society. The metaphor defined the character of that entity; it explained who owes what to whom and why, and it accounted for the inner structure and interplay of relationship within the community, here and now, constituted by Jews in their villages and neighborhoods of towns. Accordingly, "Israel" as family bridged the gap between an account of the entirety of the social group "Israel," and a picture of the components of that social group as they lived out their lives in their households and villages. An encompassing theory of society, covering all components from least to greatest, holding the whole together in correct order and proportion, derived from "Israel" viewed as extended family.

That theory of "Israel" as a society made up of persons who because they constituted a family stood in a clear relationship of obligation and responsibility to one another corresponded to what people much later would call the social contract, a kind of compact that in palpable ways told families and households how in the aggregate they formed something larger and tangible. The web of interaction spun out of concrete interchange now was formed not of the gossamer thread of abstraction and theory but by the tough hemp of family ties. "Israel" formed a society because "Israel" was compared to an extended family. That, sum and substance, supplied to the Jews in their households (themselves a made-up category that, in the end, transformed the relationship of the nuclear family into an abstraction capable of holding together quite unrelated persons) an account of the tie from household to household, from village to village, encompassing ultimately "all Israel."

The power of the metaphor of "Israel" as family hardly requires specification. If "we" form a family, then we know full well what links us: common ancestry and the obligations imposed by common ancestry on the cousins who make up the family today. The link between the commonplace interactions and relationships that make "us" into a community, on the one side, and that encompassing the entity "Israel," "all Israel," now is drawn. The large comprehends the little, the abstraction of "us" overall gains concrete reality in the "us" of the here and now of home and village, all together, all forming a "family." In that fundamental way, the metaphor of "Israel" as family therefore provided the field theory of "Israel" linking the most abstract component, the entirety of the social group, to the most mundane, the specificity of the household. One theory, framed in that metaphor of such surpassing simplicity, now held the whole together. That is how the metaphor of family provided an encompassing theory of society, an account of the social contract encompassing all social entities, Jews and gentiles as well, that no other metaphor accomplished.

"Israel" as family comes to expression in, among other writings of the fifth century, the document that makes the most sustained and systematic statement of the matter, *Genesis Rabbah*. In this theory we should not miss the extraordinary polemic utility, of which, in passing, we have already taken note. "Israel" as family also understood itself to form a nation or people. That nation-people held a land, a rather peculiar, enchanted or holy Land, one that, in its imputed traits, was as sui generis as (presently we shall see) in the metaphorical thought of the system Israel also was. Competing for the same territory, Israel's claim to what it called the Land of Israel—thus, of Israel in particular—now rested on right of inheritance such as a family enjoyed, and this was made explicit. The following passage shows how high the stakes were in the claim to constitute the genealogical descendant of the ancestors.

> *Genesis Rabbah* LXI:VII
>> 1. A. "But to the sons of his concubines, Abraham gave gifts, and while he was still living, he sent them away from his son Isaac, eastward to the east country" (Gen. 25:6):
>> B. In the time of Alexander of Macedonia the sons of Ishmael came to dispute with Israel about the birthright, and with them came two wicked families, the Canaanites and the Egyptians.
>> C. They said, "Who will go and engage in a disputation with them."
>> D. Gebiah b. Qosem [the enchanter] said, "I shall go and engage in a disputation with them."
>> E. They said to him, "Be careful not to let the Land of Israel fall into their possession."
>> F. He said to them, "I shall go and engage in a disputation with them. If I win over them, well and good. And if not, you may say, 'Who is this hunchback to represent us?'"
>> G. He went and engaged in a disputation with them. Said to them Alexander of Macedonia, "Who lays claim against whom?"
>> H. The Ishmaelites said, "We lay claim, and we bring our evidence from their own Torah: 'But he shall acknowledge the first-born, the son of the hated' (Deut. 21:17). Now Ishmael was the first-born. [We therefore claim the land as heirs of the first-born of Abraham.]"
>> I. Said to him Gebiah b. Qosem, "My royal lord, does a man not do whatever he likes with his sons?"
>> J. He said to him, "Indeed so."

K. "And lo, it is written, 'Abraham gave all that he had to Isaac' (Gen. 25:2)."

L. [Alexander asked,] "Then where is the deed of gift to the other sons?"

M. He said to him, "'But to the sons of his concubines, Abraham gave gifts, [and while he was still living, he sent them away from his son Isaac, eastward to the east country]' (Gen. 25:6)."

N. [The Ishmaelites had no claim on the land.] They abandoned the field in shame.

The metaphor as refined, with the notion of Israel today as the family of Abraham, as against the Ishmaelites, also of the same family, gives way. But the theme of family records persists. The power of the metaphor of family is that it can explain not only the social entity formed by Jews, but the social entities confronted by them. All fell into the same genus, making up diverse species. The theory of society before us thus accounts for all societies, and, as we shall see when we deal with Rome, does so with extraordinary force.

O. The Canaanites said, "We lay claim, and we bring our evidence from their own Torah. Throughout their Torah it is written, 'the land of Canaan.' So let them give us back our land."

P. Said to him Gebiah b. Qosem, "My royal lord, does a man not do whatever he likes with his slave?"

Q. He said to him, "Indeed so."

R. He said to him, "And lo, it is written, 'A slave of slaves shall Canaan be to his brothers' (Gen. 9:25). So they are really our slaves."

S. [The Canaanites had no claim to the land and in fact should be serving Israel.] They abandoned the field in shame.

T. The Egyptians said, "We lay claim, and we bring our evidence from their own Torah. Six hundred thousand of them left us, taking away our silver and gold utensils: 'They despoiled the Egyptians' (Exod. 12:36). Let them give them back to us."

U. Gebiah b. Qosem said, "My royal lord, six hundred thousand men worked for them for two hundred and ten years, some as silversmiths and some as goldsmiths. Let them pay us our salary at the rate of a denar a day."

V. The mathematicians went and added up what was owing, and they had not reached the sum covering a century before the Egyptians had to forfeit what they had claimed. They abandoned the field in shame.

W. [Alexander] wanted to go up to Jerusalem. The Samaritans said to him, "Be careful. They will not permit you to enter their most holy sanctuary."

X. When Gebiah b. Qosem found out about this, he went and made for himself two felt shoes, with two precious stones worth twenty-thousand pieces of silver set in them. When he got to the mountain of the house [of the Temple], he said to him, "My royal lord, take off your shoes and put on these two felt slippers, for the floor is slippery, and you should not slip and fall."

Y. When they came to the most holy sanctuary, he said to him, "Up to this point, we have the right to enter. From this point onward, we do not have the right to enter."

        Z. He said to him, "When we get out of here, I'm going to even
        out your hump."
      AA. He said to him, "You will be called a great surgeon and get a big
        fee."

The same metaphor serves both "Israel" and "Canaan." Each formed the latter-day heir of the earliest family, and both lived out the original paradigm. The mode of thought imputes the same genus to both social entities, and then makes it possible to distinguish between the two species. We shall see the same mode of thought—the family (but which wing of the family?)—when we consider the confrontation with Christianity and with Rome, in each case conceived in the same personal way. The metaphor applies to both and yields its own meanings for each. The final claim in the passage before us moves away from the metaphor of family. But the notion of a continuous, physical descent is implicit here as well. "Israel" has inherited the wealth of Egypt. Since the notion of inheritance forms a component of the metaphor of family (a conception critical, as we shall see in the next section, in the supernatural patrimony of the "children of Israel" in the merit of the ancestors), we survey the conclusion of the passage.

THE IMPORTANCE OF "ISRAEL" IN RABBINIC JUDAISM

If we wish to know whether "Israel" will constitute an important component in a Judaism, we ask about the categorical imperative and describe, as a matter of mere fact, the consequent composition of that system, stated as a corpus of authoritative documents. A system in which "Israel"—the social entity to which the system's builders imagine they address themselves—plays an important role will treat "Israel" as part of its definitive structure. The reason is that the system's categorical imperative will find important consequences in the definition of its "Israel." A system in which the system's builders work on entirely other questions than social ones and explore the logic of issues different from those addressing a social entity also will not yield tractates on "Israel" and will not accord to the topic of "Israel" that categorical and systemic importance that we have identified in Rabbinic Judaism in the time that Christianity began.

    What do we learn about the contrast between intransitive "Israel" in the Mishnah's stage and transitive "Israel" in the documents of the period after Constantine? System builders respond to the world in which they live, not only to the world constructed in their own minds. Extraordinary political changes, ongoing tensions of society, a religious crisis that challenges theological truth—these in time impose their definition on thought, seizing the attention and focusing the concentration of the system-building thinkers who propose to explain matters. The sages of Rabbinic Judaism made their documentary statements in reply to two critical questions: one concerned sanctification, presented by the final failure of efforts to regain Jerusalem and restore the Temple cult; the other concerned salvation, precipitated by the now-unavoidable fact of Christianity's political triumph. If sanctification is the issue imposed by events, then the Mishnah will ask a range of questions of detail, at each point providing an exegesis of the everyday in terms of the hermeneutics of the sacred: Israel as different and holy within the terms specified by Scripture. If salvation proves the paramount claim of a now-successful rival within "Israel," then the authorship of *Genesis Rabbah* will ask the matriarchs and patriarchs to spell out the rules of salvation, so far as they provide not merely precedents but also paradigms of salvation. The authorship of *Leviticus Rabbah* will seek in the picture of sanctification supplied by the book of Leviticus the rules and laws that govern the salvation of "Israel." The history of an "Israel" that is a political entity—family, sui generis, either, both, it hardly matters—will dictate for the authorship for which the Yerushalmi speaks a paramount category.

The Rabbinic sages formed that group of Jews that identified the critical issue as that of sanctification, involving proper classification and ordering of all of the elements and components of Israel's reality. Not all Jews interpreted events within that framework, however, and it follows that circumstances by themselves did not govern. The symbol change worked for those for whom it worked, and, ultimately, it changed the face of the Jews' society. But in the second and fourth centuries were Jews who found persuasive a different interpretation of events—whether the defeat of Bar Kokhba or the conversion of Constantine—and became Christian.

The upshot is that what people mean by "Israel" depends on how they see the world in general. Just as in the world today "Israel" stands for "the state of Israel," or "the Land of Israel," by reason of the prevailing theories of what it means to be a Jew, so in the setting of various Judaisms of antiquity, "Israel" takes its meaning from its context.

Chapter 9

The Chain of Tradition:
The Oral Torah

THE ORAL TORAH

When *Abot* begins, as we saw in chapter 1, with the declaration, "Moses received Torah at Sinai and handed it on to Joshua . . . ," the document boldly expresses the claim that Rabbinic Judaism sets forth the dual Torah. That is, that Judaism is comprised both by the Torah revealed at Sinai in writing and the other in memory, that is, in oral tradition. The chain of tradition refers, then, to the part of the Torah that is orally formulated, orally transmitted, and handed on in memory. It is the Torah that is memorized as against the Torah that is in writing. In the portrait of *Abot*, moreover, the chain is made up of disciples of masters, back to Moses, God's disciple and master of Joshua. The key to the chain of tradition, then, is the figure of the disciple of sages, the one who has served a master and so found a place for himself in the chain of tradition, and who then is served by disciples, who themselves are joined in that same chain. The most explicit statement of the claim that the revelation encompassed the Torah in two media, oral and written, and that, for access to God's revelation to Moses at Sinai, people must turn to disciples of sages and make themselves into disciples of sages is as follows:

Talmud of Babylonia tractate *Shabbat* 2:5.I:11–121/30b–31a

I.11

    A. *Our rabbis have taught on Tannaite authority:*

    B. There was the incident of a certain gentile who came before Shammai. He said to him, "How many Torahs do you have?"

    C. He said to him, "Two, one in writing, one memorized."

    D. He said to him, "As to the one in writing, I believe you. As to the memorized one, I do not believe you. Convert me on condition that you will teach me only the Torah that is in writing."

    E. He rebuked him and threw him out.

    F. He came before Hillel. He said to him, "Convert me. My lord, how many Torahs were given?"

    G. He said to him, "Two, one in writing, one memorized."

    H. He said to him, "As to the one in writing, I believe you. As to the memorized one, I do not believe you."

    I. On the first day he said to him, "Alef, bet, gimel, dalet." The next day he reversed the order on him.

    J. He said to him, "Well, yesterday, didn't you say it differently?"

    K. He said to him, "Didn't you depend on me then? Then depend on me when it comes to the fact of the memorized Torah too."

I.12

    A. There was another case of a gentile who came before Shammai. He said to him, "Convert me on the stipulation that you teach me the entire Torah while I am standing on one foot." He drove him off with the building cubit that he had in his hand.

    B. He came before Hillel: "Convert me."

    C. He said to him, "'What is hateful to you, to your fellow don't do.' That's the entirety of the Torah; everything else is elaboration. So go, study."

The composite goes over the same matter twice, once explicitly, as I.11, the other by inference, at I.12. That is, Hillel's "entire Torah" consists of a statement that is not found in Scripture and that the sage sets forth in Aramaic, not in the Hebrew of the Pentateuch. So Hillel does not quote a verse of Scripture. But that statement of his also goes over the ground of Leviticus 19:18: "You shall love your neighbor as yourself." It represents, therefore, a reworking of the critical saying of the Written Torah. And the story furthermore introduces the sage as a participant in the process of revelation.

THE CONTENTS OF THE ORAL TORAH

Any account of the form and contents of that chain of tradition, the Oral Torah of Sinai, must begin with the definition of matters. Precisely what do the Rabbinic sources allege concerning this Oral Torah that they set forth? What we shall now see is how the matter unfolds in the sequence of the Rabbinic documents of the early Christian centuries. Since the Mishnah is the first document, after Scripture, that speaks for Rabbinic Judaism, we begin there. The Mishnah's evidence begins with the question, Does the Oral Torah depend on the Written Torah? That is, in the end does the oral tradition taught by the sages derive from the close reading of Scripture? Or is it an autonomous tradition? In the classical statement on the matter, we find the judgment that, in some matters, the teachings of the Mishnah rest on Scripture, and in others, Scripture provides little support for the Halakhah of the Mishnah, which still forms part of the Torah. Then the oral part of the Torah is represented as autonomous of the written part:

> Mishnah tractate *Hagigah* 1:8
> A. The absolution of vows hovers in the air, for it has nothing [in the Torah] upon which to depend.
> B. The laws of the Sabbath, festal offerings, and sacrilege—lo, they are like mountains hanging by a string,
> C. for they have little Scripture for many laws ["Halakhot"].
> D. Laws concerning civil litigation, the sacrificial cult, things to be kept cultically clean, sources of cultic uncleanness, and prohibited consanguineous marriages have much on which to depend.
> E. And both these and those [equally] are the essentials of the Torah.

Authoritative laws exist even though no verse of Scripture sustains them. Then on what basis do those laws rest that lack foundations in Scripture? What is implicit is that the sages possess traditions of Sinai that fall outside of the framework of the written part of the Torah. Here is the point at which an explicit allegation that particular laws or traditions derive from Sinai but are transmitted in memory, not in writing. And here we turn to an explicit claim of verbatim revelation orally formulated and orally transmitted at Sinai:

> Mishnah tractate *Eduyyot* 8:7
> A. Said R. Joshua, "I have a tradition from Rabban Yohanan b. Zakkai, who heard it from his master, and his master from his master, as a law revealed to Moses at Sinai,
> B. "that Elijah is not going to come to declare unclean or to declare clean, to put out or to draw near,
> C. "but only to put out those who have been brought near by force, and to draw near those who have been put out by force."
> D. The family of the house of Seriphah was in Transjordan, and Ben Zion put it out by force.
> E. And there was another family there, which Ben Zion drew near by force.
> F. It is [families of] this sort that Elijah will come to declare unclean and to declare clean, to put out and to draw near.
> G. R. Judah says, "To draw near but not to put out."
> H. R. Simeon says, "To smooth out disputes."
> I. And sages say, "Not to put out or to draw near but to make peace in the world,
> J. "as it is said, 'Behold I will send you Elijah the prophet . . . and he will return the heart of the fathers to the children, and the heart of the children to the fathers'" (Mal. 4:23–24).

Here is an articulated claim that Moses received laws at Sinai that are not written down in the Torah but that are orally formulated and orally transmitted. At stake is not the status of a rule but its very substance. The oral tradition specifies that Elijah's task is to right wrongs done by force, and that involves either forcible inclusion or forcible exclusion. The passage before us raises more questions than it settles, because it allows a dispute to follow the declaration of a law revealed to Moses at Sinai. The formulation before us therefore makes puzzling exactly what people mean by a tradition from Sinai and whether some sages possess it and others do not. More to the point, when some sages supposedly announce it, others frame their opinions without regard to it.

Now, if we ignore the attributive materials and focus on what is attributed, we find a fairly standard dispute:

A. to declare unclean and to declare clean, to put out and to draw near
B. not going to come to declare unclean or to declare clean, to put out or to draw near, but to put out those who have been brought near by force, and to draw near those who have been put out by force
C. Not to put out or to draw near but to make peace in the world

Such disputes are commonplace in the Mishnah, and all that changes here is the elaborate narrative presentation of the issue. As in the other instances at which origination in oral tradition at Sinai is invoked, the allegation that a teaching derives from oral tradition produces no substantive Halakhic result. By that I mean that what is supposed to derive from Sinai fits well in form and Halakhic program with what is assigned to contemporary sages. The only disruptive aspect is the allegation concerning Sinaitic origin.

The following generalizations present themselves: First, when, in the Mishnah sages made reference to "a law revealed by God to Moses at Sinai," they had in mind specific, verbal formulations of the law at hand. At issue is not the status of a ruling or its authority, but its origin. But, second, within the myth of origin is contained the self-evident source of validation of the cited law. What sages clearly have not alleged is that a vast corpus of Halakhah derives from oral tradition, or that knowledge of that oral tradition was widely diffused among the sages themselves.

What we find is verbal formulations of rules. But at this stage, with the Mishnah of ca. 200, we detect no large concept of a Torah autonomous of the Written Torah (the Pentateuch) that exhibited counterpart traits of articulation and amplification and enjoyed equivalent status. The claim that a law comes from Moses at Sinai by oral tradition is particular to a few, specific rulings, and in the Mishnah's cases, tradition from Sinai validates what the sages have decided on their own. The further allegation, implicit but blatant, is that the outcome of the logic of the decision-making process is confirmed by Yohanan b. Zakkai's disciples, Eliezer and Joshua, in the story at Babylonian Talmud *Berakhot* 28a–b, which we met earlier. The story concerned Eliezer's and Joshua's debate on the oven of Akhnai and Joshua's insistence that while supernatural events confirm Eliezer's position, logic sustains his own contrary one, and it is sages, not Heaven, who in the end decide what the Torah will be. In the same important contexts in the Mishnah, the effect of claiming that a verbal formulation originated at Sinai is to demonstrate the reliability of sages' own decision-making processes, whether these are based on exegesis of Scripture or on their own logic.

THE PRIORITY OF THE ORAL TORAH

When we turn to the Talmud of the Land of Israel, we find an explicit claim that not just episodic rules or sayings but something constitutive of the Torah, namely, the Oral Torah, possessed by the sages and transmitted in the master-disciple-relationship, takes priority over the Written Torah. That Talmud took shape at the point at which, as we have seen, the Rabbinic sages addressed the Christian challenge. One claim of Christianity was to interpret Scripture properly; another was that "the Jews" misunderstood Scripture and that their additional teachings ("Oral Torah" to the rabbis) were spurious. In the face of that challenge, the Rabbinic sages took the position that the Oral Torah not only was authentic, revealed Torah of Sinai, but indeed superior in value to the written part of the Torah that Christians possessed along with Israel. Here is how that claim was set forth. We deal with a passage of the Mishnah in which an explicit reference to revelation of an Oral Torah to Moses at Sinai occurs and with how the Talmud of the Land of Israel then amplifies that claim. I insert comments to guide the reader through the passage.

Mishnah tractate *Peah* 2:5
(Mishnah and Yerushalmi Translation by Roger Brooks)
    A. One who sows his field with [only] one species [of seed], even if he brings the crop to the threshing floor in two lots,
    B. sets aside one [portion of produce as] peah [from the entire crop].
    C. [But if he] sowed [his field] with two species [of seeds], even if he brings [both crops] to the threshing floor in only one lot,
    D. [he] sets aside two [separate portions of produce as] peah, [one from each species of produce].
    E. He who sows his field with two [distinct] varieties of wheat [i.e., both a single species]—
    F. [if] he brings all of [the wheat] to the threshing floor in only one lot, [he] sets aside one [portion of produce as] peah.
    G. [But if he brings the wheat] to the threshing floor in two lots, [he] sets aside two [portions of produce as] peah.

The rule concerns leaving a corner of the field ("peah") for the poor. The problem is, How do we know the limits of a given field, a corner of which has to be left over and unharvested by the householder. What differentiates one field from another? Is it a physical marker, or is it the character of the crop? The particular problem concerns what happens if one sows two species of a single genus:

Mishnah tractate *Peah* 2:6

    A. Once R. Simeon of Mispah sowed [his field with two varieties of wheat].

    B. [The matter came] before Rabban Gamaliel. So they went up to the Chamber of Hewn Stone, and asked [about the law regarding sowing two varieties of wheat in one field].

    C. Said Nahum the Scribe, "I have received [the following ruling] from R. Miasha, who received it from his father, who received it from the Pairs, who received it from the Prophets, [who received] the law [given] to Moses on Sinai, regarding one who sows his field with two varieties of wheat:

    D. "If he brings [the two varieties of wheat] to the threshing floor in only one lot, [he] sets aside one [portion of produce as] peah.

    E. "If he brings [the wheat] to the threshing floor in two lots, [he] sets aside two [portions of produce as] peah."

The exact language of the Mishnah ruling turns out to preserve what was revealed at Sinai. Now the Talmud of the Land of Israel ("the Yerushalmi") takes over and comments on the matter:

Yerushalmi tractate *Peah* 2:6

    I.A. Said R. Zeira in the name of R. Yohanan, "If a ruling [on a matter of law] is transmitted to you and you do not know its rationale, do not reject it in favor of another [ruling with a lucid explanation]. For many matters of law were stated [transmitted] to Moses on Sinai, and [despite the fact that their rationale is unclear], all of them are embedded in the Mishnah!"

Here we have a clear and specific claim that laws, Halakhot, outside of the Halakhah of the Written Torah were transmitted to Moses at Sinai and are now embedded in the Mishnah. So to Yohanan is assigned the view that the Mishnah contains laws revealed by God to Moses at Sinai, and that these same laws have found their way into the Mishnah. Then the exact language of Mishnah 2:5a–d is reproduced at Mishnah 2:6d–e. The upshot is, we find the claim that we possess the exact words—ipsissima verba. What seemed to me implicit at the comparable passages of the Mishnah read separately from the Talmud, for example, at Mishnah tractates *Yadayim* and *Eduyyot* as well as here, is now made explicit: the Mishnah contains components deriving from God's revelation to Moses at Sinai, orally formulated and orally transmitted even as tractate *Abot* says.

    B. Said R. Abin, "[This advice] is proper. [For consider the ruling regarding] two varieties of wheat—were it not for the fact that Nahum [the Scribe] came along and explained [the law] to us, would we know [its rationale]? [No! Yet the rule clearly is Sinaitic, and hence has the status of authoritative law. In general, then, one should not reject a law just because its rationale is unclear.]"

That is one explanation for appeal to oral tradition from Sinai. It is a law that does not bear its own rationale and hence requires explicit articulation in oral tradition. But there are others, as are now specified.

II.A. [The Talmud now focuses on the difference between laws written at Sinai, and those transmitted orally. To this end, we consider several interpretations of Hos. 8:12]: R. Zeira in the name
of R. Eleazar: "'The many teachings I wrote for him [have been
treated as something alien]' (Hos. 8:12). Now do the Torah's
many teachings consist of written laws? [No!] Rather, [the verse
means that] those laws expounded on [the explicit authority of]
written verses [i.e., those with proof texts] are more numerous
[and so more unfamiliar and alien] than those expounded on
[the mere authority of] oral tradition [and without proof
texts]."
  B. And is this the proper [interpretation of Hos. 8:12]? [Are there
really more laws expounded with proof texts than without? No!]
Rather, this verse means that those matters expounded on [the
authority of] written sources are weightier than those
expounded merely on [the authority of] oral tradition.

The second explanation is familiar: oral tradition enjoys lower status than written. Hence what enjoys the support of proof texts is more authoritative.

  C. [Offering a different interpretation of Hos. 8:12], R. Judah ben
Pazzi says, "'The many teachings I wrote for him . . .' (Hos.
8:12)—this refers to the curses [for not following the Torah's
laws]. [This interpretation is consistent with the remainder of
the verse, which states], and even if [I wrote the curses], 'have
they not been treated as something alien?' [The point is that
God's curses only rarely are invoked on Israel, and hence are
regarded as strange by the people.]"

A third explanation appeals to the unique standing of Israel by reason of its possession of oral, as well as written, tradition. In this respect, it is claimed, Israel is
different from the nations, which have only written validation of their claims.

  D. [Providing yet another interpretation of the verse], said R. Abin,
"'Had I had written for you the bulk of my [orally transmitted]
Torah, you would be considered like a foreigner.' [For] what [is
the difference] between us and the gentiles? They bring forth
their books, and we bring forth our books; they bring forth their
national records, and we bring forth our national records." [The
only difference between Israel and the gentile nations is that a
portion of the Torah remains oral, and has a special claim upon
the nation of Israel.]

Continuing the foregoing allegation, we shall now review a demonstration that
oral tradition stands higher than written.

III.A. [The Talmud now reverts to the question posed previously at
II.B, whether laws transmitted orally or in writing are more
weighty.] R. Haggai said in the name of R. Samuel bar Nahman, "Some matters of law were transmitted orally, and some
matters of law were transmitted in writing, but we do not

know which of these are deemed more weighty. But [we can derive an answer] on the basis of that which is written [in Scripture], 'For in accordance with these commandments I make a covenant with you and with Israel' (Exod. 34:27). This proves that those [commandments] transmitted orally are more weighty."

B. R. Yohanan and R. Yudan b. R. Simeon [had a dispute over the proper interpretation of the verse just cited, Exod. 34:27]: One of them said, "If you observe [laws that are transmitted] orally and if you observe [laws that are transmitted] in writing, I shall establish a covenant with you. But if not, I shall not establish a covenant with you." [According to this view, the two types of laws are of equal weight.]

C. The other said, "[My covenant is established with you because of these orally transmitted words]. [But] if you not only observe that which is transmitted orally, but also uphold that which is transmitted in writing, [then in addition to the covenant], you will receive a reward. But if not, you will receive no reward." [According to this view, the laws transmitted orally are more weighty, because their observance leads to the establishment of God's covenant.]

Now Joshua b. Levi extends the claim of origin at Sinai to pretty much everything in the Rabbinic corpus, down to the last detail: the Torah given at Sinai included more than just the words written on the tablets, but also Scripture, the Mishnah, the Talmud, and Aggadah—and even what the experienced students in the future are going to conclude. Now the contents of the revelation at Sinai are vastly reconfigured, and the narrow limits of Oral Torah consisting of a few particular legal formulations are transcended.

IV.A. R. Joshua b. Levi said, "[The precise wording with which Scripture describes Sinaitic revelation is crucial, for Deut. 9:10 states, 'Then the Lord gave me two stone tablets, written with the finger of God; and upon them was written according to all these words that the Lord spoke with you in the mountain, out of the midst of the fire on the day of assembly.'] [Note that for] 'upon them [was written . . .],' [Scripture reads] 'and upon them [was written . . .];' [for] 'all [the words . . .],' [Scripture reads] 'according to all [the words . . .];' [for] 'words,' [Scripture reads] 'these words.' [These special formulations, including the extra particles, are meant to teach that the Torah given at Sinai included more than just the words written on the tablets, but also] Scripture, the Mishnah, the Talmud, and Aggadah. [All these types of law are deemed to have the authority of Sinai revelation.]"

B. [In fact, the verse implies that] even that which a learned student someday in the future will recite before his master has the status of a law transmitted to Moses on Sinai.

C. What reasoning [allows one to derive this point from Scripture]? "Sometimes there is a phenomenon of which they say, 'Look, this is new!' " (Qohelet/Eccl. 1:10a). His friend responds to him and says, "[There is no new teaching, for] 'It occurred long since, in ages that went before us' (Qohelet/Eccl. 1:10b)."

It would be difficult to point to a more explicit and detailed picture of what sages meant by "the Oral Torah" in the Halakhic context than the passage at hand. I see these allegations in sequence:

(1) Many matters of law were transmitted to Moses and are now embedded in the Mishnah;

(2) Such laws may prove counterintuitive, and that explains why they had to be revealed.

(3) The difference between laws deriving from Scripture and those deriving from oral tradition is that the former rest on proof texts, and the latter do not.

(4) Those resting on proof texts enjoy greater authority, or

(5) Those deriving from oral tradition are more highly valued, and

(6) Israel's own position in the hierarchy of the peoples rests on their unique possession of an oral tradition.

(7) Finally, the Torah revealed at Sinai encompasses everything: Scripture, Mishnah, Talmud, Aggadah—even what on the basis of reasoned inquiry the latest generations of disciples discern!

We have a number of freestanding statements, compositions comprising a dispute, and the like, not a systematic and coherent exposition of the topic at hand. In this full repertoire of possibilities, I find no consistent position on the matter, and I also cannot explain the program of the persons who compiled the composite; they have given us a collection of sayings on a common theme, but they have not formed them into a single argument for or against a cogent proposition.

In the Halakhic context, the claim that a law derives from oral tradition, now fully embodied in the language "Torah," and "Oral Torah," therefore has three basic components: (1) ipsissima verba from Sinai; (2) in a specific case, an assessment of the status of a given rule (parallel to demonstrations of origin via a proof text); and (3) in general circumstances, evaluation of the sages' legal processes of analysis in the context of the revelation at Sinai. Now what is at stake is fully exposed.

By "Oral Torah" sages may mean a specific teaching; or they may impute a status, higher or lower, to what lacks written validation; or they may allege that their processes of reasoning accord with those of the originally revealed Torah, so what they teach also is Torah and enjoys the standing of the Torah of Sinai.

What, in the aggregate, are the specific teachings assigned to origin at Sinai and transmission in oral tradition? They are these: The minimum number of eleven days (that by law one must reckon) between one menstrual period and another is based on a law received by Moses at Sinai. All fixed measurements enjoy the status of a law revealed to Moses at Sinai. The procession with the willow branch (Mishnah *Sukkah* 4:5), the water libation (Mishnah *Sukkah* 4:9), and the law concerning the ten saplings (*m. Shev.* 1:6) are among the rules instituted by the early prophets, but the laws originated at Sinai were forgotten and then were recovered by the prophets. In any case in which we have learned "nonetheless," we deal with a law revealed to Moses at Sinai. The manner of sewing the columns [of the scroll of the Torah] together is a law revealed to Moses at Sinai. The manner of tying *tefillin* is a law revealed to Moses at Sinai. Those letters— M, N, S, P, K—that appear in two forms were revealed as a law to Moses at Sinai. These are representative of the identified "laws revealed by God to Moses at Sinai."

A law that originates at Sinai in oral tradition is at issue, not "an entire [part of] the Torah," or "a specific Rabbinic document, the Mishnah." What makes Israel unique is its possession of the oral part of the Torah. A broader conception of orality makes its appearance as well. Not just exact wordings—for example, specific rules—or the gist of rules—for example, measurements—derive from Sinai. The very conception of an oral tradition in addition to Scripture now is broadened. Revelation itself is not limited to the exact words of the Written Torah, augmented by formulas considered to this point. "Revelation" now constitutes the results of a specified type of reasoning, so that what is in the Mishnah, Talmud, and Aggadah enjoy an autonomy, within the Torah, extending even to what a disciple will recite his master: all stand within the circle of the revelation of God to Moses at Sinai. Once the clause is included concerning a learned student and what he will someday recite before his master, we have moved from a definition of the Torah involving a specific, verbal revelation, whether transmitted in writing or in memory, to an altogether different meaning.

THE DISCIPLE OF THE SAGE AS A LIVING TORAH

The disciple of the sage now represents a figure within the framework of revelation. As part of the chain of tradition, he represents the Torah, a living being who is to be honored as the scroll of the Torah is honored:

> Yerushalmi *Megillah* 4:1.I.2
> > A. What is the law as to standing before a scroll of the Torah?
> > B. R. Hilqiah, R. Simon in the name of R. Eleazar: "Before her child [a disciple of a sage] one stands up, is it not an argument a fortiori that one stands up before the Torah itself?"
> > C. He who stands up to read in the Torah—on what count does he stand? Is it because of the honor owing to the Torah or because of the honor owing to the community?
> > D. If you say that it is because of the honor owing to the Torah, then even when one is by himself with the Torah scroll, [he must stand up to read in it].

E. If you say that it is because of the honor owing to the community still, when he is by himself with the Torah, he still should stand up on account of the honor owing to the Torah.

F. If you say so, then even when he is not engaged and not reading in the Torah [he still should stand up before the Torah]. [Accordingly, one stands up only when reading in public.]

G. R. Samuel bar R. Isaac went to a synagogue. He saw someone standing and serving as translator, leaning on a post. He said to him, "It is forbidden to you [to lean while standing]. For just as the Torah was given, originally, in fear and trembling, so we have to treat it with fear and trembling."

H. R. Haggai said R. Samuel bar R. Isaac went to a synagogue. He saw Huna standing and serving as translator and he had not set up anyone else in his stead [so he was both reading and translating himself]. He said to him, "It is forbidden to you, for just as it was given through an intermediary [namely, Moses] so we have to follow the custom of having an intermediary [so that the same person may not both read from the Torah and translate]."

I. R. Judah bar Pazzi went in and treated the matter as a question: "'The Lord spoke with you face to face at the mountain . . . while I stood between the Lord and you at that time, to declare to you the word of the Lord'" (Deut. 5:4–5).

J. R. Haggai said R. Samuel bar R. Isaac went into a synagogue. He saw a teacher [reading from] a translation spread out, presenting the materials from the book. He said to him, "It is forbidden to do it that way. Things which were stated orally must be presented orally. Things which were stated in writing must be presented in writing."

K. R. Haggai in the name of R. Samuel bar Nahman: "Some teachings were stated orally, and some teachings were stated in writing, and we do not know which of the two is more precious.

L. "But on the basis of that which is written, 'And the Lord said to Moses, "Write these words; in accordance with these words I have made a covenant with you and with Israel"' (Exod. 34:27), that is to say that the ones which are handed on orally are more precious."

M. R. Yohanan and R. Judah b. R. Simeon—one said, "[The meaning of the verse is this:] 'If you have kept what is handed on orally and if you have kept what is handed on in writing, then I shall make a covenant with you, and if not, I shall not make a covenant with you.'"

N. The other one said, "If you have kept what is handed on orally, and if you have kept what is handed on in writing, then you will receive a reward, and if not, you will not receive a reward."

O. [With reference to the following verse: "And the Lord gave me the two tablets of stone written with the finger of God; and on them were all the words which the Lord had spoken with you on the mountain, out of the midst of the fire on the day of the assembly" (Deut. 9:10),] said R. Joshua b. Levi, "[It is written,] 'on them,' 'and on them,' 'words,' 'the words,' 'all,' 'with all.' [These additional usages serve what purpose?]

P. "The reference is to Scripture, Mishnah, Talmud, and lore—and even what an experienced disciple is destined to teach in the future before his master already has been stated to Moses at Sinai."

Q. That is in line with the following verse of Scripture: "Is there a thing
of which it is said, 'this is new'? He and his fellow will reply to him,
'It has been already in the ages before us'" (Qohelet/Eccl. 1:10).

Here the oral formulation and transmission of part of the Torah are deemed to
establish a norm. What is originally oral must be transmitted only orally; so too for
what was originally written. The composite, made up of a number of distinct compositions, presents a variety of views on a range of cognate issues of orality. The issue
of orality is tangential to the main point, which has to do with the correct mode of
declaiming the Torah. The principle is established that the initially prevailing practice must govern: just as the Torah was given, originally, in fear and trembling, so we
have to treat it with fear and trembling; just as it was given through an intermediary (namely, Moses) so we have to follow the custom of having an intermediary.
Then, in an appended entry, comes the complex on orality. What was initially stated
orally must be presented orally, so too in writing. That the composite that so vastly
extends the range of the issue is put together in its own terms, not in response to the
larger issue of the construction to which it is appended, is self-evident.

I see several quite distinct positions here, and more than a single issue. Once the
fact that some traditions were formulated and transmitted in writing and others
orally, the question arises, Which is the preferred medium, as signified by the hierarchical standing of its message? That dispute, not integral to the composite, is then
worked out in its own terms, M–N. What is implicit is that a sizable corpus of
instruction is conveyed orally, not only in writing; the conception of "a law revealed
to Moses at Sinai" and handed on orally, embodying a few details of this and that,
makes no impact. On the contrary, the Torah encompasses not only Scripture but
"Mishnah, Talmud, and lore—and even what an experienced disciple is destined
to teach in the future before his master already has been stated to Moses at Sinai."
The Torah's orality now bears in its wake a much broader claim than one having to
do with specific contents, such as the Halakhic treatments define, or equivalency
or even superiority. Now the claim that part of the Torah is comprised by oral tradition serves to rationalize and validate a much larger corpus of teachings: the
entirety of the Rabbinic corpus, signified by the "even what . . ." clause.

THE FINAL ACCOUNT OF THE ORAL TORAH

Now let us survey all of the facts of the Rabbinic writings concerning the doctrine of the chain of tradition embodied in the Oral Torah set forth in the Mishnah and its companions through the two Talmuds.

What Did Rabbinic Sages Mean by the Oral Torah?

The following are the specific allegations that particular laws derive from oral formulation and oral transmission—not a huge list. (1) There are two Torahs, one

in writing, one in memory. Just as sages possess the one, so they possess the other. Sages' statement of the Torah does not cite the Written Torah but does recapitulate its main points (*b. Shabbat* 2:5.I:11/30b–31a). (2) The mode of Mishnah teaching, beginning with God's instruction of Moses and Moses' of Aaron, is to memorize a passage at a time, repeating it a number of times (*b. Erubin* 5:1.I.43/54b). God showed Moses the order of prayers as well (*b. Rosh Hashanah* 1:2.I.24/17b). (3) There are two Torahs, one in writing, the other in memory. The one is larger than the other. Traditions transmitted in the one medium are not to be transmitted in the other, a strict separation is preserved between the two (*b. Gittin* 5:8.I 9/60b). (4) A statement of an eminent authority may go over what is transmitted, also, as a law revealed to Moses at Sinai (*Baba Batra* 1:1.II.4/12a). (5) What the great sages teach is encompassed by the Torah revealed to Moses at Sinai, so that "a law given to Moses at Sinai" may include a proposition in no way articulated by the written part of the Torah. The full extent of sages' claim is contained in the phrase, "interpret on the basis of each point of the crowns heaps and heaps of laws," which means, whatever Aqiba is going to teach is deemed "a law revealed to Moses at Sinai" (*b. Menahot* 3:7.II.5/29b). (6) It is absolutely forbidden to write down decided laws; they are to be memorized only. Things that are in writing may not be transmitted in memory and vice versa (*b. Temurah* 2:1.III.1/14a–b). (7) Memorized traditions cannot be lost because the ruling of the majority will recapitulate Moses' law (*b. Temurah* 2:2.I.2/15a).

What Are the Components of the Myth?

The myth contains these principal elements: the dual Torah and the critical role of the sage in teaching the whole Torah (*b. Shabbat* 2:5.I:11/30b–31a). The process of memorization of the Mishnah in particular forms the focus of the myth, that it be done just as God did it with Moses at the outset (*b. Erubin* 5:1.I.43/54b). The division of the Torah into two parts, one in writing, the other in memory, is also carefully observed (*b. Gittin* 5:8.I 9/60b). Not providing for the oral Torah is a mark of heresy (*b. Qiddushin* 3:10–11.III.13/66a–b). Oral Torah states on the basis of its point of origin the conclusion that logic reaches on the basis of its rigorous mode of thought (*Baba Batra* 1:1.II.4/12a). "A law revealed to Moses at Sinai" need not recapitulate something Moses actually said; if it accords in logic with what originates in the Torah, it belongs in the Torah. Sages' amplification of minor details belong to the category of a "law revealed by God to Moses at Sinai" (*b. Menahot* 3:7.II.5/29b). The powerful denunciation of writing down what is supposed to be oral forms the fact at hand (*b. Temurah* 2:1.III.1/14a–b), and memorizing traditions and forgetting them is at issue (*b. Temurah* 2:2.I.2/15a).

In What Contexts Did It Serve?

Here is a summary of the contexts in the Rabbinic sources in which the myth of the dual Torah plays a role.

(1) In the encounter with outsiders to sages' circles, gentiles who wish to convert, and Jews who challenge sages' authority, the possession of the dual Torah is what defines the sages' authority and the faith of the Torah (*b. Shabbat* 2:5.I:11/30b–31a). (2) The sage teaches the disciple just as God taught Moses the Mishnah, so sages teach in that same manner to their disciples. The context is the sages' mode of instruction, the Mishnah forming the curriculum. How many times must the sage repeat the passage? Either a fixed number, or as many times as is required. While the Mishnah is not called "the Oral Torah," in context that is the intent (*b. Erubin* 5:1.I.43/54b). (3) It is not permitted to write down the traditions transmitted in memory (*b. Gittin* 5:8.I 9/60b). (4) Restoring the Torah if it is forgotten must involve recovering the oral part (*b. Qiddushin* 3:10–11.III.13/66a–b). (5) The sage gives a reason for his ruling, so if he says what the Oral Torah transmits, that is not a mere coincidence (*Baba Batra* 1:1.II.4/12a). (6) Moses does not understand Aqiba's teaching but accepts that that teaching is part of his Torah. Hence the maximalist claim of the extent of the Torah is defended on mythic grounds. That is not limited to the Mishnah, which does not figure here. The real issue is the standing of the sage's teaching and its correlation with that of Moses, and that is expressed explicitly (*b. Menahot* 3:7.II.5/29b). (7) Sages must transmit their rulings through memory, not by writing letters (*b. Temurah* 2:1.III.1/14a–b). (8) Can traditions be lost through forgetfulness? No, because through preserved practice and/or right reasoning, they can be recovered (*b. Temurah* 2:2.I.2/15a).

What Consequences Did Invoking the Myth Produce?

(1) The joining of the narrative statement of the myth with the entirety of the Torah in a saying that is not a citation of Scripture underscores the sage's centrality in the process of formulating and transmitting the Torah. (2) The preservation of the traditions via memory may fail, but the traditions will not be lost, because the accepted opinion of a majority of sages will restore the tradition in an accurate version (*b. Erubin* 5:1.I.43/54b). The liturgy is not classified as part of the Oral Torah (*b. Rosh Hashanah* 1:2.I.24/17b). (3) Some hold that the oral part of the Torah is larger than the written part; the oral Torah encompasses more traditions than the Mishnah alone. Scribal punctiliousness for the writing of the Torah extends also (*b. Gittin* 5:8.I 9/60b). (4) A heretic is someone who rejects the duality of the Torah (*b. Qiddushin* 3:10–11.III.13/66a–b). (5) At issue is the relationship between revelation and reason; they are shown to coincide (*Baba Batra* 1:1.II.4/12a). (6) Moses' own understanding of matters does not limit the extension of the Torah. The sage's allegation that a given teaching constitutes a law revealed by God to Moses at Sinai suffices. Hence the Written Torah does not stand in judgment of the Oral Torah; what governs is the sages' own reason (*b. Menahot* 3:7.II.5/29b). (7) While it is forbidden to write down what is meant to be handed on in memory, if it is necessary to do so in order to preserve the tradition, it is permitted to violate the law (*b. Temurah* 2:1.III.1/14a–b). The gen-

eral prohibition against writing down the oral part of the Torah pertains, by implication, not only to the Mishnah but to all pertinent Rabbinic traditions (*b. Temurah* 2:1.III.1/14a–b). (8) The affirmation of right reasoning, on the one side, and the reliability of common practice in restoring the revealed law of oral venue, on the other, form the polemic of this passage (*b. Temurah* 2:2.I.2/15a).

We now have exact knowledge of the components of the myth of the dual Torah, the contexts in which these find a place, severally and jointly, and the conclusions that are implicit in invoking that myth. Let us now specify the components of the myth and the meanings assigned to them, start to finish. I have identified five categories that pertain and that are to be differentiated, as indicated:

1. The component involving the name of Moses, the category "Torah," and the conception of tradition
2. The definition of "the Oral Torah" as a repository of laws set forth by God to Moses at Sinai
3. The specification of particular laws originating with Moses at Sinai, not written in the Torah or derived from the Torah
4. The matter of the status of such laws as are revealed by God to Moses at Sinai
5. The explicit myth of the dual Torah, written and oral

In the Judaism set forth in the Rabbinic literature, then, the foundations of the faith are laid by Scripture and oral tradition, with the Written Torah mediated by the sages of the Oral Torah. The Rabbinic documents represent the writing down of that originally oral Torah, and upon that doctrine was built the entire construction that is Rabbinic Judaism.

Chapter 10

Miracles in Nature: Illness and Healing

MIRACLES: RAIN MAKING

One important part of the Christian record focuses on the miracles in nature performed by Jesus, including his power of healing. About Rabbinic sages, comparable stories are told. These stories in the context of the Gospels form part of the message of Christianity, and, in the setting of the Rabbinic canon, in their own terms go over the larger theological statement of Rabbinic Judaism. There is nothing surprising in Rabbinic Judaism's invoking the record of miracles in times past and in the age of the sages themselves. For Rabbinic Judaism inherited from Scripture and greatly enhanced the record of God's intervention into nature to make his presence and will known. The plagues in Egypt and the splitting of the Sea of Reeds when the Israelites made their exodus from Egyptian slavery represent only a small part of the Scriptural heritage, and we should not find surprising that important sages likewise were credited with supernatural power.

But Rabbinic Judaism viewed as a system does not favor divine intervention into the affairs of this world, as the story about Joshua and Eliezer in the debate about the status of the oven of Akhnai has already shown us. That particular Judaism claimed to set forth a systematic account of matters, leaving little room for one-time, unique actions. To put the matter simply, for Christianity Christ was (and is) unique; for Rabbinic Judaism, the Torah of the sage was (and is) exemplary. That is why, in Rabbinic Judaism in the formative age, a general theory deriving from the logic of the Rabbinic system as a whole explains the rules that govern God's intervention, both through miracles of a salvific character and through acts of healing illness. The same theology that accounts for miraculous provision of rain also explains why people suffer illness, old age, and death. That general theory is readily summarized: God is above all just, and rational rules of justice regulate, and account for, both miracles and illness.

Any account of Judaism must begin with God's freedom to do what he wishes, without regard to the rational rules at all. Heaven has the power not only to respond to human virtue but to make its own selections of persons to be recognized and empowered and individuated. Rabbinic Judaism recognizes a class of miracle workers, favored by Heaven but not qualified by Torah-learning or distinguished by virtue. The following story indicates that the Halakhah regards with little enthusiasm the capacity of wonder-workers to accomplish what ordinary folk cannot, especially when such wonder-workers exhibit a confidence that shades over into arrogance toward Heaven—the opposite of the attitude of humility that sages identify as the distinguishing trait of the exemplary individual:

> Mishnah tractate *Ta'anit* 3:9–10
> > 3:9
> > > A. On account of every sort of public trouble—may it not happen—do they sound the shofar,
> > > B. except for an excess of rain.
> > > C. M'SH S: They said to Honi the Circle Drawer, "Pray for rain."
> > > D. He said to them, "Go and take in the clay ovens used for Passover, so that they not soften [in the rain which is coming]."
> > > E. He prayed, but it did not rain.
> > > F. What did he do?
> > > G. He drew a circle and stood in the middle of it and said before Him, "Lord of the world! Your children have turned to me, for before you, I am like a member of the family. I swear by your great name—I'm simply not moving from here until you take pity on your children!"
> > > H. It began to rain drop by drop.
> > > I. He said, "This is not what I wanted, but rain for filling up cisterns, pits, and caverns."
> > > J. It began to rain violently.
> > > K. He said, "This is not what I wanted, but rain of good will, blessing, and graciousness."
> > > L. Now it rained the right way, until the Israelites had to flee from Jerusalem up to the Temple Mount because of the rain.
> > > M. Now they came and said to him, "Just as you prayed for it to rain, now pray for it to go away."
> > > N. He said to them, "Go, see whether the stone of those who stray has disappeared [under water]."
> > 3:10
> > > A. Simeon b. Shatah said to him, "If you were not Honi, I should decree a ban of excommunication against you. But what am I

going to do to you? For you importune before the Omnipresent, so he does what you want, like a son who importunes his father, so he does what he wants.

B. "Concerning you Scripture says, 'Let your father and your mother be glad, and let her that bore you rejoice'" (Prov. 23:25).

The key language is at 3:10a. Simeon cannot favor this extraordinary resort to divine intervention, but he acknowledges that Heaven can do what it likes. The view of this story runs parallel to that of the rule about an individual's showing piety. It attests to the outer limits of individuation: those set by Heaven. The contrast between Honi and Mr. Pentakaka or the man of Kefar Immi hardly requires articulation. But the Halakhah does more than afford valid media of self-differentiation through appropriate acts of virtue. Rabbinic Judaism also makes provision for individuation through entirely personal predilections and preferences.

What, then, are the rules that explain the miracle of rainfall, on which life in the Holy Land depends? Rain falls because of the merit of the inhabitants, or fails because of their sins. Rain is better than irrigation, for specific, rational causes. The merit of the Land, loyalty, and suffering account for rain. The sins of idolatry, fornication, murder, and dissimulation account for the failure of rain.

Here are the Mishnah's rules on responding to drought, which clearly imply that Israel bears responsibility for its condition and through acts of prayer and piety can do something about it:

Mishnah tractate *Ta'anit* 3:3

    A. And so too: A town on which rain did not fall,

    B. as it is said, "And I caused it to rain upon one city and caused it not to rain upon another city, one piece was rained upon and the piece on which it rained not did wither" (Amos 4:7)

    C. that town declares a fast day and sounds the shofar.

    D. And all its neighbors fast but do not sound the shofar.

    E. R. Aqiba says, "They sound the shofar but do not fast."

Yerushalmi tractate *Ta'anit* 3:3. I:1–4

  I:1

    A. Said R. Simeon, "It is written, 'And I caused it to rain upon one city, and caused it not to rain upon another city, one piece was rained upon, and the piece on which it rained not did wither' (Amos 4:7): the merit associated with a particular field is what did it."

  I:2

    A. It is for four reasons that rain comes from above [rather than depending on water rising up from the nethermost water, or having people rely upon irrigation from wells]:

    B. It is because of high-handed men [who would divert the current of irrigation ditches and invade others' riparian rights].

    C. It is because of noxious mist.

    D. It is so that the one above will drink water as does the one below.

    E. And it is so that all will look to heaven.

  I:3

    A. It is because of the merit of three parties that rain falls:

      B. It is because of the merit of the land, the merit of steadfast loy-
         alty, and the merit of suffering.

      C. And all three derive from a single verse of Scripture: "Whether
         for correction, or for his land, or for love ['kindness'], he causes
         it to happen" (Job 37:13).

    I:4

      A. On account of four sorts of sin are rains withheld: because of the
         sins of idolatry, fornication, and murder, and because of people
         who pledge charity in public but do not hand over the money.

Events of nature, as much as of history, respond to the moral character of the community. Rain falls on those who merit it and is withheld from the wicked. The familiar order and reason pertains. The Land, the loyalty of the inhabitants, and the merit attained through suffering (and consequent atonement)—these explain why it rains. Idolatry, fornication, and murder—the cardinal sins of individuals—and failure to pay one's pledge—the sin against the community—account for withholding rain.

WHAT COMPELS DIVINE FAVOR?

If Honi's is the wrong way to bring rain, exploiting Heaven's grace beyond one's just deserts, then what accounts for a rational transaction, one in accord with rules? Rabbis acknowledge that one may pray for rain and have one's prayers answered, and they point to the exemplary character of those who possess that power. Of what does that power consist?

It consists of acts that bring Heaven's favor, because they are deeds that Heaven cannot coerce but nonetheless greatly values. God craves the love of humanity, which is precisely what he cannot coerce. So too, God responds to deeds of such nobility, such self-abnegation, that he cannot compel people to perform such deeds, but he is himself compelled to respond to them.

There is an untranslatable Hebrew word for the matter, *zekhut,* meaning, "the heritage of supererogatory virtue and its consequent entitlements." In Rabbinic Judaism *zekhut* stands for the empowerment, of a supernatural character, that derives the virtue of one's ancestry or from one's own virtuous deeds of a particular kind, specifically, deeds not commanded but impelled by utter generosity of the heart. They make a difference only when they are done without hope let alone prospect of recompense and without pressure of any kind. No single word in American English bears the same meaning, nor is there a synonym for *zekhut* in the canonical writings. But there is the antonym *sin.* Sin represents an act of rebellion; *zekhut,* an act of humble and willing, gratuitous submission. Thus the two represent binary opposites.

Honi possesses no entitlement to supernatural favor, which is gained through deeds that the law of the Torah cannot require but does favor: what one does on one's own volition, beyond the measure of the law. Here I see the opposite of sin.

A sin is what one has done by one's own volition beyond all limits of the law. So an act that generates *zekhut* for the individual is the counterpart and opposite: what one does by one's own volition that also is beyond all requirements of the law.

> Yerushalmi tractate *Ta'anit* 1:4.I
>
> L. A certain ass driver appeared before the rabbis [the context requires: in a dream] and prayed, and rain came. The rabbis sent and brought him and said to him, "What is your trade?"
>
> M. He said to them, "I am an ass driver."
>
> N. They said to him, "And how do you conduct your business?"
>
> O. He said to them, "One time I rented my ass to a certain woman, and she was weeping on the way, and I said to her, 'What's with you?' and she said to me, 'The husband of that woman [me] is in prison [for debt], and I wanted to see what I can do to free him.' So I sold my ass and I gave her the proceeds, and I said to her, 'Here is your money, free your husband, but do not sin [by becoming a prostitute to raise the necessary funds].'"
>
> P. They said to him, "You are worthy of praying and having your prayers answered."

The ass driver clearly has a powerful lien on Heaven, so his prayers are answered even while those of others are not. What did he do to get that entitlement? He did what no law could demand: impoverished himself to save the woman from a "fate worse than death."

> Q. In a dream of R. Abbahu, Mr. Pentakaka ["Five sins"] appeared, who prayed that rain would come, and it rained. R. Abbahu sent and summoned him. He said to him, "What is your trade?"
>
> R. He said to him, "Five sins does that man [I] do every day, [for I am a pimp:] hiring whores, cleaning up the theater, bringing home their garments for washing, dancing, and performing before them."
>
> S. He said to him, "And what sort of decent thing have you ever done?"
>
> T. He said to him, "One day that man [I] was cleaning the theater, and a woman came and stood behind a pillar and cried. I said to her, 'What's with you?' And she said to me, 'That woman's [my] husband is in prison, and I wanted to see what I can do to free him,' so I sold my bed and cover, and I gave the proceeds to her. I said to her, 'Here is your money, free your husband, but do not sin.'"
>
> U. He said to him, "You are worthy of praying and having your prayers answered."

Q moves us still further, since the named man has done everything sinful that one can do, and, more to the point, he does it every day. So the singularity of the act of *zekhut*, which suffices if done only one time, encompasses its power to outweigh a life of sin—again, an act of *zekhut* as the mirror image and opposite of sin. Here again, the single act of saving a woman from a "fate worse than death" has sufficed. But a larger pattern characterizes the virtuous person:

> V. A pious man from Kefar Imi appeared [in a dream] to the rabbis. He prayed for rain and it rained. The rabbis went up to him. His

householders told them that he was sitting on a hill. They went
out to him, saying to him, "Greetings," but he did not answer
them.

W. He was sitting and eating, and he did not say to them, "You
break bread too."

X. When he went back home, he made a bundle of faggots and put
his cloak on top of the bundle [instead of on his shoulder].

Y. When he came home, he said to his household [wife], "These
rabbis are here [because] they want me to pray for rain. If I pray
and it rains, it is a disgrace for them, and if not, it is a profanation of the Name of Heaven. But come, you and I will go up [to
the roof] and pray. If it rains, we shall tell them, 'We are not worthy to pray and have our prayers answered.'"

Z. They went up and prayed and it rained.

AA. They came down to them [and asked], "Why have the rabbis
troubled themselves to come here today?"

BB. They said to him, "We wanted you to pray so that it would rain."

CC. He said to them, "Now do you really need my prayers? Heaven
already has done its miracle."

DD. They said to him, "Why, when you were on the hill, did we say
hello to you, and you did not reply?"

EE. He said to them, "I was then doing my job. Should I then inter-
rupt my concentration [on my work]?"

FF. They said to him, "And why, when you sat down to eat, did you
not say to us 'You break bread too'?"

GG. He said to them, "Because I had only my small ration of bread.
Why would I have invited you to eat by way of mere flattery
[when I knew I could not give you anything at all]?"

HH. They said to him, "And why when you came to go down, did
you put your cloak on top of the bundle?"

II. He said to them, "Because the cloak was not mine. It was borrowed for use at prayer. I did not want to tear it."

JJ. They said to him, "And why, when you were on the hill, did your
wife wear dirty clothes, but when you came down from the
mountain, did she put on clean clothes?"

KK. He said to them, "When I was on the hill, she put on dirty
clothes, so that no one would gaze at her. But when I came home
from the hill, she put on clean clothes, so that I would not gaze
on any other woman."

LL. They said to him, "It is well that you pray and have your prayers
answered."

The pious man of V, finally, enjoys the recognition of the sages by reason of his
lien on Heaven, able as he is to pray and bring rain. What has so endowed him
with *zekhut?* Acts of punctiliousness of a moral order: concentrating on his work,
avoiding an act of dissimulation, integrity in the disposition of a borrowed object,
his wife's concern not to attract other men, and her equal concern to make herself attractive to her husband. None of these stories refers explicitly to *zekhut;* all
of them tell us about what it means to enjoy not an entitlement by inheritance
but a lien accomplished by one's own supererogatory acts of restraint.

The critical importance of the heritage of virtue together with its supernatural entitlements emerges in a striking claim. Even though a man was degraded, one action sufficed to win for him that heavenly glory to which rabbis in lives of Torah-study aspired. A single remarkable deed, exemplary for its deep humanity, sufficed to win for an ordinary person the *zekhut* that elicits supernatural favor enjoyed by some rabbis on account of their Torah-study. *Zekhut* represents a power that only God can ultimately grasp: the power of weakness. It is what the weak and excluded and despised can do that outweighs what the great masters of the Torah—impressed with the power of the ass driver to pray and get his prayers answered—have accomplished. *Zekhut* also forms the inheritance of the disinherited: what you receive as a heritage when you have nothing in the present and have gotten nothing in the past, that scarce resource that is free and unearned but much valued.

Now we find one antonym for *zekhut,* which, as I said just now, is sin. A person by his action brings about *zekhut* for the community, or he may by his action cause the community to sin:

Mishnah tractate *Abot* 5:18
    A. He who causes *zekhut* to the community never causes sin.
    B. And he who causes the community to sin—they never give him
       a sufficient chance to attain penitence.

Here the contrast is between causing *zekhut* and causing sin, so *zekhut* is the opposite of sin. The continuation is equally clear that a person attained *zekhut* and endowed the community with *zekhut*—or sinned and made the community sin:

    C. Moses attained *zekhut* and bestowed *zekhut* on the community.
    D. So the *zekhut* of the community is assigned to his [credit],
    E. as it is said, "He executed the justice of the Lord and his judg-
       ments with Israel" (Deut. 33:21).
    F. Jeroboam sinned and caused the community to sin.
    G. So the sin of the community is assigned to his [debit],
    H. as it is said, "For the sins of Jeroboam which he committed and
       wherewith he made Israel to sin" (1 Kgs. 15:30).

Moses through actions of his own (of an unspecified sort) acquired *zekhut,* which is the credit for such actions that accrued to him and bestowed on him certain supernatural entitlements. He, for his part, passed on as an inheritance that credit, a lien on Heaven for the performance of these same supernatural entitlements: *zekhut,* pure and simple. The upshot is to present *zekhut* as (1) an action, as distinct from a (mere) attitude, that (2) is precisely the opposite of a sinful one. It is, moreover, an action that (3) may be done by an individual or by the community at large, and one that (4) a leader may provoke the community to do (or not do). Whence then the lien on Heaven? It is through deeds of a supererogatory character—to which Heaven responds by deeds of a supererogatory character. Self-abnegation or restraint shown by man precipitates a counterpart attitude in Heaven, hence generating *zekhut*. The relationship measured by *zekhut*—Heaven's response by an act of uncoerced favor to a person's uncoerced gift, for example, act of gentility, restraint, or self-abnegation—contains an element of unpredictability for which appeal to the *zekhut* inherited from ancestors accounts. So while one cannot coerce heaven, he can through *zekhut* gain acts of favor from Heaven, and that is by doing what Heaven cannot require but only desire. Heaven then responds to man's attitude in carrying out what transcends his duties. The simple fact that rabbis cannot pray and bring rain but a simple ass driver can tells the whole story. That act of pure disinterest—giving the woman his means of livelihood—is the one that gains Heaven's deepest interest. And, we must not miss the starting point of the transaction, the woman's act of utter and tangible self-sacrifice in behalf of her husband, which wins the ass driver's empathy and provokes the action to which Heaven responds.

SICKNESS: ITS CAUSES AND ITS CURE

From the matter of miracles, represented by praying for rain and having one's prayers answered, we turn to the opposite: the Rabbinic explanation of sickness, old age, and death. Here too, sages invoke a coherent theory to deal in a consistent way with a given detail. Stated simply: they say the same thing about many things.

The general theory that explains the one accounts for the other too: God responds to the human condition and will, and while a divine purpose underlies sickness, old age, and death, still, the response accords with rational rules. Specifically, there are explanations in the Torah for whatever happens to people, and sickness is no exception. One's physical condition corresponds to one's moral condition. But the Rabbinic sages did not regard sickness, old age, and death as necessarily representing a punishment. The patriarchs themselves asked God to bestow old age, suffering, and sickness because the world needed them. These components of the human condition not only do not form challenges to the logic of God's just governance of the world, but express that very benevolence that infuses justice. So the patriarchs themselves initially beseeched God to bestow on man the blessings of old age, suffering, and sickness, each for its rational purpose.

> *Genesis Rabbah* LXV:IX.1
>> A. "When Isaac was old, and his eyes were dim, so that he could not see, he called Esau his older son, and said to him, 'My son,' and he answered, 'Here I am'" (Gen. 27:1):
>> B. Said R. Judah bar Simon, "Abraham sought [the physical traits of] old age [so that from one's appearance, people would know that he was old]. He said before him, 'Lord of all ages, when a man and his son come in somewhere, no one knows whom to honor. If you crown a man with the traits of old age, people will know whom to honor.'
>> C. "Said to him the Holy One, blessed be he, 'By your life, this is a good thing that you have asked for, and it will begin with you.'

D. "From the beginning of the book of Genesis to this passage, there is no reference to old age. But when Abraham our father came along, the traits of old age were given to him, as it is said, 'And Abraham was old' (Gen. 24:1).'"

So much for old age, but what about what goes with it, the suffering of infirmities? Here Isaac makes his contribution, now being credited with that very conception that, as we have seen, explains the justice of human suffering:

E. "Isaac asked God for suffering. He said before him, 'Lord of the age, if someone dies without suffering, the measure of strict justice is stretched out against him. But if you bring suffering on him, the measure of strict justice will not be stretched out against him. [Suffering will help counter the man's sins, and the measure of strict justice will be mitigated through suffering by the measure of mercy.]'

F. "Said to him the Holy One, blessed be he, 'By your life, this is a good thing that you have asked for, and it will begin with you.'

G. "From the beginning of the book of Genesis to this passage, there is no reference to suffering. But when Isaac came along, suffering was given to him: his eyes were dim.'"

Finally, what of sickness, the third in the components of man's fate? That is Jacob's contribution, and the wisdom and good will of God come once more to full articulation in suffering:

H. "Jacob asked for sickness. He said before him, 'Lord of all ages, if a person dies without illness, he will not settle his affairs for his children. If he is sick for two or three days, he will settle his affairs with his children.'

I. "Said to him the Holy One, blessed be he, 'By your life, this is a good thing that you have asked for, and it will begin with you.'

J. "That is in line with this verse: 'And someone said to Joseph, "Behold, your father is sick"' (Gen. 48:1)."

K. Said R. Levi, "Abraham introduced the innovation of old age, Isaac introduced the innovation of suffering, Jacob introduced the innovation of sickness."

We proceed now to a further case of the same classification, now chronic illness and its origin in the wisdom of the saints, and now Hezekiah:

L. "Hezekiah introduced the innovation of chronic illness. He said to him, 'You have kept a man in good condition until the day he dies. But if someone is sick and gets better, he will carry out a complete and sincere act of repentance for his sins.'

M. "Said to him the Holy One, blessed be he, 'By your life, this is a good thing that you have asked for, and it will begin with you.'

N. "'The writing of Hezekiah, king of Judah, when he had been sick and recovered of his sickness' (Isa. 38:9)."

O. Said R. Samuel b. Nahman, "On the basis of that verse we know that between one illness and another there was an illness more serious than either one."

Old age, suffering, and sickness do not represent flaws in creation but things to be desired. Each serves a good purpose. All form acts of divine mercy. The mode of explanation appeals to reason and practical considerations attached thereto.

Still, matters do not come out even; all die, but not everyone suffers premature death or sickness. Much more galling, sometimes wicked people live long, healthy, and prosperous lives, happily making everyone around them miserable, then die peacefully in their sleep at a ripe old age. And—then or now—one need not visit a cancer ward to find misery afflicting genuinely good and pious people. So while the doctrine of the benevolence expressed by sickness, suffering, and old age serves, it hardly constitutes a universal and sufficient justification. And, however reasonable suffering may be shown to be, in the end reason hardly suffices in the face of the raw agony of incurable illness. That is why, in sages' view, further responses to Job, Jeremiah, and Qoheleth are called for. One further effort to bring suffering within the framework of the rational, to show the justice of the matter, is called forth. Specifically, the same anomalies in the just order encompassing private life may come about for yet another reason, which is God's own plan. Specifically, when the righteous suffer, it is God who is testing them.

> *Genesis Rabbah* LV:II.1f.
> 1. A. "The Lord tries the righteous, but the wicked and him who
>   loves violence his soul hates" (Ps. 11:5).

This is now embodied in metaphors drawn from the potter, the flax maker, and the farmer:

> B. Said R. Jonathan, "A potter does not test a weak utensil, for if
>   he hits it just once, he will break it. What does the potter test?
>   He tests the strong ones, for even if he strikes them repeatedly,
>   they will not break. So the Holy One, blessed be he, does not
>   try the wicked but the righteous: 'The Lord tries the righteous'
>   (Ps. 11:5)."
> C. Said R. Yosé bar Haninah, "When a flax maker knows that the
>   flax is in good shape, then the more he beats it, the more it will
>   improve and glisten. When it is not of good quality, if he beats
>   it just once, he will split it. So the Holy One, blessed be he, does
>   not try the wicked but the righteous: 'The Lord tries the righ-
>   teous' (Ps. 11:5)."
> D. Said R. Eleazar, "The matter may be compared to a farmer
>   [Hebrew: householder] who has two heifers, one strong, one
>   weak. On whom does he place the yoke? It is on the one that is
>   strong. So the Holy One, blessed be he, does not try the wicked
>   but the righteous: 'The Lord tries the righteous' (Ps. 11:5)."

We conclude the exercise with the juxtaposition of the base verse, Genesis 22:1, and the intersecting verse, Psalm 11:5, at the meeting of which the point just now stated was triggered:

Genesis Rabbah LV:III.1
> A. Another interpretation: "The Lord tries the righteous, but the wicked and him who loves violence his soul hates" (Ps. 11:5):
> B. The cited verse speaks of Abraham: "And it came to pass after these things God tested Abraham" (Gen. 22:1).

The suffering of the righteous pays tribute to their strength and is a mark of their virtue. That is shown by appeal both to analogies (potter, flax maker, householder) and Scripture. Suffering then shows God's favor for the one who suffers, indicating that such a one is worthy of God's attention and special interest.

That suffering is a valued gift explains the critical importance of the theological principle that one should accept whatever God metes out, even suffering. In a context defined by the conviction that suffering forms a gift from a benevolent, just God, we cannot find surprising that loving God should involve accepting punishment as well as benefit. This is stated in so many words: One is obligated to bless over evil as one blesses over the good, as it is said, "And you shall love the Lord your God with all your heart, with all your soul, and with all your might" (Deut. 6:5). "With all your heart"—with both of your inclinations, with the good inclination and with the evil inclination. "And with all your soul"—even if He takes your soul. "And with all your might"—with all of your money (*m. Ber.* 9:4a–e). Accordingly, the correct attitude toward suffering entails grateful acknowledgment that what God metes out is just and merciful. The same matter is amplified in the following exegesis of the same verses of Scripture:

Sifré to Deuteronomy XXXII:V.1–12
> 1. A. R. Aqiba says, "Since it is said, 'with all your soul,' it is an argument a fortiori; that we should encompass, 'with all your might.'
> B. "Why then does Scripture say, 'with all your might'?
> C. "It is to encompass every single measure that God metes out to you, whether the measure of good or the measure of punishment."

Now we turn to the familiar position that since suffering is a medium of atonement and repentance, people should accept it thankfully:

> 5. A. And, furthermore, a person should rejoice in suffering more than in good times. For if someone lives in good times his entire life, he will not be forgiven for such sin as may be in his hand.
> B. And how shall he attain forgiveness? Through suffering.
> 6. A. R. Eliezer b. Jacob says, "Lo, Scripture says, 'For whom the Lord loves he corrects, even as a father corrects the son in whom he delights' (Prov. 3:12).
> B. "What made the son be pleasing to the father? You must say it was suffering [on account of correction]."

God punishes with love and, as we already know, some types of suffering—the ones that permit Torah-study withal—constitute suffering inflicted with love:

7. A. R. Meir says, "Lo, Scripture says, 'And you shall consider in your
      heart, that as a man chasten his son, so the Lord your God chas-
      tens you' (Deut. 8:5).
   B. "'You know in your heart the deeds that you did, and also the
      suffering that I brought upon you, which was not in accord with
      the deeds that you did at all.'"
8. A. R. Yosé b. R. Judah says, "Beloved is suffering, for the name of
      the Omnipresent rests upon the one upon whom suffering
      comes,
   B. "as it is said, 'So the Lord your God chastens you' (Deut. 8:5)."
9. A. R. Nathan b. R. Joseph says, "Just as a covenant is made through
      the land, so a covenant is made through suffering, as it is said,
      'The Lord your God chastens you' (Deut. 8:7)."
   B. "And it says, 'For the Lord your God brings you into a good
      land' (Deut. 8:7)."

The composite concludes with the familiar statement of the same matter, that suffering is precious, not as exegesis of Scripture but as a narrative of a colloquy
among the exemplary sages. This protracted composite shows the normative
standing of the conviction that comes to expression in the several media of discourse: didactic, exegetical, and even (pseudo-)narrative. Proof derives from Scripture, from analogy, from the lives and teachings of exemplary sages. The entire
intent is clear: people are expected to accept suffering as a mark of divine favor
and love, as an indication that God has special confidence in them, or that God
has a particular purpose in dealing with them as he does. Even the patriarchs asked
for sickness, old age, and other forms of suffering, all the more reason gratefully
to accept as a mark of divine justice the miseries of the human condition.

WHAT ACCOUNTS FOR ILLNESS AND SUFFERING?

It ought, then, to follow that just as a given action will precipitate, on the part of
the just God, a predictable reaction, so sages should find plausible explanations
for misfortune and reliable bases for foretelling the future as well. If one suffers
such-and-such a penalty for doing so-and-so, then under ordinary circumstances,
if one suffers so-and-so, it is because he has committed such-and-such a deed.
This is made explicit in an account of why certain calamities befall:

> Mishnah tractate *Abot* 5:8–9
>   A. There are seven forms of punishment which come upon the
>   world for seven kinds of transgression.
>   B. (1) [If] some people give tithes and some people do not give
>   tithes, there is a famine from drought.
>   C. So some people are hungry and some have enough.

The match—a pattern of some giving and some not—is that some suffer, and
some do not. Here someone ought to say that those that do not give tithes will

go hungry; that is, in fact, said in other sources. Now comes the match once more: no one gives, so everyone starves.

> D. (2) [If] everyone decided not to tithe, there is a famine of unrest
> and drought.
> E. (3) [If all decided] not to remove dough offering, there is a
> famine of totality.

We move from famine to pestilence, accounting for epidemics in the same reasonable way:

> F. (4) Pestilence comes to the world on account of the death penalties which are listed in the Torah but which are not in the hands of the court [to inflict];
> G. and because of the produce of the Seventh Year [which people buy and sell].

The sword of justice, which is rational and orderly, is replaced, when justice is delayed, by the sword of war, which is chaotic:

> H. (5) A sword comes into the world because of the delaying of justice and perversion of justice, and because of those who teach the Torah not in accord with the law.
>
> 5:9
> A. (6) A plague of wild animals comes into the world because of vain oaths and desecration of the Divine Name.

Now we move to the level of what happens to all Israel, not only to persons or communities. We invoke what we shall see as the three absolute sins, that is, actions that are sinful in any and all circumstances: idolatry, fornication, and murder. These bring about Israel's exile:

> B. (7) Exile comes into the world because of those who worship idols, because of fornication, and because of bloodshed,
> C. and because of the neglect of the release of the Land [in the year of release].

We proceed to details, worked out in response to the enumeration of the years of the seven-year cycle that governs. In specified years, a given category of tithes is required of the farmers. Then if these are not given in the years that they are required, penalties follow:

> D. At four turnings in the years pestilence increases: in the Fourth Year, in the Seventh Year, in the year after the Seventh Year, and at the end of the Festival [of Tabernacles] every year:
> E. (1) in the Fourth Year, because of the poor man's tithe of the Third Year [which people have neglected to hand over to the poor];
> F. (2) in the Seventh Year, because of the poor man's tithe of the Sixth Year;

G. (3) in the year after the Seventh Year, because of the dealing in produce of the Seventh Year;

H. and (4) at the end of the Festival every year, because of the thievery of the dues [gleanings and the like] owing to the poor [not left for them in the antecedent harvest].

Here the probative evidence derives not from Scripture but from an alleged correspondence of condition and its consequence, so, for example, *m. Abot* 5:8b–c, where the drought affects some, not others. If all are guilty, the famine is complete.

Again, we see the notion of the complement and match at 5:8h. The sword serves justice, politics standing for the legitimate exercise of violence; or it stands for injustice, that comes through war. Then if the politics of justice does not bring about justice, the sword of justice becomes the agency of the opposite. At 5:9b the standard list of mortal sins—the triplet of idolatry, fornication, and bloodshed—is invoked to match what sages deem the insufferable penalty of exile from the Holy Land—but then mistreatment of the Land itself finds its match in exile as well, measure for measure. When, at Leviticus 26:34 God through Moses threatens to penalize Israel for neglecting the Sabbatical Year that is owed to the Land through a forcible Sabbatical, Scripture says no less. The insistence on the perfect match of crime and punishment yields a collection of illustrations; the allegation then is a given, meant to be illustrated, rather than a proposition to be proved. Here then we see what it means to maintain an exact correspondence between sin and penalty, crime and punishment.

If sages had to state the logic that imposes order and proportion on all relationships—the social counterpart to the laws of gravity—they would point to justice: what accords with justice is logical, and what does not is irrational. Ample evidence derives from Scripture's enormous corpus of facts to sustain in sages' view that the moral order, based on justice, governs the affairs of men and nations. We have now seen that statements of that proposition, together with evidence characteristic of sages' entire system, comes to us from principal documents of the Oral Torah, beginning to end. In sages' discourse justice never requires explanation, but violations of justice always do. When what happens does not conform to the systemic givens but violates the expectations precipitated by them, then sages pay close attention and ask why. When what happens does conform, they do not have to: their unarticulated conviction of self-evidence is embodied, therefore, in the character of their discourse: not only the speech but the silence.

THE RESOLUTION OF THE MATTER IN
THE RESURRECTION OF THE DEAD

When the day is done, the doctrine of suffering could not encompass all cases, let alone persuade everybody who raised the questions, Why me? Why now? True, suffering is to be accepted as a mark of God's grace, a gift, an occasion, a mode of atonement and reconciliation with God. True, the patriarchs found much good in man's fate and asked God to arrange matters as they are. And yet—and yet the fact remains that some folk suffer more than others, and not uncommonly, the wicked prosper and the righteous do not. So the doctrine of suffering on its own could not, and did not, complete the Oral Torah's account of the confrontation with the key dilemma of sages' theology of world order: the anomalies that manifestly flaw private lives viewed in comparison and contrast with one another. Say what they would, sages in the end had to complete the circle: some do not get what they deserve, whether for good or for ill, and, if their time is replicated in our own, those some were very many. To that protean problem sages found in their larger theology a commensurate and predictable response.

Sages identified with the Torah the promise of life eternal and with idolatry, the extinction of being. This would come about at the last days, which will correspond with, and complete, the first days of creation. Justice will be done only when the world is perfected. With that conviction's forming the foundation of their very definition of world order, divided between those who will overcome the grave—Israel with the Torah—and those who will not—the gentiles with idolatry—sages found in hand a simple solution. The righteous suffer in this world and get their just reward in the world to come, but the wicked enjoy this world and suffer in the world to come. Since, to begin with, the theology of the Oral Torah distinguished the Torah and life from idolatry and death, what happens in this world and in this life does not tell the whole story. And when that entire story is told, the received formulation of the problem of evil no longer pertains, and the final anomalies are smoothed out.

Since that theology further contemplated a world beyond the grave—the world to come, in which individuals would resume the life they knew, but now for eternity. That conviction, critical to the system as a whole, also provided a solution to the problem of the prosperity of the wicked and the misery of the righteous. By insisting that this world does not tell the whole story of a private life, sages could promise beyond the grave what the here and now denied. The simplest statement of that position is as follows:

> Talmud of Babylonia tractate *Horayot* 3:3, I.11a
> 6. A. Expounded R. Nahman bar Hisda, "What is the meaning of the verse of Scripture, 'There is a vanity that occurs on the earth, for there are the righteous who receive what is appropriate to the deeds of the wicked, and there are the wicked who receive what is appropriate to the deeds of the righteous' (Qoh. 8:14).
> B. "Happy are the righteous, for in this world they undergo what in the world to come is assigned as recompense for the deeds of the wicked, and woe is the wicked, for in this world they enjoy the fruits of what is assigned in the world to come to the deeds of the righteous."

The righteous will enjoy the world to come all the more, and the wicked will suffer in the world to come all the more; the one has saved up his reward for eternity, the other has in this transient world already spent such reward as he may ever get. But that still begs the question:

> B. Said Raba, "So if the righteous enjoy both worlds, would that be so bad for them?"

Raba acts in the model of Abraham facing God before Sodom! But he has a better solution, making a still more radical claim:

> C. Rather, said Raba, "Happy are the righteous, for in this world they get what is set aside for the [meritorious] deeds of the wicked in this world, and woe to the wicked, for in this world they get what is assigned for the deeds of the righteous in this world."

Raba's solution takes account of the theory of atonement through suffering. The righteous atone in the here and now; that is why they suffer. Then the world to come is all the more joyful. Now follows a story that shows how disciples of sages enjoy in this world such benefit as the wicked ought to have had in the world to come, and the rest follows. To grasp how, in massive detail, ultimate justice pervades the here and now, the premise of this passage should not be missed. It is that of a steady-state moral economy: a finite store of rewards and punishments awaits the righteous and the wicked alike, so what comes to the one is denied the other. The sages expressed a powerful yearning for a world of stability and hierarchical order. To them world order defined by reasoned justice serves to justify—show God's justice in—even humble, everyday experience. It follows that the rules that govern and account for everyday experience are supposed to make sense of the nonsense of miracles, on the one side, and sickness, old age, and death, on the other. The resurrection of the dead and the life of the world to come form a fundamental component of the Judaic religious system set forth in the dual Torah, and we shall return to the same matter in chapter 13—with much the same result.

Chapter 11

Sacred Space:
The Land and Pilgrimage

WHY IS THE LAND OF ISRAEL DIFFERENT
FROM ALL OTHER LANDS? WHY IS JERUSALEM
DIFFERENT FROM ALL OTHER CITIES?

In Rabbinic Judaism pilgrimage means a voyage to the Holy Land, and, in the Land, it means the ascent to Jerusalem, and, in Jerusalem, the entry into the condition of purification required for those who climb to the Temple mount and enter the courtyard and participate in the Temple offerings. The sole focus of pilgrimage is Land, Jerusalem, Temple, and the purpose of pilgrimage is to present offerings to God and to partake of the meat of some of those offerings in the Temple courtyard: to eat meat with God.

So, for purposes of pilgrimage (and all other contexts as well), the only territories differentiated in world geography are the Land of Israel and, therein, the only city that is differentiated from all other cities is the metropolis—the mother of cities—of Jerusalem. These are heavily differentiated, for example, as to levels of sanctification, while no other territory or city in the world is differentiated in any way at all. These are holy, and no other territory or city is holy. That explains

135

why they are different from all other lands and cities, as Holy Israel is different in genus from all other social entities in humanity.

The Land of Israel is that territory that God promised to Abraham and gave to the children of Israel on condition that they keep the covenant; so Scripture made clear. Still more indicative of its enchanted standing, as we have seen at many points, the Land of Israel is the counterpart of Eden, as Israel is the counterpart of Adam. Israel can make of the Land of Israel its own Eden. But losing the Land is the counterpart to the Fall from Eden. Separation of Israel from the Land of Israel through exile marks the divine penalty for Israel's violating the covenant, and return of Israel to the Land of Israel will signify the end of history, the last judgment, the resurrection of the dead, and the advent of the age to come. So the land of Israel forms a critical component and a native category of classical Judaism.

The question of the borders of the Land at various points in the history of Judaism is moot; for Judaism the religion, what matters is the holiness of the Land, which is enhanced when the Land is occupied by the Holy People. The union of Land and People marked Israel's attainment of Eden when Joshua led Israel into the Land. That union would have stood forever had Israel not sinned. By sinning, Israel lost the Land. The restoration for good will take place, classical Judaism teaches, when Israel has repented its sin, atoned, attained reconciliation with God, and been forgiven. Then the Messiah will gather in the exiles of Israel and restore the People of Israel to the Land of Israel, the new Eden of the world to come. At that time, humanity at large will acknowledge the unity of God and enter into the condition of Israel too. So the Land in concrete and in theological terms defines a principal component of classical Judaism. In that context, the pilgrimage at the specified seasons of the year marked a foretaste of the restoration to Eden.

Why pilgrimage only to the Land of Israel in particular? The election of Israel is matched by the election of the Land. Election is particular to the one that is chosen: God examined all the nations and chose Israel among them; all generations and chose the generation of the wilderness to receive the Torah; and all lands and chose the Land of Israel.

Leviticus Rabbah XIII:II.1

1. A. R. Simeon b. Yohai opened [discourse by citing the following verse:] "'He stood and measured the earth; he looked and shook [YTR = released] the nations; [then the eternal mountains were scattered as the everlasting hills sank low. His ways were as of old]' (Hab. 3:6).

   B. "The Holy One, blessed be he, took the measure of all the nations and found no nation but Israel that was truly worthy to receive the Torah.

   C. "The Holy One, blessed be he, further took the measure of all generations and found no generation but the generation of the wilderness that was truly worthy to receive the Torah.

   D. "The Holy One, blessed be he, further took the measure of all mountains and found no mountain but Mount Moriah that was truly worthy for the Presence of God to come to rest upon it.

E. "The Holy One, blessed be he, further took the measure of all cities and found no city but Jerusalem that was truly worthy in which to have the house of the sanctuary built.

F. "The Holy One, blessed be he, further took the measure of all mountains and found no mountain but Sinai that was truly worthy for the Torah to be given upon it.

G. "The Holy One, blessed be he, further took the measure of all lands and found no land but the Land of Israel that was truly worthy for Israel.

H. "That is in line with the following verse of Scripture: 'He stood and took the measure of the earth.'"

The question that is answered is, Why did God choose Israel, the generation that received the Torah, Moriah, Sinai, the Land of Israel, and so on? The answer is that there was no better, more worthy choice, because of Israel's willingness to receive the Torah, just that generation, just that location being added.

How is the priority of the Land actualized in concrete law? The holiness of the Land expresses its election and its place in the entire hierarchy of sanctification, on the one side, and uncleanness, on the other. Here is how the Land fits into the laws governing sanctification and its opposite, uncleanness. Hierarchization organizes the data of both sanctification and uncleanness in a single structure, even though there is no correspondence of the details of the one to those of the other. The points of differentiation, both as to sanctification and as to uncleanness, are the same, arrayed in sets of opposites. We start with the descent into uncleanness and proceed to the matching ascent into sanctification, the ascent being marked out in the hierarchy of parts of the Holy Land:

Mishnah tractate *Kelim* 1:5–9

    1:5

A. Ten levels of uncleanness pertain to man:

B. (1) He whose atonement [sacrifice] is incomplete [solely in respect to the purificatory sacrifice] is prohibited in regard to Holy Thing(s) but permitted in regard to heave offering and in regard to tithe.

C. (2) He [who] [became unclean so as] to be a *tebul-yom* [who awaits sunset to complete his purification] is prohibited in regard to Holy Thing(s) and in regard to heave offering but permitted in regard to tithe.

D. (3) He [who] [became unclean so as] to be one who had suffered a pollution is prohibited in regard to all three.

E. (4) He [who] [became unclean so as] to be one who has intercourse with a menstruating woman conveys uncleanness to what lies [far] beneath him [in like degree as he conveys uncleanness to a spread that lies] above [it and directly underneath him].

F. (5) [If] he [became unclean so as] to be a Zab who has suffered two appearances [of flux], he renders the couch and the chair [on which he sits or lies] unclean and needs bathing in running water but is free of the offering.

G. (6) He [who] saw three [appearances of flux] is liable for the offering.

H. (7) He [who] [became unclean so as] to be a leper that is shut up [for examination to see whether signs of uncleanness will appear] conveys uncleanness through coming [into a house] but is exempt from loosening [the hair], and tearing [the clothes], and from shaving, and from the bird [offering].

I. (8) And if he was certified [as a leper], he is liable for all of them.

J. (9) [If] a limb on which there is not an appropriate amount of flesh separated from him, it renders unclean through contact and through carrying but does not render unclean in the tent.

K. (10) And if there is on it [the limb] an appropriate amount of flesh, it renders unclean through contact and through carrying and through the tent.

L. The measure of flesh that is appropriate is sufficient to bring about healing.

We now systematically situated the geography of the world in relationship to the Land and the city, respectively, the whole signified by location and distance from the center:

1:6

A. There are ten [degrees of] holiness(es):

B. (1) The land of Israel is holier than all lands.

C. And what is its holiness? For they bring from it the omer, and the firstfruits, and the Two Loaves, which they do not bring (thus) from all lands.

1:7

A. (2) The cities surrounded by a wall are more holy than it [the land].

B. For they send from them the lepers, and they carry around in their midst a corpse so long as they like. [But once] it has gone forth, they do not bring it back.

1:8

A. (3) Within the wall [of Jerusalem] is more holy than they.

B. For they eat there lesser sanctities and second tithe.

C. (4) The Temple mount is more holy than it.

D. For Zabim, and Zabot, menstruating women [all dealt with at Leviticus 15], and those that have given birth [in line with Leviticus 12] do not enter there.

E. (5) The rampart is more holy than it.

F. For gentiles and he who is made unclean by a corpse do not enter there.

G. (6) The court of women is more holy than it.

H. For a *tebul-yom* does not enter there, but they are not liable on its account for a sin offering.

I. (7) The court of Israel is more holy than it.

J. For one who [yet] lacks atonement [offerings made in the completion of his purification rite] does not enter there, and they are liable on its account for a sin-offering.

K. (8) The court of the priests is more holy than it.

L. For Israelite(s) do not enter there except in the time of their [cultic] requirements: for laying on of hands, for slaughtering, and for waving.

1:9
  A. (9) [The area] between the porch and the altar is more holy than
     it.
  B. For those [priests] who are blemished or whose hair is unloosed
     do not enter there.
  C. (10) The sanctuary is more holy than it.
  D. For [a priest] whose hands and feet are not washed does not enter
     there.
  E. (11) The Holy of Holies is more holy than they.
  F. For only the high priest on the Day of Atonement at the time of
     the service enters there.

The pattern for sanctification is clear: a set of available facts is organized and laid
out in the established pattern of ascension to ever higher levels; but the facts are
available, not established through any program of investigation. The single standard pertains: relationship to the same locus of sanctification. The centrality of
the Land of Israel in the hierarchical sanctification of Israel the people is self-
evident. And the spatial relationships introduced into the hierarchy of sanctification upward, uncleanness downward, make inevitable the focus on pilgrimage:
a journey to some one, holy place.

PILGRIMAGE: THE PARTICULAR OCCASION

Israelites are represented in the Temple offerings every day, when the public
atonement offerings, sustained by the contribution of a half-sheqel required of
all Israelite men and accepted from women as well, are presented. Individual
Israelites also may make the journey and present atonement offerings for sins
inadvertently committed and discovered later on; or various other votive offerings. But only on the pilgrim festivals is all Israel summoned to make the pilgrimage. That is when the individual Israelites form part of the corporate
community, the holy people appearing en masse. The three requirements—
appearing before God, keeping a feast to the Lord, and rejoicing—are made
explicit in Scripture, Exodus 23:17, Deuteronomy 16:15, and Deuteronomy
16:14, respectively. These then form the concrete occasion for Israel's most immediate and tangible encounter with God.

The encounter of Holy Israel with God takes place, in particular, in the Temple
in Jerusalem at the pilgrim festivals: Passover, which falls on the first full moon after
the vernal equinox; Pentecost, fifty days later; and Tabernacles, on the first full
moon after the autumnal equinox. Then—at the turning of the seasons—Israelites
are called to Jerusalem to be seen by and rejoice before the Lord. Now the engagement entails not repentance and atonement but celebration, each of the festivals
devoted to the enjoyment of creation and Israel's own formation. And the act of
rejoicing encompasses the eating of meat. The three pilgrim festivals entail the individual's appearance before God within the entire community. That is not required
at the Day of Atonement, which effects atonement for all Israel, wherever located.

Then the high priest stands for Israel in the rites of the Day of Atonement. On the pilgrim festivals, by contrast, Israel, encompassing all of its genealogical strata, meets God, exactly when and where and how God wishes to be met. Israel is seen by God, or, in accord with the writing out of the Hebrew letters for the same passage, Israel sees God—in the holiness of the Temple, in the savor of its offerings to heaven, in its music and song and bloody rites in celebration of life.

In tractate *Hagigah*, the pilgrimage is given concreteness through law, as we should expect in Rabbinic Judaism. There the religious occasion is defined and actualized. The Halakhah takes up the pilgrims' complementary obligations of sacrifice and cultic purity. The Israelite is to be seen in the Temple court on the feast with a whole offering (birds or cattle) and that is obligatory: "None shall appear before me empty" (Exod. 23:15). Keeping the feast furthermore means presenting a peace offering when one makes an appearance on the first festival day of the feast. The duty of rejoicing involves a peace offering in addition to the festal peace offering: "the peace offering of rejoicing in the feast," in line with Deuteronomy 27:7: "And you shall sacrifice peace offerings and shall eat there and you shall rejoice before the Lord your God."

The Halakhah of *Hagigah* accordingly deals with two closely related topics on a single theme, the occasions on which common folk come to the Temple, that is, the pilgrim festivals. That Halakhah is also devoted to two matters: the festival offerings and the conditions of cultic cleanness that pertain and govern the right to consume part of the meat of those offerings. The following three offerings are called for by the pilgrimage: an appearance offering that involves a burnt offering, which yields no food for the sacrifier [the one who benefits from the atonement offering] or sacrificer [the priest who actually conducts the rite and tosses the blood of the sacrifice onto the altar fires]; a festal offering (*Hagigah*), which falls under the rules of peace offerings and does yield meat for the sacrifier; and peace offerings of rejoicing, subject to the same law as the festal offering. Since the ordinary folk are going to eat sacrificial meat, they have to make themselves ready to consume food in the status of Holy Things. The Halakhah then encompasses not only the pertinent offerings but the rules of cleanness that govern on the occasion of the festivals.

As to the offerings themselves, on Passover, Pentecost, and Tabernacles, families present the appearance offering and the festal offering, an obligatory burnt offering and peace offerings, respectively. The obligatory appearance offering is located by sages in the following verses:

> You shall rejoice in your feast, you and your son and your daughter, your manservant and your maidservant, the Levite, the sojourner, the fatherless and the widow who are within your towns. For seven days you shall keep the feast to the Lord your God at the place that the Lord will choose, because the Lord your God will bless you in all your produce and in all the work of your hands, so that you will be altogether joyful.
>
> Three times a year all your males shall appear before the Lord your God at the place which he will choose: at the feast of unleavened bread, at the

feast of weeks, and at the feast of booths. They shall not appear before the Lord empty-handed; every man shall give as he is able, according to the blessing of the Lord your God which he has given you.

(Deut. 16:14–17)

The passages that refer to celebrating a festival are deemed to pertain to the festal offering (*Hagigah*). What concerns the Halakhah is two matters: first, the details of the pilgrims' offerings; second, the attainment, by pilgrims, of cultic cleanness to permit their participation in the cult and their eating their share of the Holy Things of the altar.

PILGRIMS AND THEIR OFFERINGS

When it comes to the festival seasons, ordinary people are assumed to preserve cultic cleanness, even though at other times of the year, they do not do so. That is because everyone is assumed to understand that the condition for entering the Temple is cultic cleanness. The same assumption that people in general will preserve cultic cleanness where it is required pertains to produce destined for the Temple: in Judah people are deemed trustworthy in regard to the preservation of the cleanness of wine and oil for use on the altar—that is, food in the status of Holy Things throughout the year. But only in the time of pressing the wine and crushing the olives also for the purposes of heave offering are they deemed trustworthy. When it comes to the status of clay utensils that one finds, within the locale of Jerusalem, people are assumed to preserve the cultic cleanness of clay utensils, and if they claim they are cultically clean, that claim is accepted. In Jerusalem, even tax collectors searching a house for valuables are assumed to respect the rules of cultic cleanness. At the time of festivals, then, all are assumed to observe the rules of cultic cleanness.

All persons possessed of autonomy of will are liable to bring an appearance offering, that is, to make the pilgrimage. Excluded is the standard list: those who are impaired in body or mind, and those subject to the will of another: (1) a deaf mute, (2) an idiot, (3) a minor, (4) one without pronounced sexual characteristics, (5) one who exhibits the sexual traits of both sexes, (6) women, (7) slaves who have not been freed, (8) the lame, (9) the blind, (10) the sick, (11) the old, (12) and one who cannot go up on foot. An unclean person does not appear in the Temple either. For one reason or another, these persons do not possess autonomy of will, or they are unable to carry out the physical obligation involved in making a pilgrimage.

The pilgrimage involved the forming in the Temple courtyard of a vast congregation of Israel. As to the definition of, and differentiation among, the appearance offering and the festal offering, these are offerings that were presented in the Temple courtyard, not merely on the Temple mount.

Tosefta tractate *Hagigah* 1:4
F. Three religious requirements [involving sacrifices] apply to a Festival, these are they:

G. the appearance-offering, the festal-offering, and the [peace-offerings of] rejoicing.

H. There is a rule applying to the appearance-offering which does not apply to the other two of them.

I. The appearance-offering is wholly offered up to the Most High, which does not apply to the other two of them.

J. The festal-offering applies both before the revelation [of the Torah at Mount Sinai] and after the revelation [of the Torah at Mount Sinai], which does not pertain to the other two of them.

K. The requirements of peace-offerings of rejoicing on the Festival apply to men and women, and apply for all seven days [of Tabernacles and Passover], which is not the case for the other two of them.

L. What is the definition of an appearance-offering? These are the burnt-offerings which are brought for [designated as] the appearance-offering.

M. What is the definition of a festal-offering? These are the peace-offerings which are brought for [designated as] the festal-offering.

N. If a person has sufficient [funds] to bring such an offering from his own resources, lo, this person does so. But if not, he joins together with others,

0. on condition that he should not provide less than the required measure.

P. This one and that one fall under the title of festal-offering.

The appearance offering, which yields no meat for the pilgrim, is purchased with unconsecrated funds. But the offerings that yield meat, that is, peace offerings for the festal offering, may be purchased from funds in the status of second tithe, and, in the same theory, the same rule applies to the offering for the first festival day of Passover. So too people may fulfill their obligation through animals brought in fulfillment of vows, or as thank offerings, or through tithe of cattle. People are permitted to vary the classification of their offerings—burnt offerings as against peace offerings—by reference to their resources and the number of their dependents. If they have many dependents and limited resources, they classify their offerings as peace offerings and not as whole offerings, beyond the stated minimum. People do as they are able, which is the governing principle when it comes to the cult; and the Written Torah said no less.

The pilgrims' offerings in respect to Sabbath restrictions are treated in accord with the Temple's rule in general. That is to say, just as the public offerings override the restrictions of the Sabbath, so the pilgrims' offerings, though for personal purposes, do the same. The pilgrim presents both offerings that yield meat for his family and those that do not (peace offerings, whole offerings, respectively) and lays hands on them. The restrictions of the Sabbath do not intervene. The normative reasoning is as follows: "Now if at a time at which you are permitted to prepare food for an ordinary person, you are permitted to prepare food for the Most High for on the Sabbath, one is not permitted to prepare food for himself, but one is permitted to offer up daily whole-offerings and additional offerings, at a time at which you are permitted to prepare food for an ordinary person for on the Festival day one is permitted to prepare food, should you not be permitted to prepare food for the Most High?" On that basis, the pilgrims may make the pertinent offerings.

ENTERING THE STATE OF CLEANNESS ON THE PILGRIM FESTIVALS

On the pilgrim festivals, Israelites—not priests, not Levites—undertake the condition of cultic cleanness just like the designated castes. An unclean person is exempt from the requirement of making an appearance (Exod. 23:14; Deut. 16:16), since it is said, "And you will come there and you will bring there" (Deut. 12:6). The requirement applies to one who is suitable to come into the Temple courtyard, excluding the unclean person, who is not suitable to come into the Temple courtyard. To attain cultic cleanness for eating Holy Things, people had to immerse, not just wash hands. If one immerses for eating unconsecrated food, that does not suffice for eating tithe; if one is confirmed as suitable for eating tithe, he still has not immersed for the purpose of eating heave offering, and if one immerses for eating heave offering, he still has to immerse to eat Holy Things. This is stated in the following language:

> Mishnah tractate *Hagigah* 2:5–6
> *m.* 2:5
>> [For purposes of cultic purification, it is sufficient if] they wash the hands for eating unconsecrated food, tithe, and heave offering; and for eating food in the status of Holy Things [it is sufficient only if] they immerse; and as to [the preparation of] purification water [through the burning of the red cowl, if one's hands are made unclean, his entire body is deemed to be unclean as well].
>
> *m.* 2:6
>> He who immerses for the eating of unconsecrated food and is thereby confirmed as suitable for eating unconsecrated food is prohibited from eating tithe. [If] he immersed for eating tithe and is thereby confirmed as suitable for eating tithe, he is prohibited from eating heave offering. [If] he immersed for eating heave offering and is thereby confirmed as suitable for eating heave offering, he is prohibited from eating food in the status of Holy Things. [If] he immersed for eating food in the status of Holy Things and is thereby confirmed as suitable for eating food in the status of Holy Things, he is prohibited from engaging in the preparation of purification water. [If, however], one immersed for the matter requiring the more stringent rule, he is permitted to engage in the matter requiring the less stringent rule. [If] he immersed but was not confirmed, it is as though he did not immerse.

Hence whatever the normal domestic practice of the pilgrim, in connection with his visit to the cult, he must immerse with the intention of attaining cleanness for Holy Things. Hence a clear distinction is drawn between cleanness in the household, where some people maintained cultic purity even in connection with everyday food, and cleanness in the Temple. There everyone must immerse and remain on the alert to avoid sources of uncleanness, and, should they impinge, to remove the uncleanness through immersion. The one—keeping cultically clean at home—represented an act of intent and conviction; the other—becoming clean for entry into the Temple—an act of substance.

SHARING A MEAL WITH GOD

The upshot is, on the pilgrim festivals, all Israel, not only the priest who is the sacrificer of the offering but also the individual Israelite who is the sacrifier—the one who benefits from the offering, for example, who is atoned for—eat God's meat. Rejoicing on the festival means eating meat at God's place, in the condition in which God eats his meals as well: cultic cleanness. It is then that the Israelite appears before God and is seen by God. The nexus of the encounter is the meal, in which the Israelite accepts the rules of cleanness that pertain to God's table, the altar. Even though some may preserve cultic cleanness at home, standards for the Temple are much higher. The main point is that whatever is done at home serves in the household, but the cult is clearly differentiated from the household, with special reference for those that preserve cultic cleanness even within the household. That is expressed in connection with persons and utensils alike. One may immerse a utensil for purposes of cultic cleanness, but, when it comes to use in the cult, a utensil has to be processed to begin with in a state of insusceptibility to uncleanness and so must be cultically clean when it becomes susceptible, and still it must be immersed for use in the cult, that is, in connection with Holy Things. So too, for the cult one must wash hands even if the food that the hands will touch is insusceptible to uncleanness, which is not the case with heave offering: With unclean hands they eat food which has not been wet down in the case of heave offering, but not in the case of Holy Things.

The attitude of the pilgrim governs. The effect of his act of purification through immersion is dictated by the attitude with which he immerses. If one was unclean and immersed with the intention of becoming clean, that serves. He who immerses in order to rise up from uncleanness to cleanness, lo, this person is clean for all purposes. He who immerses—if he had the intention of becoming clean—becomes clean. And if not, he remains unclean. If he immersed for eating food in the status of Holy Things and is thereby confirmed as suitable for eating food in the status of Holy Things, he is prohibited from engaging in the preparation of purification water. If, however, one immersed for the matter requiring the more stringent rule, one is permitted to engage in the matter requiring the less stringent rule. If he immersed but was not confirmed, it is as though he did not immerse. But there are realms to which the attitude of the Israelite gains no access. The area within the veil excludes all but the priesthood, so the intentionality of Israelites is null therein. Thus, just as that which is within the veil is exceptional, in that it is not subject to the knowledge and consent of the Israelites, so are excluded heave offering, heave offering of tithe, and dough offering, which are subject to the knowledge and consent of the Israelites.

Here is where the rules of hierarchical purification embody the motif of the pilgrimage: the ascent to the holy place, the ascent to purity, thence to sanctification. That is captured in another context altogether, which places into moral and eschatological context the entry into the state of cultic cleanness:

> Mishnah tractate *Sotah* 9:15
>
> R. Pinhas b. Yair says, "Heedfulness leads to cleanliness, cleanliness leads to cultic cleanness, cleanness leads to abstinence, abstinence leads to holiness, holiness leads to modesty, modesty leads to the fear of sin, the fear of sin leads to piety, piety leads to the Holy Spirit, the Holy Spirit leads to the resurrection of the dead, and the resurrection of the dead comes through Elijah, blessed be his memory, Amen."

While the pilgrimage does not figure, the context of cleanness, a state attained by corporate Israel on the festivals, does. It is at that point that corporate Israel enters into the condition that will lead to the coming of Elijah and the resurrection of the dead. So what is at stake on the pilgrimage is readiness for the realization of the messianic promises. No wonder, then, that various traditions identify the time of the coming of the Messiah and the resurrection of the dead with one or another of the festivals.

But in Rabbinic Judaism, these matters come to expression in concrete deeds of a palpable character. What emerges is the hierarchization of the rules that govern the sanctity and sanctification of Israel, from the household upward to the Temple courtyard and the altar in Jerusalem. It is, in particular, for the occasion of the ascent to the city and the Temple that the hierarchization of sanctity and uncleanness is required. Then the Halakhah has to answer the question, Is cleanness at home equivalent to cleanness in the cult? Is the cult differentiated from the household, even while both are deemed sanctified? And the Halakhah answers that question in an explicit way: attitude has its limits, and the facts of sanctification override the attitude of the pious person. However much one wishes to attain cultic cleanness and actually does so in the household, still, the cult preserves its own rules and requirements. The recognition that levels of cleanness, depending on circumstance and attitude, differentiate one's suitability for eating food at various levels of sanctification yields a broader judgment. It is that there is a match between levels of sanctification and levels of uncleanness, with the hierarchy of the one matched by the hierarchy of the other, ascending, descending, respectively. Thus as we saw earlier, Mishnah tractate *Kelim* 1:6–9 spells out the hierarchy of sanctification in locative terms.

It is in connection with the pilgrimage for which *Hagigah* provides that these matters become urgent. And, we note, on that occasion, the limits of intentionality and its power are reached. The intentionality to attain cleanness in the domestic household now does not suffice, nor do the rules and regulations that pertain when ordinary folk in their homes eat their food as though they were in the Temple in Jerusalem. The Halakhah embodies the difference between imagination and intention, on the one side, and actuality, on the other. What suffices in the pretense that one's table forms the altar; the members of the household, the priesthood; and its ménage, the home, the Temple, now does not serve. Actuality intervenes: the real Temple imposes its own, very strict rules, and all of the proper intentions in the world will not serve now. The table compares to the Temple; the household to the priesthood; the boundaries of the home to the Temple—but in a hierarchical structure, encompassing rules of both sanctification and uncleanness. The pilgrimage sets the stage: the occasion, the location, and the participants intersect, where Israel meets God.

Chapter 12

Sacrifice, Repentance, and Atonement

SACRIFICE IN THE CONTEXT OF ATONEMENT: CORPORATE ISRAEL AND THE DAILY WHOLE OFFERING

When the Temple of Jerusalem stood, sacrifice served as the medium of atonement for sin, just as Scripture insists, and, when the Temple was destroyed, deeds of loving kindness took the place of sacrifice:

Fathers According to Rabbi Nathan IV:V.2
> A. One time [after the destruction of the Temple] Rabban Yohanan ben Zakkai was going forth from Jerusalem, with R. Joshua following after him. He saw the house of the sanctuary lying in ruins.
>
> B. R. Joshua said, "Woe is us for this place which lies in ruins, the place in which the sins of Israel used to come to atonement."
>
> C. He said to him, "My son, do not be distressed. We have another mode of atonement, which is like [atonement through sacrifice], and what is that? It is deeds of loving kindness.
>
> D. "For so it is said, 'For I desire mercy and not sacrifice, [and the knowledge of God rather than burnt offerings]' (Hos. 6:6)."

But Judaism as set forth in the Torah, written mediated by oral, maintained the hope that the Temple would be rebuilt and the offerings restored to the altar, as God had commanded Moses to instruct Israel to begin with. And a principal purpose of those offerings was to atone for sin.

First comes atonement for the entire community of Israel. That community was deemed a moral entity, responsible collectively for its deeds. How did the Torah afford the occasion for individual Israelites to participate en masse in the Temple offerings, and which offerings atoned for all Israel? It is to contribute the half-sheqel to support the public offerings of the Temple. Each Israelite male must contribute his share of those offerings, which are described from Scripture forward as atonement for all Israel:

> The Lord said to Moses, "When you take the census of the people of Israel, then each shall give a ransom for himself to the Lord when you number them, that there be no plague among them when you number them. Each who is numbered in the census shall give this: half a sheqel, according to the sheqel of the sanctuary . . . half a sheqel as an offering to the Lord. Every one who is numbered in the census, from twenty years old and upward, shall give the Lord's offering. The rich shall not give more, and the poor shall not give less, than the half-sheqel, when you give the Lord's offering to make atonement for yourselves. And you shall take the atonement money from the people of Israel and shall appoint it for the service of the tent of meeting; that it may bring the people of Israel to remembrance before the Lord, so as to make atonement for yourselves."
>
> (Exod. 30:11–16)

What the Halakhah of the Oral Torah contributes is the articulation of the analogous relationship of the half-sheqel to tithes and heave offering. It is through this particular medium that all Israel, not only the enlandised components of Israel, relate directly and concretely to God. The conception that, through the half-sheqel, everyone acquires a share in the atonement offering is explicit. Here is the medium of Israel's relationship with God that transcends place, genealogy, and condition; the half-sheqel, unlike firstfruits, comes from any location, even beyond the Land, and comes from all Israelites:

Tosefta tractate *Sheqalim* 1:6
> They exact pledges from Israelites for their sheqels, so that the public offerings might be made of their [funds]. This is like a man who got a sore on his foot, and the doctor had to force it and cut off his flesh so as to heal him. Thus did the Holy One, blessed be he, exact a pledge from Israelites for the payment of their sheqels, so that the public offerings might be made of their [funds]. For public offerings appease and effect atonement between Israel and their father in heaven. Likewise we find of the heave-offering of sheqels which the Israelites paid in the wilderness, as it is said, "And you shall take the atonement money from the people of Israel and shall appoint it for the service of the tent of meeting; that it may bring the people of Israel to remembrance before the Lord, so as to make atonement for yourselves" (Exod. 30:16).

The conception that through the obligatory half-sheqel paid to the Temple by all Israelite males, everyone acquires a share in the daily whole offerings,, which serve as atonement offerings for Israel viewed whole, is explicit. In the daily whole offerings corporate Israel is incorporated: an atoning community. These and certain counterpart offerings, for example, the atonement offerings of the Day of Atonement (Leviticus 16) effect atonement for the community as a whole. So the social entity, corporate Israel, embodies a sinful community. Israelites become party to the community of Israel because all together they sinned and all together they share in the task of collective atonement.

Accordingly, all Israel, everywhere, relates to God through support of the public offerings in expiation of collective guilt. In the obligation to provide that support all are equal, rich and poor, priest and convert, resident of the Land and of the exile alike. The half-sheqel that is paid itself is sanctified in the way in which the heave offering or tithe is sanctified, and the analogy to second tithe, on the one side, and the heave offering paid to the priests, on the other, is Halakhically explicit. The half-sheqel moreover is taken up in the consecrated manner—randomly, through an act of raising up—and then is used for the purchase of animals in behalf of all Israel and for certain other purposes connected with the cult and the building where it was located.

What, exactly, is done with the half-sheqels? A random sample of the collection is raised up and devoted to the purchase of the daily whole offerings (and other cultic tasks as we shall see). As the farmer relies on chance to indicate God's choice as to the particular portion of the crop to be designated as heave offering or tithe, so chance defines the selection process when the priests in the Temple take up a heave offering of the "crop" of coins. They were careful to sample the collection in such a way that once a batch of coins has been subjected to the taking up of coins, that batch is not sampled a second time. And so too, as heave offering of a given batch of produce may serve for other batches, so too the heave offering of the sheqel coins is deemed to represent a random sample of an entire batch of such coins, even including those not physically present when the heave offering of the sheqel chamber is taken up. The action covers that which is subject to a pledge from what already has been collected but which got lost en route to the Temple, and, in the opinion of some, also what is going to be collected in the future. But once the span of time in which a given coin serves has passed, the coin itself is no longer sanctified. Its value is used for the upkeep of the Temple house. So the half-sheqels are "raised up" in the manner of heave offering, in a random sample, out of the sheqel chamber, and, with the funds, appropriate offerings of atonement were purchased. The stress throughout reprises Scripture's emphasis on atonement for collective Israel through the daily whole offerings and their counterparts.

What about votive offerings, for example, from those not obligated to contribute, such as gentiles or women? These are accepted for the purchase of the public offerings, so long as the donors assign title of their funds to the community at large:

Tosefta tractate *Sheqalim* 2:7
> If people volunteered the funds on their own, they are valid, on con-
> dition that they [to begin with, explicitly] donate the funds to the
> community for public use.

It is the donation to the community for public use that supplies the key. And, it
follows, not only do Israelites sin and atone one by one. Israel as a whole sins and
corporately requires atonement, and that is the purpose of the daily whole offerings, as Scripture makes explicit. The public offerings—the daily whole offerings—atone for Israel's sin: public offerings appease and effect atonement
between Israel and its father in heaven, just as is stated in the Written Torah. It
is the collectivity of Israel that is embodied in the half-sheqel offering. And that
statement of the corporate character of Israel comes to expression in the half-
sheqel in particular. No wonder the half-sheqel forms the counterpart to the agri-
cultural tithes and offerings, representing as they do enlandised Israel. But then
the difference cannot be missed: the half-sheqel embodies the offering of all Israel
equally, wherever located, however situated within the genealogical and social
order.

So the corporate action, transcending individual householders, priests, and
the poor, represents the entire social entity. Capable of sinning collectively, Israel
also atones collectively. That in detail the sheqel tax derives from, and stands for,
all Israel, both within and without the Land, is stated explicitly:

Tosefta tractate *Sheqalim* 2:4
> He took up the heave-offering of sheqels the first time and said, "Lo,
> this is from the Land of Israel in behalf of the whole people of Israel."
> Then he took up the heave-offering the second time and said, "Lo,
> this is from the lands of Ammon and Moab and from the cities sur-
> rounded by a wall in the Land of Israel." He took up the heave-
> offering the third time and said, "Lo, this is from Babylonia and
> Medea and from places distant from the Land of Israel, in behalf of
> all Israelites." But he did not cover it up. This was the richest fund
> of all of them, for in it were golden istras and golden darics.

The upshot is simple. As signified by the daily whole offerings supported by
every Israelite male, Israel is formed as the sinning, therefore also the atoning,
community. Collective sin, collective atonement—the capacity for the one and
for the other together define corporate Israel—demarcate the "Israelness" of
Israel, as we shall see at the end in another context altogether. These categories
of the relationship of the community, viewed whole and all together, with God,
defined by Scripture from the story of the Golden Calf forward—transcend class,
genealogy, and location. To be Israel, wherever one is situated geographically and
socially, is to participate in the collective character of Israel, its capacity to sin, its
vocation of atonement. God views Israel as a collectively and mutually responsible social entity, not as a collection of individuals of shared convictions and origins. Israel, unique in humanity, not only encompasses individuals but forms of

them something else, something other than what, as individuals, they comprise. Among the innumerable statements of that view, Amos 3:2 suffices in its use of the plural: "Only you have I known of all the families of Man, therefore I will visit on you all your iniquities." The half-sheqel serves as the indicator because it provides for that collective guilt and collective atonement that makes Israel into Israel. But what about individual Israelites?

SACRIFICE AND THE ATONEMENT
OF INDIVIDUALS' INADVERTENT SINS

A person who has sinned inadvertently and realizes it presents a sin offering, which atones for sins not committed in rebellion against God's will. The action does not mean to express an attitude of defiance or an intention to rebel against God's will. The Written Torah explicitly imputes guilt even for actions committed inadvertently and not with the intention of violating the Torah. A sin offering is required in the case of an action, the deliberate commission of which is penalized by extirpation (early death, before the age of sixty), and a suspensive guilt offering in the case of doubt. The principal interest then is in animal offerings that expiate sin. The Written Torah contributes to the topic the following statement:

> If any one sins, doing any of the things that the Lord has commanded not to be done, though he does not know it, yet he is guilty and shall bear his iniquity. He shall bring to the priest a ram without blemish out of the flock, valued by you at the price for a guilt offering, and the priest shall make atonement for him for the error that he committed unwittingly, and he shall be forgiven. It is a guilt offering; he is guilty before the Lord.
>
> (Lev. 5:17–19)

Three divisions make up the topical presentation: occasions on which the sin offering or extirpation, as the case may be, is required; a single sin offering and multiple sins; and the suspensive guilt offering, required where one inadvertently may or may not have committed a sin. The order is logically necessary, since the suspensive guilt offering cannot come before the sin or guilt offering for what one is certain he has done. The governing principle is stated as follows:

> Mishnah tractate *Keritot* 1:2
> Tosefta tractate *Keritot* 1:6
> *m.* 1:2
>> For those [thirty-six classes of transgressions] are people liable, for deliberately doing them, to the punishment of extirpation, and for accidentally doing them, to the bringing of a sin offering, and for not being certain of whether or not one has done them, to a suspensive guilt offering [Lev. 5:17]—[except for] the one who blasphemes, as it is said, "You shall have one law for him that does anything unwittingly" (Num. 15:29)—excluding the blasphemer, who does no concrete deed.

t. 1:6

> This is the general principle: [For violation of] any negative com-
> mandment containing within itself a concrete deed do [violators]
> receive the penalty of forty stripes. And for the violation of any which
> does not contain within itself a concrete deed they do not receive the
> penalty of forty stripes. And as to all other negative commandments
> in the Torah, lo, these are subject to warning. He who transgresses
> them violates the decree of the King.

Extirpation—death before age sixty—is inflicted for deliberate violation of the
Torah; presentation of a sin offering is the sanction for inadvertently committing
any of the thirty-six classes. These are the pertinent transgressions:

Mishnah tractate *Keritot* 1:1

m. 1:1

> Thirty-six [classes of] transgressions set forth in the Torah are sub-
> ject to extirpation: he who has sexual relations with (1) his mother,
> and (2) with his father's wife, and (3) with his daughter-in-law; he
> who has sexual relations (4) with a male, and (5) with a beast; and
> (6) the woman who has sexual relations with a beast; he who has sex-
> ual relations (7) with a woman and with her daughter, and (8) with
> a married woman; he who has sexual relations (9) with his sister, and
> (10) with his father's sister, and (11) with his mother's sister, and (12)
> with his wife's sister, and (13) with his brother's wife, and (14) with
> his father's brother's wife, and (15) with a menstruating woman (Lev.
> 18:6ff.); (16) he who blasphemes (Num. 15:30), and (17) he who
> performs an act of blasphemous worship (Num. 15:31), and (18) he
> who gives his seed to Moloch (Lev. 18:21), and (19) one who has a
> familiar spirit (Lev. 20:6); (20) he who profanes the Sabbath day
> (Exod. 31:14); and (21) an unclean person who ate a Holy Thing
> (Lev. 22:3), and (22) he who comes to the sanctuary when unclean
> (Num. 19:20); he who eats (23) forbidden fat (Lev. 7:25), and (24)
> blood (Lev. 17:14), and (25) remnant (Lev. 19:6–8), and (26) refuse
> (Lev. 19:7–8); he who (27) slaughters and who (28) offers up [a sac-
> rifice] outside [the Temple court] (Lev. 17:9); (29) he who eats leaven
> on Passover (Exod. 12:19); and he who (30) eats and he who (31)
> works on the Day of Atonement (Lev. 23:29–30); he who (32) com-
> pounds anointing oil [like that made in the Temple (Exod.
> 30:23–33)], and he who (33) compounds incense [like that made in
> the Temple], and he who (34) anoints himself with anointing oil
> (Exod. 30–32); [he who transgresses the laws of] (35) Passover
> (Num. 9:13) and (36) circumcision (Gen. 17:14), among the posi-
> tive commandments.

The key doctrine before us concerns the distinction between an act that is
deliberate and one that is inadvertent. In its principal divisions—the sin offering
as against extirpation, the suspensive guilt offering as against the unconditional
guilt offering—the Halakhah treats in concrete terms the distinction between
deliberate, intentional sin and unintentional law violation. Nowhere else in the
Halakhah do we find so sharp a line distinguishing the unintentional sin, penal-

ized by an offering, and the intentional one, penalized by extirpation. The reason that that critical distinction concerns us in the particular Halakhah at hand is self-evident. Here is where God intervenes, and it is God above all who knows what is in man's heart and can differentiate intentional from unintentional actions. And it also is God who has the heaviest stake in the matter of intentional sin, for intentional sin represents rebellion against the Torah and God's rule through the Torah.

Offerings then expiate those sins that are not committed as an act of rebellion against God. These God accepts, graciously, as an appropriate act of atonement for an act for which one bears responsibility that was not meant as defiance of God. The ones that embody an attitude of rebellion, by contrast, can be expiated not through the surrogate, the blood of the beast, but through the sinner, who is put to death by the court here on earth or is flogged by the court's agents or is cut off in the prime of life. So God sees into man's heart.

REPENTANCE

That God sees into a person's heart explains the centrality of "repentance" in the process of atonement: the restoration of the sinner's right relationship with God. The word "repentance" renders into English the Hebrew theological word *teshuvah*, or "turning," in the sense of a turning away from sin, a turning toward God. Repentance in Judaism, when properly carried out, erases the consequences of sin and reconciles God and the sinner. That means that, the one who has sinned regrets the sin and resolves not to repeat it, and, further, when the occasion to repeat the sinful deed comes once more, the penitent does not then revert to the prior sinful action or condition. The power of repentance or *teshuvah* is unlimited, for a remarkable statement shows that sin is not indelible either upon one's family or upon oneself.

> Talmud of Babylonia tractate *Gittin* 57b
> Grandsons of Haman [who tried to wipe out all the Jews, as the Scroll of Esther relates] studied Torah in Bene Beraq.
> Grandsons of Sisera [who made war against Israel] taught children in Jerusalem.
> Grandsons of Sennacherib [who conquered Northern Israel] taught Torah in public. And who were they? Shemaiah and Abtalion [teachers of Hillel and Shammai].

To understand the power of this statement, we have only to say, "Adolf Hitler's grandson teaches Torah in a yeshiva of Bene Beraq." Or "Adolf Eichmann's grandson sits in a Jerusalem yeshiva, reciting prayers and psalms and learning Talmud." Since Judaism is a living religion, it is worth noting that in fact a cousin of Adolf Hitler has converted to Judaism, and today does teach Judaism at an Israeli university.

If the sinner repents the sin, atones, and attains reconciliation with God, the sin is wiped off the record, the sinner forgiven, and the sinners' successors rendered blameless. The mark of repentance comes to the surface when the one-time sinner gains the chance to repeat the sinful deed but does not do so; then the repentance is complete. True, Scripture says ". . . visiting the guilt of the parents upon the children, upon the third and upon the fourth generations of those who reject me" (Exod. 20:5). But the Torah—the Oral Torah reading the Written Torah—qualifies that judgment: if the third and fourth generations continue the tradition of the fathers in rejecting the Lord, they too suffer punishment—for their own sins.

The sins of the fathers reach closure with the repentance of the children and their determination to make their own future. That is what the sinner who repents also does. Such statements represent the outcome of repentance, which is moral regeneration for oneself based on genuine regret and fully realized in deed, and they instruct the current generation of Judaism, in the aftermath of the unique Holocaust, on its moral duties to those of its enemies who repent and seek reconciliation. The message declares that sinners who repent are to be forgiven.

The concept of *teshuvah* is generally understood to mean a returning to God from a situation of estrangement. The turning is not only from sin, for sin serves as an indicator of a deeper pathology, that is, utter estrangement from God. *Teshuvah* then involves not humiliation but reaffirmation of the self in God's image, after God's likeness. It follows that repentance in Judaism forms a theological category encompassing moral issues of action and attitude—wrong action, arrogant attitude, in particular. Repentance forms a step in the path to God that starts with the estrangement represented by sin: doing what I want, instead of what God wants, thus rebellion and arrogance. Sin precipitates punishment, whether personal for individuals or historical for nations, and punishment brings about repentance for sin, which, in turn, leads to atonement for sin and, it follows, reconciliation with God. That sequence of stages in the moral regeneration of sinful humanity, individual or collective, defines the context in which repentance finds its natural home.

Judaism's conception of repentance—regretting sin, determining not to repeat it, seeking forgiveness for it—defines the key to the moral life with God. No single component of the human condition takes higher priority in establishing right relationship with God, and none bears more profound implications for this-worldly attitudes and actions. The entire course of a human life—filled as it is with the natural propensity to sin, that is, to rebel against God, but comprised also by the compelled requirement of confronting God's response, punishment for sin—takes its direction, finds its critical turning, at the act of repentance, the first step in the regeneration of the human condition as it was meant to be. The concept takes on specificity when atonement comes to the fore: in the Temple, atonement involved correct offerings for sin; for the prophets, repentance would characterize the entire nation, Israel, come to its senses in the aftermath of God's punishment. And, as we shall see, in the oral part of that one Torah—revelation—that defines Judaism, repentance takes on a profoundly this-worldly, social sense. But in all statements of the matter, the single trait proves ubiquitous: repentance defines a stage in the relationship of Man and God, inclusive of repentance to one's fellow for sin against him or her.

The matter is best set forth in the presentation of the moral dimensions of the Day of Atonement (Yom Kippur):

> Mishnah tractate *Yoma* 8:8–9
>
> *m.* 8:8
>> A. A sin offering and an unconditional guilt offering atone.
>> B. Death and the Day of Atonement atone when joined with repentance.
>> C. Repentance atones for minor transgressions of positive and negative commandments.
>> D. And as to serious transgressions, [repentance] suspends the punishment until the Day of Atonement comes along and atones.
>
> *m.* 8:9
>> A. He who says, "I shall sin and repent, sin and repent"—
>> B. they give him no chance to do repentance.
>> C. [If he said,] "I will sin and the Day of Atonement will atone,"— the Day of Atonement does not atone.
>> D. For transgressions done between man and the Omnipresent, the Day of Atonement atones.
>> E. For transgressions between man and man, the Day of Atonement atones, only if the man will regain the good will of his friend.

We recall that a sin offering in the Temple in Jerusalem, presented for unintentional sins, atones, and therein we find the beginning of the definition of repentance. It lies in the contrast between the sin offering at A, that is, atonement for unintentional sin and those things that atone for intentional sin (which are two events) on the one side, and the expression of right attitude, *teshuvah*, returning to God, on the other. The role of repentance emerges in the contrast with the sin offering; what atones for what is inadvertent has no bearing on what is deliberate. The willful sin can be atoned for only if repentance has taken place, that is to say, genuine regret, a turning away from the sin, after the fact therefore transforming the sin from one that is deliberate to one that is, if not unintentional beforehand, then at least unintentional afterward. Then death, on the one side, or the Day of Atonement, on the other, work their enchantment.

As much as mercy completes the principle of justice, so repentance forms the complement to sin; without mercy, represented here by the possibility of repentance, justice as God defines justice cannot endure. For were man to regret sin and see things in God's way without a corresponding response from God, God would execute justice but not mercy, and, from sages' perspective, the world would fall out of balance. To them, therefore, it is urgent that God have his own distinctive message to the sinner, separate from the voices of wisdom, prophecy, and even the Pentateuch (the Torah narrowly defined) of the Written Torah:

Yerushalmi tractate *Makkot* 2:6.I:4/10a

> A. Said R. Phineas: "'Good and upright [is the Lord; therefore he instructs sinners in the way]' (Ps. 25:8).
> B. "Why is he good? Because he is upright.
> C. "And why is he upright? Because he is good.
> D. "'Therefore he instructs sinners in the way—that is, he teaches them the way to repentance.'"

Now we interrogate the great compendia of God's will, wisdom and prophecy, then turn to God himself, and ask how to treat the sinner:

> E. They asked wisdom, "As to a sinner, what is his punishment?"
> F. She said to them, "Evil pursues the evil" (Prov. 13:21).
> G. They asked prophecy, "As to a sinner, what is his punishment?"
> H. She said to them, "The soul that sins shall die" (Ezek. 18:20).
> I. They asked the Holy One, blessed be he, "As to a sinner, what is his punishment?"
> J. He said to them, "Let the sinner repent, and his sin will be forgiven for him."
> K. This is in line with the following verse of Scripture: "Therefore he instructs sinners in the way" (Ps. 25:8).
> L. "He shows the sinners the way to repentance."

The response of wisdom presents no surprise; it is the familiar principle of measure for measure, and prophecy concurs, but God has something more to say. Accordingly, the proposition concerns the distinctive mercy of God, above even the Torah. The data for the composition, E–L, respond to the question that is addressed to the components of the Torah, that is, What does prophecy say about the punishment of the sinner? But the question is prior, and the question forms part of the systemic plan: to demonstrate the uniquely merciful character of God, the way in which God is God.

ATONEMENT

Repentance is the precondition of atonement; there is no atonement without the statement of remorse and appropriate, confirming action. If one rebels against God's rule and does not repent, no atonement is possible. But if he does repent,. then the Day of Atonement effects atonement for him:

Talmud of Babylonia tractate *Shebu'ot* 1:1ff. XVI.2/13a
> D. Rabbi says, "For all of the transgressions that are listed in the Torah, whether one has repented or not repented, the Day of Atonement attains atonement, except for one who breaks the yoke [of the kingdom of heaven from himself, meaning, denies God] and one who treats the Torah impudently, and the one who violates the physical mark of the covenant. In these cases if

one has repented, the Day of Atonement attains atonement, and if not, the Day of Atonement does not attain atonement."

Now come the facts to validate the proposition:

> E. What is the scriptural basis for the position of Rabbi?
>
> F. It is in line with that which has been taught on Tannaite authority:
>
> G. "Because he has despised the word of the Lord": This refers to one who is without shame in interpreting the Torah.
>
> H. "And broken his commandment": This refers to one who removes the mark of the covenant.
>
> I. "That soul shall utterly be cut of 'Be cut off'"—before the Day of Atonement. "Utterly"—after the Day of Atonement.
>
> J. Might one suppose that that is the case even if he has repented?
>
> K. Scripture says, "His iniquity shall be upon him" (Num. 15:31)—I say that the Day of Atonement does not effect atonement only when his iniquity is still upon him.

While repentance is required, in a system of hierarchical classification such as this one, the other components of the process, prayer in this case, have to be situated in relationship to one another. Whether or not repentance accomplishes the whole of atonement is subject to some uncertainty, since prayer retains a critical role in the process:

> *Leviticus Rabbah* X:V.1
>
> 1. A. Judah b. Rabbi and R. Joshua b. Levi:
>
>   B. Judah b. Rabbi said, "Repentance achieves [only] part, while prayer achieves the complete [atonement]."
>
>   C. R. Joshua b. Levi said, "Repentance achieves the whole [of atonement], while prayer achieves only part [of atonement]."

The two views now have to be sustained by fact, and the facts of Scripture serve. But both parties are clear that repentance forms a stage in the path to atonement, with or without the necessity of prayer.

> D. In the view of R. Judah b. Rabbi, who has said that repentance achieves [only] part [of the needed atonement], from whom do you derive proof?
>
> E. It is from Cain, against whom a harsh decree was issued, as it is written, "A fugitive and a wanderer will you be on the earth" (Gen. 4:12). But when Cain repented, part of the harsh decree was removed from him.
>
> F. That is in line with the following verse of Scripture: "Then Cain went away from the presence of the Lord and dwelt in the land of the wanderer [Nod], east of Eden" (Gen. 4:16). "In the land of a fugitive *and* a wanderer" is not written here, but rather, only "in the land of the wanderer." [The matter of being a fugitive is thus annulled.]
>
> M. When he had left [God], the first man met him, saying to him, "What happened at your trial?"

N. He said to him, "I repented and copped a plea."

Here Cain illustrates the total power of repentance, meaning, confession and a statement of remorse:

> O. When the first man heard this, he began to slap his own face, saying, "So that's how strong repentance is, and I never knew!"
> P. At that moment, the first man pronounced [this Psalm], "A Psalm, the song for the Sabbath day" (Ps. 92:1) [which says, "It is a good thing to make a confession to the Lord" (Ps. 92:2)].
> Q. Said R. Levi, "It was the first man who made up that psalm."

Above all, death marks the final atonement for sin, which bears its implication for the condition of man at the resurrection, as we saw in chapter 10. Because one has atoned through sin (accompanied at the hour of death by a statement of repentance, "May my death be atonement for all my sins," in the liturgy), when he is raised from the dead, his atonement for all his sins is complete. The judgment after resurrection becomes for most a formality. That is why "all Israel has a portion in the world to come," with the exception of a few whose sins are not atoned for by death, and that is by their own word. The Day of Atonement provides atonement, as the Written Torah makes explicit, for the sins of the year for which one has repented, and that accounts for the elaborate rites of confession that fill the day.

The process of reconciliation with God—"at-one-ment" so to speak—encompasses a number of steps and components, not only repentance; and repentance, for its part, does not reach concrete definition in the formulation of the process. This is how the Babylonian Talmud deals with precisely the problem of intransigence on the part of the victim:

> Talmud of Babylonia tractate *Yoma* 8:8–9. VI.1–2/87a–b
> VI.1
> A. [Citing the Mishnah rule:] For transgressions done between man and the Omnipresent, the Day of Atonement atones. For transgressions between man and man, the Day of Atonement atones, only if the man will regain the good will of his friend.

The matter of reconciling the other is now spelled out:

> 2. A. Said R. Isaac, "Whoever offends his fellow, even if through what he says, has to reconcile with him, as it is said, 'My son, if you have become surety for your neighbor, if you have struck your hands for a stranger, you are snared by the words of your mouth . . . do this now, my son, and deliver yourself, seeing you have come into the power of your neighbor, go, humble yourself, and urge your neighbor' (Prov. 6:1–3). If it is a money-claim against you, open the palm of your hand to him [and pay him off], and if not, send a lot of intermediaries to him."

B. Said R. Hisda, "He has to reconcile with him through three sets of three people each: 'He comes before men and says, I have sinned and perverted that which was right and it did not profit me' (Job 33:27)."

C. Said R. Yosé bar Hanina, "Whoever seeks reconciliation with his neighbor has to do so only three times: 'Forgive I pray you now . . . and now we pray you' (Gen. 50:17).

D. "And if he has died, he brings ten people and sets them up at his grave and says, 'I have sinned against the Lord the God of Israel and against this one, whom I have hurt.'"

Specific cases exemplifying the working of the law now are set forth:

3. A. R. Abba had a complaint against R. Jeremiah, [Jeremiah] went and sat at the door of R. Abba. In the interval his serving girl threw out slops. Some drops fell on his head. He said, "They've made a dung heap out of me," and about himself he cited the verse, "He raises up the poor out of the dust" (1 Sam. 2:8).

B. R. Abba heard and came out to him, saying, "Now I must come out to seek reconciliation with you: 'Go, humble yourself and urge your neighbor' (Prov. 6:1)."

Here is how a sage gave the offending man an opportunity of reconciliation:

4. A. When R. Zira had a quarrel with someone, he would pass by him repeatedly, so as to show himself to him, so that the other might come forth to seek reconciliation with him.

But that provision for reconciliation even after the fact raises the question of deliberate and willful violation of the law, encompassing repentance before the fact. And that is the point at which repentance loses its power. If, to begin with, one has insinuated repentance into the sinful act itself, declaring up front that afterward one will repent, the power of repentance is lost, the act of will denying the post facto possibility altogether. That is the point of Mishnah tractate *Yoma* 8:9A–C, which is now amplified. For, we now observe, the issue of attitude takes over, and it is in the end the fundamental attitude that governs: if, to begin with, the willful act is joined to an act of will affecting the post facto circumstance, all is lost; one's attitude to begin with nullifies all further possibilities.

Fathers According to Rabbi Nathan XL:V.1

A. He who says, "I shall sin and repent" will never suffice to carry out repentance.

B. "I will sin and the Day of Atonement will accomplish atonement"—the Day of Atonement will not accomplish atonement.

C. "I shall sin and the day of death will wipe away the sin"—the day of death will not wipe away the sin.

D. R. Eliezer b. R. Yosé says, "He who sins and repents and then proceeds in an unblemished life does not move from his place before he is forgiven.

> E. "He who says, 'I shall sin and repent' is forgiven three times but
> no more."

That is why there is no such thing as preemptive repentance, that is, planning in advance to atone for a sin. We shall presently take up atonement in its own terms; at this point it suffices to register that repentance leads to atonement, at which point God and man reconcile.

SACRIFICE, REPENTANCE, ATONEMENT

How do these media of reconciliation of sinful Israel and God work together? The principal categorical component is the atonement brought about by the advent of the Day of Atonement, as set forth at Leviticus 16. So, for instance, on that day the high priest, representing all Israel, brings about atonement through the rites of the Day of Atonement, beginning with the confession. Scripture presents diverse facts on a given sin, the penalty thereof, and the media of remission of the penalty, and reason and exegesis then make possible the classification of those facts into a coherent whole:

> Tosefta tractate *Kippurim* 4:6–8
> A. R. Ishmael says, "There are four kinds of atonement.
> B. "[If] one has violated a positive commandment but repented,
> he hardly moves from his place before they forgive him,
> C. "since it is said, 'Return, backsliding children. I will heal your
> backsliding' (Jer. 3:22).
> 4:7
> A. "[If] he has violated a negative commandment but repented,
> repentance suspends the punishment, and the Day of Atone-
> ment effects atonement,
> B. "since it is said, 'For that day will effect atonement for you' (Lev.
> 16:30).
> 4:8
> A. "[If] he has violated [a rule for which the punishment is] extir-
> pation or death at the hands of an earthly court, but repented,
> repentance and the Day of Atonement suspend [the punish-
> ment], and suffering on the other days of the year will wipe away
> [the sin],
> B. "since it says, 'Then will I visit their transgression with a rod'
> (Ps. 89:32).
> C. "But he through whom the Name of Heaven is profaned delib-
> erately but who repented—repentance does not have power to
> suspend [the punishment], nor the Day of Atonement to atone,
> D. "but repentance and the Day of Atonement atone for a third,
> suffering atones for a third, and death wipes away the sin, with
> suffering,
> E. "and on such a matter it is said, 'Surely this iniquity shall not be
> purged from you until you die' (Isa. 22:14)."

The four kinds of atonement are worked out in their own systematic and logical terms, but the verses of Scripture then contribute to the validation of the classification scheme. There is a grid established by positive and negative commandments, intersecting with the matter of repentance; then there is the grid established by the kind of penalty—extirpation or the earthly court's death sentence. Here repentance and the Day of Atonement form the intersecting grid. Then there is the matter of the profanation of the divine name, in which case repentance and the Day of Atonement come into play along with suffering and death. So the point of differentiation is established by appeal to the type of sin, on the one side, and the pertinent penalties, on the other, and the effects of media of atonement—repentance, death, Day of Atonement, suffering.

Clearly, then, what is at stake in repentance and atonement vastly transcends issues of this world. Time and again we have noted that repentance, along with atonement, forms the condition of the restoration of world order. Even in the here and now, Israel is able through repentance to reconcile itself with God, and in God's own time, the reconciliation—Israel's will now voluntarily conform to God's word—will mark the end of the world as man knows it and the beginning of the time of restoration. That is why repentance forms the bridge between the analysis of the imperfection of world order and the account of the restoration of world order at the last. In so many words repentance is linked to the salvation of the individual Israelite and the redemption of Holy Israel, for these mark the return to Eden.

Chapter 13

Death and Afterlife

DEATH

As we saw in chapter 10, death is natural to the human condition; sages in no way deemed death a challenge to the doctrine of God's goodness but encompassed within that doctrine the fact that man dies. Death came about by reason of Adam's and his descendants' sins. We noted in chapter 12 how integral to the doctrines of sacrifice, sin, repentance, and atonement is the presence of death:

> *Genesis Rabbah* IX:V.2–3
>
> 2. A. R. Hama bar Hanina and R. Jonathan:
>
> B. R. Hama bar Hanina said, "The first man was worthy not to have to taste the taste of death. And why was the penalty of death applied to him? The Holy One, blessed be he, foresaw that Nebuchadnezzar and Hiram were destined to turn themselves into gods. Therefore the penalty of having to die was imposed upon man. That is in line with this verse of Scripture: 'You were in Eden, the garden of God' (Ezek. 28:13). And was Hiram actually in Eden? But he said to him, 'You are the one who caused that one in Eden to have to die.'"

C. [Said R. Jonathan to him, "If so, God should have decreed death only for the wicked, but not for the righteous. Rather, it was so that the wicked should not be able hypocritically to pretend to repent, so that they should not have occasion to say, 'Are not the righteous living on and on? It is only because they form a treasure of merit accruing on account of the practice of doing religious duties as well as good deeds. We too shall lay up a treasure of merit accruing from doing religious duties and good deeds.' What would come out is that the things they do would not be done sincerely, [for their own sake, but only for the sake of gaining merit]. [That is what is good about death. It prevents the wicked from perverting the holy life by doing the right thing for the wrong reason. Everyone dies, so there is no point in doing religious duties only so as to avoid dying.]"

Death is essential to the divine plan for creation. It would not be possible to find a more powerful and one-sided endorsement of that position.

The more important question, then, is, What happens after death? When Israelites die, they go for judgment for conduct in this life. And that fact brings us to the other aspect of the good death as well as the Torah's picture of what happens then—the good death as the statement of acceptance, submission to God's will, and humility in the face of divine judgment and justice. For we shall now see how the great sage died in an attitude of uncertainty and humility, not taking for granted that even through a life of study and practice of the teachings of the Torah, he has forced his way into the Garden of Eden. Rather, the great sage dies in an attitude of humility and awareness of sin. Here we see, moreover, the theory of what happens after death. A broad range of opinions makes its way in the written and oral parts of the Torah, but three points emerge as authoritative:

1. We are judged.
2. We are rewarded or penalized for our life on earth by being sent to either the Garden of Eden or Gehenna.
3. When the Messiah comes, we will all be raised from the dead.

Individual judgment takes place upon death, and the resurrection of the dead forms part of the end of time inaugurated by the coming of the Messiah. Here is the classic account of how sages view that matter and of what is at stake in it:

Fathers According to Rabbi Nathan XXV:II.1
    A. At the time that Rabban Yohanan ben Zakkai was departing from this life, he raised up his voice and wept. His disciples said to him, "Lord, tall pillar, eternal light, mighty hammer, why are you weeping?"
    B. He said to them, "Now am I going to appear before a mortal king, who, should he be angry with me, is angry only in this world, and if he should imprison me, imposes imprisonment only in this world, and if he should put me to death, imposes death only in this world, and not only so, but whom I can appease with words and bribe with money?

C. "Lo, I am going to appear before the King of kings, the Holy One, blessed be he, who, should he be angry with me, is angry both in this world and in the world to come, whom I cannot appease with words or bribe with money.

D. "And furthermore, before me are two paths, one to the Garden of Eden, the other to Gehenna, and I do not know on which road, whether I shall be drawn down to Gehenna or whether I shall be brought into the Garden of Eden."

E. And in this regard it is said, "Before him shall be sentenced all those who go down to the dust, even he who cannot keep his soul alive" (Ps. 22:30).

After a life of Torah-study, deeds of compassion, and love of God, Yohanan still trembles at the judgment he faces, for the Torah teaches never to be certain of oneself until death but to live a life of repentance and prayer. Yohanan therefore does not claim to know whether he will go to the Garden of Eden or to Gehenna. But that is typical of someone who asks no more than that his disciples fear God as much as they fear man—that is, someone with a solid grasp of ordinary reality.

AFTERLIFE: RESURRECTION

In Rabbinic Judaism, death does not mark the end of the individual human life, nor exile the last stop in the journey of Holy Israel. Israelites will live in the age or the world to come; Israel will be restored to the Land of Israel; and in the end along with Israel all of humanity will know the one true God. So far as the individual is concerned, beyond the grave, at a determinate moment, a person (1) rises from the grave in resurrection, (2) is judged, and (3) enjoys the world to come.

For the entirety of Israel, congruently, all Israel participates in the resurrection, which takes place in the Land of Israel, and enters the world to come. The two principal components of the Oral Torah's theology of last things—(1) resurrection and judgment, and (2) the world to come and eternal life—as laid out in the several documents do not fit together seamlessly. First comes the resurrection of individuals, and, with it, judgment of individuals one by one. Then, those chosen for life having been identified, "the world to come" takes place, and that final restoration of perfection, involving all Israel in place of Adam, lasts forever. "Israel" is not, however, an ethnic category but a supernatural social entity. The Israel of Judaism is defined as the cohort of those chosen for life, and Israelites are those restored to life in the Land of Israel.

On what bases did Rabbinic Judaism found the doctrine of resurrection? They required evidence from Scripture and from nature, both sources of truth in their system. For sages, the issue was not that the dead would be raised, but that the Torah proved that the dead would be raised. In the following story, *minim*, that is, heretic Jews, wished to deny that claim and to demonstrate that the Torah contained no such teaching:

Talmud of Babylonia tractate *Sanhedrin* 11:1.I.5/90a

I.5

    A. Minim asked Rabban Gamaliel, "How do we know that the Holy One, blessed be he, will resurrect the dead?"

    B. He said to them, "It is proved from the Torah, from the Prophets, and from the Writings." But they did not accept his proofs.

    C. "From the Torah: for it is written, 'And the Lord said to Moses, Behold, you shall sleep with your fathers and rise up' (Deut. 31:16)."

    D. They said to him, "But perhaps the sense of the passage is, 'And the people will rise up' (Deut. 31:16)?"

    E. "From the Prophets: as it is written, 'Thy dead men shall live, together with my dead body they shall arise. Awake and sing, you that live in the dust, for your dew is as the dew of herbs, and the earth shall cast out its dead' (Isa. 26:19)."

    F. "But perhaps that refers to the dead whom Ezekiel raised up."

    G. "From the Writings, as it is written, 'And the roof of your mouth, like the best wine of my beloved, that goes down sweetly, causing the lips of those who are asleep to speak' (Song 7:9)."

    L. [The minim would not concur in Gamaliel's view] until he cited for them the following verse: "'Which the Lord swore to your fathers to give to them' (Deut. 11:21)—to them and not to you, so proving from the Torah that the dead will live."

At the same time, sages had to take up the challenge of reasonable gentiles, who found the belief implausible. For them, questions of rational proof, not demonstrations of truth based on the Torah, had to be devised, and in the following stories we see how appeal to nature, not to revelation, was set forth:

Talmud of Babylonia tractate *Sanhedrin* 11:1.I:10–12/90b–91a

I.10

    A. Queen Cleopatra asked R. Meir, saying, "I know that the dead will live, for it is written, 'And [the righteous] shall blossom forth out of your city like the grass of the earth' (Ps. 72:16).

    B. "But when they rise, will they rise naked or in their clothing?"

    C. He said to her, "It is an argument a fortiori based on the grain of wheat.

    D. "Now if a grain of wheat, which is buried naked, comes forth in many garments, the righteous, who are buried in their garments, all the more so [will rise in many garments]!"

I.11

    A. Caesar said to Rabban Gamaliel, "You maintain that the dead will live. But they are dust, and can the dust live?"

    B. [91A] His daughter said to him, "Allow me to answer him:

    C. "There are two potters in our town, one who works with water, the other who works with clay. Which is the more impressive?"

    D. He said to her, "The one who works with water."

    E. She said to him, "If he works with water, will he not create even more out of clay?"

I.12

    A. A Tannaite authority of the house of R. Ishmael [taught], "[Res-

urrection] is a matter of an argument a fortiori based on the case
of a glass utensil.

B. "Now if glassware, which is the work of the breath of a mortal
man, when broken, can be repaired,

C. "A mortal man, who is made by the breath of the Holy One,
blessed be he, how much the more so [that he can be repaired,
in the resurrection of the dead]."

The resurrection of the dead therefore forms a principal component of the
Judaic theology of death and the afterlife. It comes to critical expression, moreover, in the liturgy of the synagogue. The prayers of petition, recited three times
a day, include at the head the following blessing:

> Your might, O Lord, is boundless. Your loving kindness sustains the living,
> your great mercies give life to the dead. You support the falling, heal the ail-
> ing, free the fettered. You keep your faith with those that sleep in the dust.
> Whose power can compare with yours? You are the master of life and death
> and deliverance. Faithful are you in giving life to the dead. Praised are you,
> Lord, master of life and death.[8]

The logic of the Judaic view proves blatant here: master of life also is lord over
death, and who gives life once can and will bestow life a second time.

The absolute given, a logical necessity of a theology revealing God's justice,
maintains that individual life goes forward from this world, past the grave, to
the world to come, and people are both judged and promised eternal life. That
is a necessary doctrine for a system that insists on the rationality and order of
the universe under God's rule. Without judgment and eternal life for the righteous, this world's imbalance cannot be righted, nor can God's justice be
revealed. Monotheism without an eschatology of judgment and the world to
come leaves unresolved the tensions inherent in the starting point: God is one;
God is just. That is why the starting point of the theology dictates its conclusion: the deeds one does in this world bear consequences for his situation in the
world to come, and the merit attained through this-worldly deeds, for example, of generosity, persists. Individuals retain their status as such through all
time to come. So the basic logic of the system requires the doctrine of personal
resurrection, so that the life of this world may go onward to the next. Indeed,
without the conception of life beyond the grave the system as a whole yields a
mass of contradictions and anomalies: injustice to the righteous, prosperity to
the wicked, never recompensed. That explains why, at one point after another,
the path to the future passes through, and beyond, the grave and the judgment
that, for all Israel with few exceptions, leads to eternity. The principal continues and yields interest, or punishment may take place in this world, while eternal punishment goes onward as well, especially for the trilogy of absolute sins:
idolatry, incest (or fornication), and murder, capped by gossip. But how all of
this squares with the conception of "all Israel" that transcends individual
Israelites remains to be seen.

"ALL ISRAEL HAS A PORTION IN THE WORLD TO COME"

The first component of the doctrine of the resurrection of the dead—belief both that the resurrection of the dead will take place and that it is the Torah that reveals that the dead will rise—is fundamental to the Oral Torah. It is fully exposed in a fundamental composition devoted by the framers of the Mishnah to that subject. The components of the doctrine fit together, in that statement, in a logical order: (1) In a predictable application of the governing principle of measure for measure, those who do not believe in the resurrection of the dead will be punished by being denied what they do not accept. Some few others bear the same fate. (2) But to be Israel means to rise from the grave, and that applies to all Israelites. The given of the condition of Israel is that the entire holy people will enter the world to come, that is, will enjoy the resurrection of the dead and eternal life. "Israel" then is anticipated to be the people of eternity. (3) Excluded from the category of resurrection and the world to come, then, are only those who by their own sins have denied themselves that benefit. These are those that deny that the teaching of the world to come derives from the Torah, or those who deny that the Torah comes from God, or hedonists. Exegesis of Scripture also yields the names of three kings who will not be resurrected, as well as four commoners and these specified generations: the flood, the dispersion, Sodom, the generation of the wilderness, the party of Korah, and the Ten Tribes:

> Mishnah tractate *Sanhedrin* 10:1
> A. All Israelites have a share in the world to come,
> B. as it is said, "Your people also shall be all righteous, they shall inherit the land forever; the branch of my planting, the work of my hands, that I may be glorified" (Isa. 60:21).

That single statement serves better than any other to define Israel in the Oral Torah. Now we forthwith take up exceptions:

> C. And these are the ones who have no portion in the world to come:
> D. He who says, the resurrection of the dead is a teaching which does not derive from the Torah, and the Torah does not come from Heaven; and an Epicurean.
> E. R. Aqiba says, "Also: He who reads in heretical books,
> F. "and he who whispers over a wound and says, 'I will put none of the diseases upon you which I have put on the Egyptians, for I am the Lord who heals you' (Exod. 15:26)."
> G. Abba Saul says, "Also: He who pronounces the divine Name as it is spelled out."

From classes of persons, we turn to specified individuals who are denied a place within Israel and entry in the world to come; all but one are Israelites, and the exception, Balaam, has a special relation to Israel as the gentile prophet who came to curse but ended with a blessing:

Mishnah tractate *Sanhedrin* 10:2

    A. Three kings and four ordinary folk have no portion in the world to come.

    B. Three kings: Jeroboam, Ahab, and Manasseh.

    C. R. Judah says, "Manasseh has a portion in the world to come,

    D. "since it is said, 'And he prayed to him and he was entreated of him and heard his supplication and brought him again to Jerusalem into his kingdom' (2 Chron. 33:13)."

    E. They said to him, "To his kingdom he brought him back, but to the life of the world to come he did not bring him back."

    F. Four ordinary folk: Balaam, Doeg, Ahitophel, and Gehazi.

Then come entire generations of gentiles before Abraham, who might have been considered for eternal life outside of the framework of God's self-manifestation, first to Abraham, then in the Torah. These are the standard sets: the generation of the flood, the generation of the dispersion, and the men of Sodom:

Mishnah tractate *Sanhedrin* 10:3

    A. The generation of the flood has no share in the world to come,

    B. and they shall not stand in the judgment,

    C. since it is written, "My spirit shall not judge with man forever" (Gen. 6:3)

    D. neither judgment nor spirit.

    E. The generation of the dispersion has no share in the world to come,

    F. since it is said, "So the Lord scattered them abroad from there upon the face of the whole earth" (Gen. 11:8).

    G. "So the Lord scattered them abroad"—in this world,

    H. "and the Lord scattered them from there"—in the world to come.

    I. The men of Sodom have no portion in the world to come,

    J. since it is said, "Now the men of Sodom were wicked and sinners against the Lord exceedingly" (Gen. 13:13)

    K. "Wicked"—in this world,

    L. "And sinners"—in the world to come.

    M. But they will stand in judgment.

    N. R. Nehemiah says, "Both these and those will not stand in judgment,

    O. "for it is said, 'Therefore the wicked shall not stand in judgment [108A], nor sinners in the congregation of the righteous' (Ps. 1:5)

    P. "'Therefore the wicked shall not stand in judgment'—this refers to the generation of the flood.

    Q. "'Nor sinners in the congregation of the righteous'—this refers to the men of Sodom."

    R. They said to him, "They will not stand in the congregation of the righteous, but they will stand in the congregation of the sinners."

    S. The spies have no portion in the world to come,

    T. as it is said, "Even those men who brought up an evil report of the land died by the plague before the Lord" (Num. 14:37)

    U. "Died"—in this world,

    V. "By the plague"—in the world to come.

What about counterparts in Israel, from the Torah forward? The issue concerns the generation of the wilderness, which rejected the Land; the party of Korah; and the

Ten Tribes. These match the gentile contingents. But here there is a dispute, and no normative judgment emerges from the Mishnah's treatment of the matter:

> Mishnah tractate *Sanhedrin* 10:4
> A. "The generation of the wilderness has no portion in the world to come and will not stand in judgment,
> B. "for it is written, 'In this wilderness they shall be consumed and there they shall die' (Num. 14:35)," the words of R. Aqiba.
> C. R. Eliezer says, "Concerning them it says, 'Gather my saints together to me, those that have made a covenant with me by sacrifice' (Ps. 50:5)."
> D. "The party of Korah is not destined to rise up,
> E. "for it is written, 'And the earth closed upon them'—in this world.
> F. "'And they perished from among the assembly'—in the world to come," the words of R. Aqiba.
> G. And R. Eliezer says, "Concerning them it says, 'The Lord kills and resurrects, brings down to Sheol and brings up again' (1 Sam. 2:6)."

> Mishnah tractate *Sanhedrin* 10:5
> A. "The ten tribes [of northern Israel, exiled by the Assyrians] are not destined to return [with Israel at the time of the resurrection of the dead],
> B. "since it is said, 'And he cast them into another land, as on this day' (Deut. 29:28). Just as the day passes and does not return, so they have gone their way and will not return," the words of R. Aqiba.
> C. R. Eliezer says, "Just as this day is dark and then grows light, so the ten tribes for whom it now is dark—thus in the future it is destined to grow light for them."

Scripture thus contributes the details that refine the basic proposition; the framer has found the appropriate exclusions. But the prophet, in Scripture, also has provided the basic allegation on which all else rests, that is, "Israel will be entirely righteous and inherit the land forever." Denying the stated dogmas removes a person from the status of "Israel," in line with the opening statement, so to be Israel means to rise from the dead, and Israel as a collectivity is defined as those persons in humanity who are destined to eternal life, a supernatural community.

What evidence do the sages present to prove their point? The certainty of resurrection derives from a simple fact of their restorationist theology: God has already shown that he can do it, so *Genesis Rabbah* LXXVII:I.1: "You find that everything that the Holy One, blessed be he, is destined to do in the age to come he has already gone ahead and done through the righteous in this world. The Holy One, blessed be he, will raise the dead, and Elijah raised the dead." The paramount composite on the subject derives its facts, demonstrating the coming resurrection of the dead, from the Written Torah, which, as we realize, serves as counterpart to nature for philosophy, the source of actualities. Sages deem urgent the task of reading outward and forward from Scripture, and at the critical conclusion of their theological system the Oral Torah focuses on Scripture's evidence, the regularization of Scripture's facts. But the doctrine of resurrection as defined by the principal (and huge) composite of the Talmud of Babylonia contains a number of components: (1) origin of the doctrine in the Written Torah; (2) the gentiles and the resurrection of the dead; (3) the distinction between the days of the messiah and the world to come; (4) the restoration of Israel to the Land of Israel. Here is the beginning of the systematic exposition:

> Talmud of Babylonia tractate *Sanhedrin* 11:1–2.I.22ff/91b
> I.22
>> A. R. Simeon b. Laqish contrasted [these two verses]: "It is writ-
>> ten, 'I will gather them . . . with the blind and the lame, the
>> woman with child and her that travails with child together'
>> (Jer. 31:8), and it is written, 'Then shall the lame man leap as
>> a hart and the tongue of the dumb sing, for in the wilderness
>> shall waters break out and streams in the desert' (Isa. 35:6).
>> How so [will the dead both retain their defects and also be
>> healed]?
>> B. "They will rise [from the grave] bearing their defects and then
>> be healed."

The first inquiry deals with the problem of the condition of the body upon resurrection and finds its resolution in the contrast of verses, yielding the stated doctrine: the dead rise in the condition in which they died and then are healed.
Among the components of that doctrine, that resurrection of the dead is a doctrine set forth by the Written Torah and demonstrable within the framework of
the Torah, occupies a principal place in the Oral Torah's exposition of the topic.
That proposition is demonstrated over and over again. Evidence from the Torah
concerning the resurrection of the dead is ubiquitous:

> *Sifré* to Deuteronomy CCCVI:XXVIII.3
>> A. And so did R. Simai say, "There is no passage [in the Torah]
>> which does not contain [clear evidence concerning] the resur-
>> rection of the dead, but we have not got the power of exegesis
>> [sufficient to find the pertinent indication].
>> B. "For it is said, 'He will call to the heaven above and to the earth,
>> that he may judge his people' (Ps. 50:4).
>> C. "'He will call to the heaven above': this refers to the soul.
>> D. "'and to the earth': this refers to the body.
>> E. "'that he may judge his people': who judges with him?
>> F. "And how on the basis of Scripture do we know that Scripture
>> speaks only of the resurrection of the dead?
>> G. "As it is said, 'Come from the four winds, O breath, and breathe
>> upon these slain, that they may live' (Ezek. 37:9)."

Further proofs of the same proposition are abundant, with the following
instances representative of the larger corpus. First, we note the recurrent formula,
"How on the basis of the Torah do we know . . . ?" Then we are given a sequence
of cases, each one of them, as noted earlier, deriving from an individual, none of
them appealing to the eternity of the collectivity of Israel.

THE MESSIAH

When Israel really wants the Messiah to come, he will come. Then he will raise the dead, restore Israel to the Land of Israel, and prepare the way for judgment and the recovery of Eden. But we are now aware of the special weight attached to the words "want" or "will." What Israel must want is only what God wants. What Israel must do is give up any notion of accomplishing on its own, by its own act of will, the work of redemption. It is only through the self-abnegation of repentance that Israel can accomplish its goal. Specifically, when Israel's will conforms to the will of God, then God will respond to the act of repentance by bringing about the time of restoration and eternal life. This is expressed in a colloquy which announces that the Messiah will come when all Israel keeps a single Sabbath. And that will take place when Israel wants it to take place. It requires only an act of will on the part of Israel to accept one of the Ten Commandments. Then in a broader restatement of matters, the entire redemptive process is made to depend on Israel's repentance:

> Yerushalmi tractate *Ta'anit* 1:1.II:5
> G. The Israelites said to Isaiah, "O our Rabbi, Isaiah, What will come for us out of this night?"
> H. He said to them, "Wait for me, until I can present the question."
> I. Once he had asked the question, he came back to them.
> J. They said to him, "Watchman, what of the night? What did the Guardian of the ages say [a play on 'of the night' and 'say']?"
> K. He said to them, "The watchman says: 'Morning comes; and also the night. [If you will inquire, inquire; come back again]'" (Isa. 21:12).
> L. They said to him, "Also the night?"
> M. He said to them, "It is not what you are thinking. But there will be morning for the righteous, and night for the wicked, morning for Israel, and night for idolaters."

Now comes the main point in the exchange: when will this happen? It will happen when Israel wants. And what is standing in the way is Israel's arrogance, to be atoned for by Israel's remorseful repentance:

> N. They said to him, "When?"
> O. He said to them, "Whenever you want, He too wants [it to be]—if you want it, he wants it."
> P. They said to him, "What is standing in the way?"
> Q. He said to them, "Repentance: 'come back again'" (Isa. 21:12).

This is stated in the clearest possible way: one day will do it.

> R. R. Aha in the name of R. Tanhum b. R. Hiyya, "If Israel repents for one day, forthwith the son of David will come.
> S. "What is the scriptural basis? 'O that today you would hearken to his voice!'" (Ps. 95:7).

Now comes the introduction of the Sabbath as a test case:

> T. Said R. Levi, "If Israel would keep a single Sabbath in the proper
> way, forthwith the son of David will come.
> U. "What is the scriptural basis for this view? 'Moses said, Eat it
> today, for today is a Sabbath to the Lord; [today you will not
> find it in the field]' (Exod. 16:25).
> V. "And it says, '[For thus said the Lord God, the Holy One of Israel],
> In returning and rest you shall be saved; [in quietness and in trust
> shall be your strength. And you would not]'" (Isa. 30:15). By means
> of returning and [Sabbath] rest you will be redeemed.

The main point, then, is the linkage of repentance to the coming restoration of Israel to the Land, the dead to life, by the Messiah. But the advent of the messiah depends wholly on Israel's will. If Israel will subordinate its will to God's, all else will follow.

Israel's own repentance will provide the occasion, and God will do the rest. It is when Israel has repented. It follows that the messiah's advent and activity depend on Israel, not on the messiah's own autonomous decision, character, and behavior. Israel decides issues of its own attitude toward God and repents; God decides to respond to the change in will. But not a comparable, categorical imperative, the messiah only responds to Israel's decision regarding when he should make his appearance to signal the change in the condition of mankind, and the messiah responds to God's decision, taking a part within that sequence that comes to an end with Elijah. That accounts for the heavy emphasis not on the Messiah's intervention but on Israel's own responsibility.

What about the gentiles in all this? By "gentiles," Rabbinic Judaism understood "idolaters." Naturally, as soon as the category "Israel and the Torah" is invoked, its counterpart and opposite "the gentiles and idolatry" complements and balances the discussion. So too, when it comes to the messiah, the gentiles are given a role. Specifically, the nations will bring gifts to the messiah, and it will be a great honor to them that they are permitted to do so. Here is the judgment of the nations: "In the age to come the Holy One, blessed be He, will bring a scroll of the Torah and hold it in his bosom and say, 'Let him who has kept himself busy with it come and take his reward'"—leading to the exclusion of the gentiles from the world to come. So too, their participation in the messiah's activities only underscores Israel's centrality to the human drama:

> Talmud of Babylonia tractate *Pesahim* 10:7.II.22/118b
> A. Said R. Kahana, "When R. Ishmael b. R. Yosé fell ill, Rabbi sent
> word to him: 'Tell us two or three of the things that you said to
> us in the name of your father.'
> B. "He sent word to him, 'This is what father said: "What is the mean-
> ing of the verse of Scripture, 'Praise the Lord all you nations' (Ps.
> 117:1)? What are the nations of the world doing in this setting?
> This is the sense of the statement, 'Praise the Lord all you nations'
> (Ps. 117:1) for the acts of might and wonder that he has done with
> them; all the more so us, since 'his mercy is great toward us.'"'"

Now the nations take a more specific role in relationship to the messiah, each claiming a relationship to the messiah on account of its dealings with Israel:

> C. "'And further: "Egypt is destined to bring a gift to the Messiah. He will think that he should not accept it from them. The Holy One, blessed be He, will say to the Messiah, 'Accept it from them, they provided shelter for my children in Egypt.' Forthwith: 'Nobles shall come out of Egypt, bringing gifts' (Ps. 68:32).
>
> D. "The Ethiopians will propose an argument a fortiori concerning themselves, namely: 'If these, who subjugated them, do this, we, who never subjugated them, all the more so!' The Holy One, blessed be He, will say to the Messiah, 'Accept it from them.' Forthwith: 'Ethiopia shall hasten to stretch out her hands to God' (Ps. 68:32).""'

Rome always comes at the climax, and, in any sequence of the nations, will always mark the end of the discussion. Here Rome evokes its descent from Esau, a given for the Oral Torah, or from Edom, thus becoming part of the extended family of Israel:

> E. "Wicked Rome will then propose the same argument a fortiori in her own regard: 'If these, who are not their brethren, are such, then we, who are their brethren, all the more so!' The Holy One, blessed be He, will say to Gabriel, 'Rebuke the wild beast of the reeds, the multitude of the bulls' (Ps. 68:32)—'rebuke the wild beast and take possession of the congregation.'
>
> F. "Another interpretation: 'Rebuke the wild beast of the reeds'—who dwells among the reeds, 'the boar out of the wood [Rome] ravages it, that which moves in the field feeds on it' (Ps. 80:14).""'

Here, the messiah accords honor to the nations, except for Rome, the empire that will fall at the redemption of Israel now at hand. The governing concern—the nations relate to the messiah only through Israel—registers. The messiah then plays a part in the resurrection of the dead, on the one side, and the restoration of Israel, on the other.

The theme of death and afterlife in Judaism brings to an end the story of how God created an orderly world but at the climax of creation made man, in his image, after his likeness. Man both complements and corresponds to God, and it is man's freedom, meaning, his effective will and power of intentionality, that match God's will. When these conflict, man's arrogance leads him to rebellion against God, sin resulting. And from sin comes the imperfection of world order, change, inequity, imbalance. Punished and remorseful, man gives up his arrogant attitude and conforms his will to God's. God responds with mercy, freely accepting the reformation that is freely offered. Then world order is restored; that perfection effected at the outset is regained for Israel, which means, for God's part of mankind. Eden, now the Land of Israel, is recovered; Adam, now embodied in Israel, is restored to his place. For the Israelite, death dies; man rises from the grave to life eternal. For Israel, the gentiles' rule comes to an end, and Israel regains the Land. Repentance then marks the recovery of the world as God wanted it to be, which is to say, the world in which Israel—defined as those that know the one and only God and love him with all their heart, soul, and might—regains its promised place in paradise for eternity.

Chapter 14

The Representation of the Faith: Art and Symbol in Judaism

THE ART OF THE SYNAGOGUES
AND SYMBOLIC DISCOURSE IN JUDAISM

Most synagogues built from the third to the seventh century, both in the land of Israel and abroad, had decorated floors or walls. Some iconic symbols out of the religious life of Judaism or of Greco-Roman piety occur nearly everywhere. Other symbols, available, for example, from the repertoire of items mentioned in Scripture, or from the Greco-Roman world, never make an appearance at all. We find representations of these symbols of Judaic origin: *shofar* (ram's horn, for the New Year), a *lulab* ("branches of palm trees, boughs of leafy trees, and willows" [Lev. 23:40] for Tabernacles), *etrog* ("the fruit of goodly trees" [Lev. 23:40], also for Tabernacles), and a *menorah* (candelabrum). In addition, synagogue art encompassed such pagan symbols as a Zodiac. All of these form part of the absolutely fixed symbolic vocabulary of the synagogues of late antiquity. By contrast, symbols of other elements of the Judaic calendar year, at least as important as those that we do find, never make an appearance. And, obviously, a vast number of pagan symbols proved useless to Judaic synagogue artists. It follows that the artists of the synagogues spoke through a certain set of symbols and ignored other

175

available ones. That simple fact makes it highly likely that the symbols they did use meant something to them, represented a set of choices, and delivered a message important to the people who worshipped in those synagogues.

Now, as a matter of fact, the second commandment forbids the making of graven images of God:

> You shall not make yourself a graven image or any likeness of anything that is in heaven above or that is in the earth beneath or that is in the water under the earth; you shall not bow down to them or serve them . . .
>
> (Exod. 20:4–5)

Therefore people have long taken for granted that Judaism should not produce an artistic tradition. Some held that if Judaic settings yielded iconic representations, these should be essentially abstract and nonrepresentational, much like the rich decorative tradition of Islam. But from the beginning of the twentieth century, archaeologists began to uncover in the Middle East, North Africa, the Balkans, and the Italian peninsula synagogues of late antiquity richly decorated in representational art. For a long time historians of Judaism did not find it possible to accommodate the newly discovered evidence of an ongoing artistic tradition. Today the testimony of archaeology, especially of the art of the synagogues of antiquity, finds a full and ample hearing. In understanding the way in which art contributes to the study of the history of a religion, we find in Judaism in late antiquity a fine example of the problems of interpretation and how they are accommodated and solved.

SYNAGOGUE ICONOGRAPHY:
THE DISTRIBUTION OVER TIME

Before the fourth century, it was uncommon to decorate synagogues with iconic representations, afterward, it became routine. Synagogue decoration in the fifth and sixth centuries C.E. used iconic symbols for the communication of religious sentiments. A restricted vocabulary of symbols served. Not only so, but a strikingly limited repertoire of symbols predominated. A few components of the symbolic vocabulary recur very broadly, and many possible ones (out of the same corpus) not at all. Signs meant to serve as symbols are distinguished, in iconic form, by three traits:

1. The function and provenance, within a synagogue
2. The combination or relationship with other representations of things
3. The selection of those few things among many that can have been represented

We shall now see that these conditions are met by synagogue iconic representation in the fourth, fifth, and sixth centuries, so it would appear that symbolic discourse as a medium for the expression of religious feeling served not only the authors of compositions and compilers of composites but also the patrons and artists responsible for the decoration of synagogues.

If synagogues were decorated at all before the fifth and sixth centuries (and many were), they exhibited diverse iconic representations, and, so far as we can see, no severely limited repertoire of iconic items governed. By contrast, most synagogues were decorated in the fifth and sixth centuries, and among them, most used a severely restricted symbolic vocabulary. By the criteria just now set forth, therefore, the marks of symbolic discourse are exhibited by the iconic evidence of Judaism in the fifth and sixth centuries. What symbols recur most commonly are these: the *lulab* and *etrog* (nearly always together, so not to be differentiated as two distinct symbols), the *shofar*, and the *menorah* (variously represented, with five or seven or nine branches). If any iconic representations are to be deemed symbolic merely by reason of frequent appearance in a wide variety of settings, they are those. The three symbols appear to form, on the average, between one fourth and one third of all iconic representations. Since, as a rough guess, we may count upward of one hundred different items represented on the sites that are examined, the three items occur a disproportionate number of times. The appearance of these particular items is therefore highly unlikely to have occurred by chance alone. No such result favoring one item is likely to have appeared randomly, and the probability of three items' forming a traveling unit is still more remote. These results therefore seem to me to point toward these propositions:

1. The *etrog, lulab,* and *shofar* travel together, and the *menorah* goes with them. Among the sites in which the *etrog, lulab,* and *shofar* occur, the *menorah* is always portrayed. Where there is an *etrog* and a *lulab,* there is ordinarily a *shofar* as well (eighteen sites for the *etrog* and *lulab,* and eighteen sites for the *shofar,* with only two discrepancies).
2. While, by a rough guess, any other symbol may occur at two or at most three sites by chance or randomly, the grouping of *etrog* and *lulab, shofar,* and *menorah* is very unlikely to have occurred by chance alone. If the *etrog, lulab,* and *shofar* occur, it will always be with a *menorah.*

It follows that, by the same criteria imposed on the literary evidence, we may conclude that

1. Symbolic discourse went forward through use of combinations of symbols in iconic form.
2. Single combinations of iconic symbols circulated broadly.
3. That set of symbols in iconic form represents a clear-cut selection among a much larger repertoire of available symbols.

Whether or not the ninety-seven other objects that are represented in synagogue art (a rough count at best!) were symbolic and not decorative I do not claim to know. But the *etrog* and *lulab*, *shofar,* and *menorah* do form a repertoire of icons that clearly served to carry on symbolic discourse.

The data, however raw, prove that the *shofar, lulab, etrog,* and *menorah* (1) occur very routinely in synagogues, and (2) they occur together. They clearly have been selected out of a large repertoire of candidates—one hundred or more. By the criteria offered here, in function and provenance, these four items are syna-gogue symbols. They combine with one another. They occur with dispropor-tionate frequency, in most synagogues of the fourth, fifth, and sixth centuries. None of the other items that occur in the synagogues assigned to the period at hand exhibit these traits, at all or in equivalent proportion. If therefore we wish to claim that symbolic discourse was carried on in synagogue iconography as much as in canonical writing, it was through the four items identified here. We have now to ask whether the symbols in iconic form and those in verbal form comprise a single symbolic structure.

INTEGRATING SYMBOLIC DISCOURSE
IN ICONIC AND VERBAL FORMS

How does the iconic symbolic vocabulary of the synagogues compare with the counterpart usages of the Rabbinic canon? What we shall now see is that in ver-bal form, in the writings of the Rabbinic sages, the *lulab* and *etrog, shofar,* and *menorah,* if they occur at all, do not occur in the combination(s) common in syn-agogue art. To state the question in concrete form: When in writing people refer to the *lulab,* do they forthwith think also of the *menorah* and *shofar?* And when they refer to the *shofar,* do they think of the *lulab* and *menorah?* Or do they think of other things—or of nothing? As a matter of fact, they think of other things. The combinations that people make in writing are not of the same symbols as the combinations that people make iconically. I state categorically that in no case of symbolic discourse in verbal form that I have examined do we find the com-binations of the *etrog* and *lulab, shofar,* and *menorah.*

To satisfy ourselves that the distinctive combination of symbols characteristic of the synagogue—the *etrog* and *lulab, shofar,* and *menorah*—does not occur in the literary form of discourse we consider how the Rabbinic writings treat the first and second of the three items. Here we see that the persistent manipulation of the three symbols as a group finds no counterpart in writing. The connections are different. We begin with the *lulab* and ask whether representation of that sym-bol provokes discourse pertinent, also, to the symbols of the *shofar* and of the *menorah,* or even only of the *menorah.* The answer is no. Other matters, but not those matters, are invoked. *Leviticus Rabbah,* devoted to the exegesis of the book of Leviticus, treats the Festival of Tabernacles (*Sukkot*), the sole point in the litur-gical calendar at which the *etrog* and *lulab* pertain. The base verse that is treated is Leviticus 23:39–40, and that statement is taken to refer, specifically, to the *lulab.* When sages read that verse, they are provoked to introduce the considera-

tion of Torah-study; the opening and closing units of the pertinent unit tell us
what is important:

Leviticus Rabbah XXX:I.1, 6

    1. A. "[On the fifteenth day of the seventh month, when you have
        gathered in the produce of the land, you shall keep the feast of
        the Lord seven days . . .] And you shall take on the first day [the
        fruit of goodly trees, branches of palm trees and boughs of leafy
        trees and willows of the brook, and you shall rejoice before the
        Lord your God for seven days]" (Lev. 23:39–40).
      B. R. Abba bar Kahana commenced [discourse by citing the fol-
        lowing verse]: "Take my instruction instead of silver, [and
        knowledge rather than choice gold]" (Prov. 8:10).
      C. Said R. Abba bar Kahana, "Take the instruction of the Torah
        instead of silver.
      D. "'Why do you weigh out money? Because there is no bread' (Isa.
        55:2).
      E. "'Why do you weigh out money to the sons of Esau [Rome]? [It
        is because] "there is no bread," because you did not sate your-
        selves with the bread of the Torah.'
      F. "'And [why] do you labor? Because there is no satisfaction' [Isa.
        55:2].
      G. "'Why do you labor while the nations of the world enjoy plenty?
        Because there is no satisfaction,' that is, because you have not
        sated yourselves with the wine of the Torah.
      H. "For it is written, 'Come, eat of my bread, and drink of the wine
        I have mixed'" (Prov. 9:5).
    6. A. Said R. Abba bar Kahana, "On the basis of the reward paid for
        one act of 'taking,' you may assess the reward for [taking] the
        palm branch [on the festival of Tabernacles].
      B. "There was an act of taking in Egypt: 'You will take a bunch of
        hyssop' [Exod. 12:22].
      C. "And how much was it worth? Four *manehs.*
      D. "Yet that act of taking is what made Israel inherit the spoil at the
        sea, the spoil of Sihon and Og, and the spoil of the thirty-one
        kings.
      E. "Now the palm-branch, which costs a person such a high price,
        and which involves so many religious duties—how much the
        more so [will a great reward be forthcoming on its account]!"
      F. Therefore Moses admonished Israel, saying to them, "And you
        shall take on the first day . . ." (Lev. 23:40).

Whatever the sense of *lulab* to synagogue artists and their patrons, the combination with the *etrog, menorah,* and *shofar* was critical, yet nothing in these words
invokes any of those other symbols. What would have led us to suppose some sort
of interchange between iconic and verbal symbols? If we had an association, in
iconic combinations, of the Torah shrine and the *etrog* and *lulab*, we might have
grounds on which to frame the hypothesis that some sort of association—com-
parison/contrast for instance—between the symbols of the Festival of Tabernacles and Torah-study was contemplated. Here there is no basis for treating the

iconic symbols as convergent with the manipulation of those same symbols in propositional discourse. It suffices to say that nowhere in *Leviticus Rabbah* do we find reason to introduce the other iconic symbols.

What about the *shofar?* If we speak of that object, do we routinely introduce the *etrog, lulab, menorah?* The answer is again no. We introduce other things, but not those things. *Pesiqta deRab Kahana, pisqa* 23, addresses the New Year:

> In the seventh month on the first day of the month you shall observe a day of solemn rest, a memorial proclaimed with blast of trumpets.
>
> (Lev. 23:24)

The combination of judgment and the end of days is evoked in the following. I give two distinct statements of the same point, to show that it is in context an important motif.

Pesiqta deRab Kahana XXIII:II
    2. A. "For I will make a full end of all the nations" (Jer. 30:11): As to the nations of the world, because they make a full end (when they harvest even the corner of) their field, concerning them Scripture states: I will make a full end of all the nations among whom I scattered you.
       B. But as to Israel, because they do not make a full end (when they harvest, for they leave the corner of) their field, therefore: "But of you I will not make a full end" (Jer. 30:11).
       C. "I will chasten you in just measure, and I will by no means leave you unpunished" (Jer. 30:11). I shall chasten you through suffering in this world, so as to leave you unpunished in the world to come.
       D. When?
       E. "In the seventh month, [on the first day of the month]" (Lev. 23:24).

Pesiqta deRab Kahana XXIII:V
    1. A. R. Jeremiah commenced [discourse by citing the following verse]: "The wise man's path of life leads upward, that he may avoid Sheol beneath" (Prov. 15:24).
       B. [He said,] "The path of life: The path of life refers only to the words of the Torah, for it is written, as it is written, 'It is a tree of life' (Prov. 3:18).
       C. "Another matter: The path of life: The path of life refers only to suffering, as it is written, 'The way of life is through rebuke and correction' (Prov. 6:23).
       D. "'[The wise man's path]' . . . leads upward refers to one who looks deeply into the Torah's religious duties, [learning how to carry them out properly].
       E. "What then is written just prior to this same matter (of the New Year)?
       F. "'When you harvest your crop of your land, you will not make a full end of the corner of your field' (Lev. 23:22).
       G. "The nations of the world, because they make a full end when they harvest even the corner of their field, [and the rest of the mat-

ter is as is given above: 'I will make a full end of all the nations
among whom I have driven you' (Jer. 30:11). But Israel, because
they do not make a full end when they harvest, for they leave the
corner of their field, therefore, 'But of you I will not make a full
end' (Jer. 30:11). I will chasten you in just measure, 'and I will by
no means leave you unpunished' (Jer. 30:11).

H. "When? 'In the seventh month, on the first day of the month,
[you shall observe a day of solemn rest, a memorial proclaimed
with blast of trumpets' (Lev. 23:24)]."

What is now linked is Israel's leaving the corner of the field for the poor (Lev.
23:22); the connection between that verse and the base verse here is what is
expounded. Then there is no evocation of the *menorah* or the *lulab* and *etrog*—
to state the obvious. We can explain what is combined, and we also can see clearly
that the combination is deliberate. That means that what is joined elsewhere but
not here bears another message but not this one. An elaborate investigation of
the role of *lulab* and *etrog, shofar* and *menorah* in the literary evidence of the
Midrash compilations hardly is required to demonstrate what we now know: we
find no evidence of interest in the combination of those items in literary evidence.

SYMBOLS IN VERBAL FORM

Now that we have identified the iconic symbols that occur together in a given manner, let me set forth an already-familiar example of what I conceive to be a fine
statement of the symbolic structure of Judaism, for symbols in verbal form set
forth such a structure. This will serve as an example of the kinds of symbols we
find in general in symbolic discourse in verbal form. Our further experiments will
then draw on the symbolic repertoire that a single passage—counterpart to a single synagogue—has supplied. The character of the passage will explain why I have
chosen it as representative. I have abbreviated the passage as much as possible:

Genesis Rabbah LXX:VIII

2. A. "As he looked, he saw a well in the field":

B. R. Hama bar Hanina interpreted the verse in six ways [that is,
he divides the verse into six clauses and systematically reads each
of the clauses in light of the others and in line with an overrid-
ing theme:

C. "'As he looked, he saw a well in the field': this refers to the well
[of water in the wilderness (Num. 21:17)].

D. "'. . . and lo, three flocks of sheep lying beside it': specifically,
Moses, Aaron, and Miriam.

E. "'. . . for out of that well the flocks were watered': from there
each one drew water for his standard, tribe, and family."

H. [Reverting to Hama's statement:] "'. . . and put the stone back
in its place upon the mouth of the well': for the coming journeys. [Thus the first interpretation applies the passage at hand
to the life of Israel in the wilderness.]

3. A. "'As he looked, he saw a well in the field': refers to Zion.

   B. "'. . . and lo, three flocks of sheep lying beside it': refers to the three festivals.

   C. "'. . . for out of that well the flocks were watered': from there they drank of the holy spirit.

   D. "'. . . The stone on the well's mouth was large': this refers to the rejoicing of the house of the water-drawing."

   F. [Resuming Hama b. Hanina's discourse:] "'. . . and when all the flocks were gathered there': coming from 'the entrance of Hamath to the brook of Egypt' (1 Kgs. 8:66).

   G. "'. . . the shepherds would roll the stone from the mouth of the well and water the sheep': for from there they would drink of the Holy Spirit.

   H. "'. . . and put the stone back in its place upon the mouth of the well': leaving it in place until the coming festival. [Thus the second interpretation reads the verse in light of the Temple celebration of the Festival of Tabernacles.]

4. A. "'. . . As he looked, he saw a well in the field': this refers to Zion.

   B. "'. . . and lo, three flocks of sheep lying beside it': this refers to the three courts, concerning which we have learned in the Mishnah: There were three courts there, one at the gateway of the Temple mount, one at the gateway of the courtyard, and one in the chamber of the hewn stones [Mishnah tractate *Sanhedrin* 11:2].

   C. "'. . . for out of that well the flocks were watered': for from there they would hear the ruling.

   D. "'The stone on the well's mouth was large': this refers to the high court that was in the chamber of the hewn stones.

   E. "'. . . and when all the flocks were gathered there': this refers to the courts in session in the Land of Israel.

   F. "'. . . the shepherds would roll the stone from the mouth of the well and water the sheep': for from there they would hear the ruling.

   G. "'. . . and put the stone back in its place upon the mouth of the well': for they would give and take until they had produced the ruling in all the required clarity." [The third interpretation reads the verse in light of the Israelite institution of justice and administration.]

5. A. "'As he looked, he saw a well in the field': this refers to Zion.

   B. "'. . . and lo, three flocks of sheep lying beside it': this refers to the first three kingdoms [Babylonia, Media, Greece].

   C. "'. . . for out of that well the flocks were watered': for they enriched the treasures that were laid upon up in the chambers of the Temple.

   D. "'. . . The stone on the well's mouth was large': this refers to the merit attained by the patriarchs.

   E. "'. . . and when all the flocks were gathered there': this refers to the wicked kingdom, which collects troops through levies over all the nations of the world.

   F. "'. . . the shepherds would roll the stone from the mouth of the well and water the sheep': for they enriched the treasures that were laid upon up in the chambers of the Temple.

   G. "'. . . and put the stone back in its place upon the mouth of the well': in the age to come the merit attained by the patriarchs will

stand [in defense of Israel]." [So the fourth interpretation interweaves the themes of the Temple cult and the domination of the
four monarchies.]

Further readings of the same verse find in it symbolic reference to the Sanhedrin
and to Israel at Sinai. The six themes read in response to the verse cover (1) Israel
in the wilderness, (2) the Temple cult on festivals with special reference to Tabernacles, (3) the judiciary and government, (4) the history of Israel under the four
kingdoms, (5) the life of sages, and (6) the ordinary folk and the synagogue. The
whole is an astonishing repertoire of fundamental themes of the life of the nation
Israel: at its origins in the wilderness, in its cult, in its institutions based on the
cult, in the history of the nations, and, finally, in the twin social estates of sages
and ordinary folk, matched by the institutions of the master-disciple circle and
the synagogue. The vision of Jacob at the well thus encompassed the whole of the
social reality of Jacob's people, Israel. If we wished a catalogue of the kinds of topics addressed in passages of symbolic, as distinct from propositional, discourse,
the present catalogue proves compendious and complete.

SYMBOLIC DISCOURSE IN ICONIC AND IN
VERBAL FORM: CONVERGENCE OR DIVERGENCE?

A simple set of indicators will now permit us to compare the character of symbolic discourse in verbal form with that in iconic form. The question is now a
simple one. Let us represent the Judaism—way of life, worldview, theory of who
or what is "Israel" as we saw in chapter 1—set forth by symbolic discourse in
iconic form effected by the *lulab* and *etrog, shofar,* and *menorah.* Let us further
represent the Judaism set forth by symbolic discourse in verbal form, treating as
exemplary a discourse that will appeal to visual images appropriate to the themes
of Israel in the wilderness, the Temple cult, the judiciary and government, Israel
under the four kingdoms and at the end of time, the life of sages, ordinary folk
and the synagogue. How do these statements relate?

The shared program will cover the standard topics that any symbolic structure of representing a religion should treat: holy day, holy space, holy word, holy
man (or person), and holy time or the division of time.

	ICONIC SYMBOLS	*VERBAL SYMBOLS*
Holy day	New Year/Tabernacles/ Hanukkah	Tabernacles/Pentecost/Passover
Holy space	Temple	Temple/Zion
Holy man/person	No evidence	The sage and disciple
Holy time	Messiah (*shofar*)	Four kingdoms/Israel's rule
Holy event	Not clear	Exodus from Egypt

The important point of convergence is unmistakable: holy space for both symbolic structures is defined as the Temple and Mount Zion. That is hardly surprising; no Judaic structure beyond 70 ignored the Temple, and all Judaisms, both before and after 70, found it necessary to deal in some way with, to situate themselves in relationship to, that paramount subject. So the convergence proves systemically inert, indeed trivial.

Both structures—the iconic and the literary—point toward the end of time; but they speak of it differently. So far as the *shofar* refers to the coming of the Messiah, the gathering of the exiles, and the restoration of the Temple, as is the case, in the synagogue liturgy, then the iconic representation of the messianic topic and the verbal representation of the same topic diverge. For the latter frames the messianic topic in terms of Israel's relationship with the nations, and the principal interest is in Israel's rule over the world as the fifth and final monarchy. That theme is repeated in symbolic discourse in verbal form, and if the *shofar* stands in synagogue iconography for what the synagogue liturgy says, the message, if not an utterly different one, is not identical with that delivered by symbols in verbal form. So here matters are ambiguous.

The unambiguous points of divergence are equally striking. The most important comes first. Symbolic discourse in verbal form privileges the three festivals equally and utterly ignores Hanukkah. So far as the *menorah* stands for Hanukkah—and in the literary evidence, the association is firm—we may suppose that, just as the *lulab* and *etrog* mean to evoke Tabernacles, and the *shofar,* the New Year and Day of Atonement, so the *menorah* speaks of Hanukkah. Then we find a clear and striking divergence. That the *menorah* also serves as an astral symbol is well established, and if that is the fact, then another point of divergence is registered. In symbolic discourse in verbal form, I find not one allusion to an astral ascent accessible to an Israelite, for example, through worship or Torah-study. A survey of the cited passages yields not a trace of the theme of the astral ascent.

The second point of divergence seems similarly unambiguous. Critical to the symbolic vocabulary of the Rabbinic compilations is study of the Torah, on the one side, and the figure of the sage and disciple, on the other. I do not find in the extant literary sources a medium for identifying the figure of the sage and the act of Torah-study with the symbols of the *lulab, etrog, shofar,* or *menorah.* Quite to the contrary, the example given earlier from *Leviticus Rabbah* counterpoises the *lulab* with words of Torah. The fact that these are deemed opposites, with the former not invoking but provoking the latter, by itself means little. But it does not sustain the proposition that the combined symbols before us, the *lulab, etrog, shofar,* and *menorah,* somehow mean to speak of Torah-study and the sage.

When we compare the symbols that reach us in two distinct forms, the verbal and the iconic, we find ourselves at an impasse. The verbal symbols serve in one way; the iconic in another, and while they occasionally converge, the points of convergence are few whereas those of divergence are overwhelming. No evidence permits us to describe a single Judaism. Some scholars claim that there is a "Judaism out there" beyond any one document, to which in some way or other all documents in various ways and proportions are supposed to attest. If such evidence is to be located, however, then nonverbal data such as we have examined should have provided it. Here, by definition, in iconic and verbal symbols alike, we should have been able to demonstrate that, whatever verbal explanations people attached to symbols, a fundamentally uniform symbolic structure served all Judaisms that our evidence attests. If we had been able to show that a single symbolic vocabulary and a single syntax and grammar of symbolic discourse served in all extant testimonies to all Judaisms—iconic, literary evidence alike—then we should have begun to pursue the problem of defining that Judaism through the principles of symbolic discourse.

Why choose the symbolic data? Because it is through the study of what is inchoate and intuitive—a matter of attitude and sentiment and emotion rather than of proposition and syllogism, therefore through the analysis of symbolic structure—that we should be able to discern and set forth the things on which everyone agreed. But that is the opposite of what we find out when we compare the symbolic discourse of synagogue iconography with that of the Rabbinic writings. The art of the synagogues employs a symbolic vocabulary, deriving from Scripture, that intersects only partially with the symbolic vocabulary of the writings of the Rabbinic sages. That fact underscores the point at which we started, the diversity of Judaic religious systems that flourished in antiquity, all of them resting on Scripture.

CONCLUSION: FROM SCRIPTURE TO JUDAISM

What we see at the end is what we saw at the outset: Judaic religious systems rest squarely on the Hebrew Scriptures of ancient Israel. The Rabbinic sages read from the Written Torah forward to the Oral Torah. Any outline of Scripture's account begins with Creation and tells about the passage from Eden via Sinai and Jerusalem to Babylon—and back. It speaks of the patriarchal founders of Israel, the Exodus, Sinai, the Torah, covenants, Israel, the people of God, the priesthood and the tabernacle, the possession of the Land, exile and restoration. And so too does Rabbinic Judaism focus on these same matters. Sages' Judaism, that is, their theological structure and system, appeals to the perfection of Creation and accounts for imperfection by reference to the fall of man into sin by reason of arrogant rebellion and Adam's and Eve's descent into death in consequence. The Rabbinic sages, then, tell Scripture's story of the formation of holy Israel as God's part in humanity, signified by access to knowledge of God through God's self-manifestation in the Torah. They then present the exile of Israel from and to the Land of Israel as the counterpart to the exile of Adam from Eden and the return of Israel to the Land. Therefore main beams of the Hebrew Scripture's account of matters define the structure of the Oral Torah's theology. The generative tensions of the Hebrew Scripture's narrative empower the dynamics of that theology.

A few obvious facts suffice. Take the principal propositions of Scripture read in sequence and systematically—meaning, as exemplary—from Genesis through Kings. Consider the story of the exile from Eden and the counterpart exile of Israel from the Land. Sages did not invent that paradigm. Scripture's framers did. Translate into propositional form the prophetic messages of admonition, rebuke, and consolation—the promise that as punishment follows sin, so consolation will come in consequence of repentance. Sages did not fabricate those categories and make up the rules that govern the sequence of events. The prophets said them all. Sages only recapitulated the prophetic propositions with little variation except in formulation. All sages did was to interpret within the received paradigm the exemplary events of their own day, the destruction of Jerusalem and Israel's subjugation in particular. But even at that they simply asked Scripture's question of events that conformed to Scripture's pattern. Identify as the dynamics of human history the engagement of God with man, especially through Israel, and what do you have if not the heart of sages' doctrine of the origins and destiny of man. Review what Scripture intimates about the meaning and end of time, and how much do you miss of sages' eschatology of restoration? Details, amplifications, clarifications, an unsuccessful effort at systematization—these do not obscure the basic confluence of sages' and Scripture's account of last things (even though, as I said, the word "last" has its own meaning for sages).

Nor do I have to stress the form that sages impart to their propositions. As we have seen, nearly everything they say is joined to a verse of Scripture. That is not a formality. Constant citations of scriptural texts cited as authority serve merely to signal the presence of a profound identity of viewpoint. The cited verses are not solely pretexts or formal proof texts. Sages cite and interpret verses of Scripture to show where and how the Written Torah guides the oral one, supplying the specificities of the process of recapitulation. And what sages say about those verses originates not in the small details of those verses (such as Aqiba was able to interpret to Moses' stupefaction) but in the large theological structure and system that sages framed.

Sages read Scripture as a letter written that morning to them in particular about the world they encountered. That is because for them the past was forever integral to the present. So they looked into the Written Torah to construct the picture of reality that is explained by worldview set forth in the Oral Torah. They found their questions in Scripture; they identified the answers to those questions in Scripture; and they then organized and interpreted the contemporary situation of holy Israel in light of those questions and answers. Scripture's corpus of facts, like nature's, was deemed to transcend the bonds of time. That timelessness accounts for the fact that, in the heavenly academy to which corner of Eden imagination carried them, the great sages could amiably conduct arguments with God and with Moses. Not only so, but they engage in ongoing dialogue with the prophets and psalmists and the other saints of the Written Torah as well as with those of their masters and teachers in the oral tradition who reached Eden earlier. A common language joined them all, for in their entire engagement with the written part of the Torah, sages mastered every line, every word, every letter, sorting matters of the day out in response to what they learned in the written tradition.

Accordingly, on every page of the writings of the Oral Torah we encounter the sages' encompassing judgment of and response to the heritage of ancient Israel's Scripture. There they met God; there they found God's plan for the world of perfect justice—the flawless, eternal world in stasis—and there in detail they learned what became of that teaching in ancient times and in their own day, everything seen in the same way. The result is the Rabbinic sages' account of the Torah revealed by God to Moses at Sinai and handed on in tradition through the ages.

So if we ask, What if, in the timeless world of the Torah studied in the same heavenly academy, Moses and the prophets, sages, and scribes of Scripture were to take up the results of oral tradition produced by their heirs and successors in the Oral Torah? The answer is clear. They would have found themselves hearing familiar words, their own words, used by honest, faithful men in familiar, wholly legitimate ways. When, for example, Moses heard in the tradition of the Oral Torah that a given law was a law revealed by God to Moses at Sinai, he may have kept his peace, though puzzled, or he may have remembered that, indeed, that is how it was, just so. In very concrete, explicit language the sages themselves laid their claim to possess the Torah of Moses. We recall how impressed Moses is by Aqiba, when he observed, from the rear of the study hall, how Aqiba was able to interpret on the basis of each point of the crowns heaps and heaps of laws. But he could not follow the debate and felt faint until he heard the later master declare, "It is a law given to Moses from Sinai," and then he regained his composure:

Talmud of Babylonia tractate *Menahot* 3:7, II.5/29b
- A. Said R. Judah said Rab, "At the time that Moses went up on high, he found the Holy One in session, affixing crowns to the letters [of the words of the Torah]. He said to him, 'Lord of the universe, who is stopping you [from regarding the document as perfect without these additional crowns on the letters]?'
- B. "He said to him, 'There is a man who is going to arrive at the end of many generations, and Aqiba b. Joseph is his name, who is going to interpret on the basis of each point of the crowns heaps and heaps of laws.'
- C. "He said to him, 'Lord of the Universe, show him to me.'
- D. "He said to him, 'Turn around.'
- E. "He went and took a seat at the end of eight rows, but he could not grasp what the people were saying. He felt faint. But when the discourse reached a certain matter, and the disciples said, 'My lord, how do you know this?' and he answered, 'It is a law given to Moses from Sinai,' he regained his composure.
- F. "He went and came before the Holy One. He said before him, 'Lord of the Universe, how come you have someone like that and yet you give the Torah through me?'
- G. "He said to him, 'Silence! That is how the thought came to me.'
- H. "He said to him, 'Lord of the Universe, you have shown me his Torah, now show me his reward.'

I. "He said to him, 'Turn around.'

J. "He turned around and saw his flesh being weighed out at the butcher-stalls in the market.

K. "He said to him, 'Lord of the Universe, such is Torah, such is the reward?'

L. "He said to him, 'Silence! That is how the thought came to me.'"

Then are the rabbis of the Oral Torah right in maintaining that they have provided the originally oral part of the one whole Torah of Moses our rabbi? To answer that question in the affirmative, sages would have only to point to their theology in the setting of Scripture's as they grasped it. The Rabbinic sages' Torah, oral and written, tells a simple, sublime story.

1. God created a perfect, just world and in it made man in his image, equal to God in the power of will.
2. Man in his arrogance sinned and was expelled from the perfect world and given over to death. God gave man the Torah to purify his heart of sin.
3. Man educated by the Torah in humility can repent, accepting God's will of his own free will. When he does, man will be restored to Eden and eternal life.

In our terms, we should call it a story with a beginning, middle, and end. In sages' framework, we realize, the story embodies an enduring and timeless paradigm of humanity in the encounter with God: man's powerful will, God's powerful word, in conflict and, ultimately, in concert.

Notes

Chapter 4

1. Webster's *Seventh Collegiate Dictionary* (Springfield, Mass.: G. & C. Merriam Co., 1965), s.v. "system."

Chapter 5

2. W. Lee Humphreys, *Crisis and Story: Introduction to the Old Testament* (Palo Alto, Calif.: Mayfield Publishing Co., 1979), 217.

Chapter 7

3. Brevard S. Childs, *Memory and Tradition in Israel* (London: SCM Press, 1962), 85.
4. Norman Maclean, *Young Men and Fire* (Chicago: University of Chicago Press, 1992), 257.
5. Ibid., 261.
6. Ibid., 262.
7. Ibid., 267.

Chapter 13

8. Translation: Jules Harlow, in *Mahzor for Rosh Hashanah and Yom Kippur* (New York: Rabbinical Assembly, 1972), pass.

Index of Ancient Sources

Non-Biblical Writings

AGGADAH,   70, 110, 111,
                   112

AUGUSTINE

CONFESSIONS,   16–17, 88

BABYLONIAN TALMUD
                   92

ABODAH ZARAH
3b   40

BABA BATRA
1:1.II.4/12a   115, 116

BABA MESIA
59a-b   21–22

BERAKHOT
6   41–42
28a-b   106

ERUBIN
5:1.I.43/54b   115, 116
54b   8–9

GITTIN
5:8.I9/60b   115, 116
57b   153

HORAYOT
3:3, I/11a   133–34

MAKKOT
23b-24a   26–27

MENAHOT
3:7.II.5/29b   115, 116,
                   187–88

PESAHIM
10:7.II.22/118b   173–74

QIDDUSHIN
3:10–11.III.13/66a-b   115,
                   116
70a-b   11–13

ROSH HASHANAH
1:2.I.24/17b   115, 116

SANHEDRIN
11:1–2.I.22ff/91b   171
11:1.I:10–12/90b-91a
                   166–67
11:1.I.5/90a   166
111a-b, VI   38–39

SHABBAT
2:5.I:11–121/30b-31a 104
2:5.I:11/30b-31a   115, 116
39a   77
89a   40–41

SHEBU'OT
1:1ff. XVI.2/13a   156–57

SOTAH
48B   22–23

TEMURAH
2:1.III.1/14a-b 115, 116–17
2:2.I.2/15a   115, 116, 117

YOMA
8:8–9. VI.1–2/87a-b 158–59

BAVLI. SEE BABYLONIAN
TALMUD

FATHERS ACCORDING TO
RABBI NATHAN
IV:V.2   147
XL:V.1   159–60
XXV:II.1   164–65

GENESIS RABBAH   101
IX:V.2–3   163–64
LV:II.1f.   128
LV:III.1   129
LXI:VII   98–100
LXV:IX.1   126–27
LXX:VIII   88–90, 181–83
LXXVII:I.1   170
VIII:X   29–30
XIX:IX.1–2   56
XLII:II   86

HALAKHAH, 67–78, 105,
   106, 108, 114, 120, 121,
   140, 145, 148, 152–53

ERUBIN,   72–76, 78

HAGIGAH, 140–41, 145–46

SHABBAT,   72–78

SHEBI'IT,   73, 78

LEVITICUS RABBAH,
       101, 178, 180, 184
X:V.1   157–58
XI:VII.3   20
XIII:II.1   136–37
XIII:V   84–85
XXX:I.1   179
XXX:I.6   179

MEKHILTA OF R. ISH-
MAEL SHIRATA
Chap. 1 = XXIX:2   31

MISHNAH,   6, 7–9, 33,
       35–36, 48, 50, 54, 76,
       83, 92, 93–94, 100, 101,
       104–12, 114–17, 168

ABOT,   108
3:13–14   43
5:8–9   130–32
5:18   125

BABA MESIA
4:10.I.15   21–22

BER.
9:4a-e   129

EDUYYOT   108
Hagigah,   140–41, 145
1:8   105
2:5–6   143
7   105

KELIM,   51, 54
1:5   137–38
1:5–9   137–39
1:6–9   145

1:6	138	*HAGIGAH*		SEE BABYLONIAN	
1:9	139	2:1.2ff.	37	TALMUD	
5:10	21	*HORAYOT*		TALMUD OF THE LAND	
KERITOT		3:5.III.PP	37	OF ISRAEL. SEE	
1:1	152	*MAKKOT*		PALESTINIAN TALMUD	
1:2	151	2:6.I:4/10a	156	TOSEFTA	50, 76
MAKKOT		*MEGILLAH*		*HAGIGAH*	
3:16.II.1	26	4:1.I.2	112–14	1:4	141–42
OHALOT,	54	*PEAH*		*KERITOT*	
PEAH		2:6	108	1:6	152
2:5	107, 108	*SANHEDRIN*		*KIPPURIM*	
2:6	108	1:1.IV.Q	37	4:6–8	160
QIDDUSHIN		5:1.IV.E	37	4:7	160
4	94	10:1.IX	36	4:8	160
4:1–2, V:5	11–13	*TA'ANIT*		*MENAHOT*	
SANHEDRIN		1:1.II:5	172–73	6:20	71
10:1	168	1:1.X.E ff.	37	*NEGA'IM*	
10:2	169	1:1.X.U	37	6:7	49
10:3	169	1:4.I	123–24	*SHEQALIM*	
10:4	170	3:3 I:1–4	121–22	1:6	148
10:5	170	*PESIQTA DE RAB KAHANA*		2:4	150
11:2	182	VII:XI.3	87	2:7	150
SHEV		XII:XXV	31–32	*SOTAH*	
1:6	112	XXI:V	86	13:3	22
Sotah		XXIII:II	180	YERUSHALMI. SEE PALES-	
9:12	22–23	XXIII:V	180–81	TINIAN TALMUD	
9:15	50, 145	*PIRQÉ ABOT*			
SUKKAH		1:1–2	6–7, 17, 22, 103	**Hebrew Bible/Old**	
4:5	112	1:12	7	**Testament (Septuagint)**	
4:9	112	1:13–15	7–8		
TA'ANIT		3:6	18	**Genesis**	3, 15, 58, 82
3:3	121	*QOHELET*		1 73	
3:9–10	120–21	8:14	133	1:1	86
TOHOROT	51, 54	*QOHELET/ECCL.*		1:26	29
UQSIN,	51	1:10a-b	110–11, 114	2:1–3	67
				2:3	48
YADAYIM,	54, 108	*SIFRA*		2:15	56
YOMA		CCXLV:I.2	70–71	2:16	56
8:8–9	155	CLV:I.8 49		3:9	56
8:9A-C	159	CXCV:I.1-CC:III.6	46–48	3:11	56
PALESTINIAN TALMUD,		*SIFRÉ TO DEUTERONOMY*		3:23	56
	6, 94–96	CCCVI:XXVIII.3	171	3:24	56
'ABOD.ZAR.		XXXII:V.1–12	129–30	4:12	157
3:1.II.AA	37	*SIFRÉ TO DEUTERONOMY*		4:16	157
		TO EQEB		5:1	48
BERAKHOT		XLIII:III.7	80–81	6:3	169
9:1.VII.E	37–38	TALMUD OF BABYLON.		9:6	43
				9:25	99

11:8	169	34:27	110, 113	21:17	89, 181
13:13	169	**Leviticus**	3, 58, 101	**Deuteronomy**	4, 15, 58, 76
14:9	86	5:17–19	151	4:34	41
15:12	85	7:25	152	5:4–5	113
15:13–14	63	11:1–8	84	6:4	36
17:1	26	11:4–8	85	6:4a-b	41
17:14	152	11:34	50	6:4–9	24
18:19	26	11:37	50	6:5	129
18:25	18	12	138	8:5	130
22:1	128, 129	13–14	48	8:7	130
24:1	127	14:35	49	9:10	110, 113
25:2	99	15	49, 51, 138	11:21	166
25:6	98, 99	16	149, 160	12:6	143
27:1	126	16:30	160	14:1	43
27:12	26	17:9	152	14:7	85
48:1	27	17:14	152	15:1–3	68
50:17	159	18:6ff.	152	16:14	139
		18:21	152	16:14–17	140–41
Exodus,	3, 58, 76	19	45–47	16:15	139
3	15, 30	19:1–4	46	16:16	143
8:12	87	19:2	45	21:17	98
12:12	37	19:6–8	152	24:80	49
12:19	152	19:7–8	152	26:17	41
12:22	179	19:15–16	47	26:18	41
12:36	99	19:17–18	47	26:19	41
14	15	19:18	104	29:28	170
15:3	30–31	20:6	152	30:12	21
15:26	168	22:3	152	31:16	166
16:25	173	23:22	180, 181	31:19	9
16:29–30	72	23:24	180	32:39	31
16:31	32	23:29–30	152	33:21	125
20	46	23:39–40	178–79	33:29	41
20:2	31, 32	23:40	175, 179	**Ruth,**	6
20:4–5	176	24:2	56		
20:5	154	25:1–8	73	**1 Samuel**	
20:7	46	25:2–7	68	1:13	38
20:8	67	25:8–10	69	2:6	170
20:11	67	26:34	132	2:8	159
20:24	18				
23:2	21	**Numbers**	3, 58	**Kings,**	82
23:14	143	1:51	80	**1 Kings**	
23:15	140	9:13	152	8:66	89, 182
23:17	139	11:8	32		
24:10	31	12:2	49	**2 Kings**	
27:20	56	12:12	49	15:30	125
30–32	152	14:17	39		
30:11–16	148	14:35	170	**1 Chronicles**	
30:16	148	14:37	169	17:21	41
30:23–33	152	15:29	151	**2 Chronicles**	
31:1	9	15:30	152	26:16	49
31:14	152	15:31	152, 157	33:13	169
34:6	30	19	51, 52, 54	**Esther,**	6
34:7	38, 39	19:20	152	7:4	85
34:8	38				

Job

3:3	87
33:27	159
37:13	122

Psalms

1:5	169
11:5	128, 129
15	26
22:30	165
25:8	156
29:4	32
42:9	40
50:4	171
68:32	174
72:16	166
80:14	174
82:1	18
89:2	37
89:32	160
92:1	158
92:2	158
95:7	172
104:	26 40
117:1	173
147:8	85
147:17	37

Proverbs

3:12	129
3:18	180
4:2	43
6:1	159
6:1–3	158
6:23	180
6:25–26	25
8:10	179
9:5	179
13:21	156
15:24	180
23:25	121

Song of Solomon | 6

7:9	166

Isaiah

2:22	30
7:1	20
8:2	81
8:16	20
9:12	20
21:12	172
22:14	160
26:19	166
28:9	40
30:15	173
33:25–26	26
34:6–7	87
34:9	87
34:11	87
35:6	171
38:9	127
41:4	31
51:16	86
55:2	179
56:1	27
56:7	42
60:21	168
63:11	36
66:6	87

Jeremiah, | 83

2:7	56
3:22	160
4:23	86
15:1	56
23:24	181
26:18	81
30:11	180, 181
31:8	171
49:21	85

Lamentations, | 6, 83

1:1	56
5:17–18	81

Ezekiel

16:19	32
18:20	156
28:13	163

37:9	171
38:22	87
39:17–19	87

Daniel

3:19	85
7:9	31
7:10	31
9:11	56

Hosea

6:6	147
6:7	56
8:12	109
9:15	56

Amos

3:2	92, 151
4:7	121
9:6	18

Micah

6:8	26

Habakkuk

2:4	27
3:6	136

Zechariah

8:4	81
14:12	87

Malachi

3:16	18
3:22	41
4:23–24	105

New Testament

Matthew

5:17–20	23
5:21–22	24
5:27–28	24
5:33–34	24
5:38–39	24
5:43–44	24
5:48	24

Index of Subjects and Names

Aaron, 7, 8, 9, 10, 24, 48–49, 89, 115, 181
Abba, Rabbi, 13, 159
Abba bar Kahana, Rabbi, 179
Abbahu, Rabbi, 56, 123
Abba Saul, 168
Abin, Rabbi, 86, 108, 109
Abraham
  evil kingdoms and, 84–85
  family of, 60, 91, 92, 95–99
  on God's commandments, 26
  God's relationship with, 18, 91, 129, 136
  God's revelation to, 15, 169
  Israel and, 91, 92, 95–99
  on justice, 18
  old age of, 126, 127
  Sodom and, 134
  and sons of concubines, 98, 99
Adam, 5–57, 29–30, 70, 74, 76, 80, 88, 90, 136, 174, 185
afterlife. See resurrection of the dead
Aggadah, 70, 110, 111, 112. See also Index of Ancient Sources
Aha, Rabbi, 41–42, 172
Ahab, 169
Ahaz, 20
Ahitophel, 169
Alexander of Macedonia, 98–99
alienation. See exile and return
Amos, 27
angels, 29–30
animal sacrifice. See sacrifice
apocryphal books of Hebrew Scriptures, 9

Aqiba, Rabbi, 8–9, 43, 80–83, 116, 121, 129, 168, 170, 186, 187
archaeology, 10, 176
art of synagogues, 10, 175–81, 183–85
Ashi, Rabbi, 41–42
Assyrians, 15, 170
atonement, 129, 132–34, 136–40, 147–53, 156–61. See also repentance
Augustine, 16–17, 88
Avery-Peck, A. J., 69–70

Babylonia, 10, 15, 57, 58, 60, 61, 62, 66, 84, 85, 86, 89, 182
Babylonian Talmud, 6. See also Index of Ancient Sources
Balaam, 168, 169
Bar Kokhba, 83, 101
bat yisra'el (woman), 94
Bible, 3, 5
blasphemy, 151, 152
Brooks, Roger, 107
Buddhism, 5

Caesar, 166
Cain, 157–58
Canaan and Canaanites, 98, 99–100
chain of tradition, 7–8, 16–18, 22, 103–17, 112–14
Childs, B., 79–80, 82
Christianity
  beginning of, 6
  church as body of Christ, 95
  compared with Judaism, 3, 4
  diversity in, 4–5
  as established religion of Roman state, 95

  and God of Old Testament, 30
  Israel and, 93–96
  Jesus Christ as Last Adam of, 57
  Jesus Christ as prophet of, 4, 5, 23–24
  Jews' conversion to, 101
  and miracles of Jesus, 119
  as monotheistic religion, 3, 4–6
  Nicaean Creed and, 9
  salvation and, 95
  Scripture and, 3, 5, 16, 107
  unique role of Christ in, 120
  writings of, 9
circumcision, 92
cleanness. See sanctification; uncleanness
Cleopatra, Queen, 166
Conservative Judaism, 4
Constantine, 95, 101
converts
  to Christianity, 101
  to Judaism, 92, 97, 104, 116, 153
corpse uncleanness, 48, 49, 50, 52, 54, 138
Creation, 67–70, 72, 76, 77, 78, 185
cultic cleanness, 49
Cyrus, 57

Darius, 85
David, 26
Day of Atonement, 139–40, 149, 155, 156–61, 184
Dead Sea Scrolls, 9, 50
death
  extirpation as consequence of sins, 151, 152, 153

death *(continued)*
    as final atonement for
        sin, 158
    judgment after, 164–65
    as natural, 163–65
    Rabbinic explanation of,
        120, 126, 128, 134,
        163–65
    as unclean, 48, 49, 50,
        51, 52, 54, 138
    See also resurrection of
        the dead
Diaspora, 62–63
disciples of sages, 103–4,
    112–14, 116
diversity in religions, 4–6, 57
divinity of God, 43
Doeg, 169
dual Torah, 7–8, 103–17,
    185–87. *See also* Oral
    Torah; Torah
Dura Europos, 10

eating. *See* food and eating
Eden
    Adam and Eve in, 29–30
    Land of Israel compared
        with, 68, 70–71, 78,
        80, 88, 90, 136, 172,
        174, 185–86
    repentance and restora-
        tion of, 188
    Sabbath and restoration
        of, 67–68, 73, 74,
        75–76
    See also Adam; Eve
Edom, 96, 174
Egypt and Egyptians, 86, 87,
    98, 99, 100, 119, 174, 179,
    182
Eleazar, Rabbi, 8, 109, 112,
    128
Eleazar b. Azariah, Rabbi,
    80–81
Eliezer, Rabbi, 8, 21, 106,
    119, 170
Eliezer b. Jacob, Rabbi, 129
Eliezer b. R. Yosé, Rabbi, 159
Elijah, 15, 21–22, 30, 50,
    105, 106, 145, 173
    'erub (commingling), 73,
        74–75
Esau, 96, 126, 174, 179

Essenes, 50
Esther, 85
ethical monotheism, 3,
    45–48. *See also* monothe-
    ism
Ethiopia, 174
etrog, 177–81, 183–84
Euphrates, 10
Eve, 30, 55–57, 74, 185. *See
    also* Adam
evil, 55, 133, 156. *See also*
    exile and return; sin
exile and return
    Adam and Eve compared
        with Israel, 55–57,
        185
    Babylonian captivity of
        Israel, 57, 60, 66
    invention of paradigm
        of, 59–63
    Israelites in Sinai wilder-
        ness, 62, 89, 119,
        181–83
    lessons learned from, 60
    Pentateuchal construc-
        tion of, 58–59,
        61–66, 185–86
    persistence of paradigm
        of, 63–66
    Sabbath and sacred time,
        67–78
    separation from Land of
        Israel as penalty, 136
    See also Moses
extirpation, 151, 152, 153
Ezra, 22, 57, 58, 61, 65

family metaphor for Israel,
    95, 96–100, 101
famine, 131–32
farmer metaphor, 128, 129
festivals, 45, 50, 139–46, 183.
    See also specific festivals
flax maker metaphor, 128,
    129
flood, 168, 169
fluids. *See* liquids
food and eating, 49–54, 72,
    84–85, 135, 141, 142–46,
    152
fornication, 121, 131, 132,
    167
Freedman, H., 39

funerals, 50, 54

Gamaliel, Rabbi, 17, 80–81,
    108, 166
Gebiah b. Qosem, 98–100
Gehazi, 169
genealogy, 96
generative myth and
    metaphors, 6–9, 78
gentiles
    as converts to Judaism,
        92, 97, 104, 116, 153
    and family metaphor for
        Israel, 98
    messiah and, 173–74
    as "not-Israel" and idola-
        tors, 91, 94, 173
    Oral Torah and, 104,
        109
    and resurrection of the
        dead, 166–69
    Rome as, 96, 174, 179
    Temple not accessible to,
        138
    votive offerings by,
        149–50
God
    characterization of,
        30–33
    choice of Israel and Land
        of Israel by, 136–37
    Creation by, 67–70, 72,
        76, 77, 78
    divine favor of, 122–26
    divinity of, 43
    "eating-like-God," 53
    freedom of, 120
    as Holy One, 45
    humanity as mirror
        image of, 18, 29–30,
        32, 43, 188
    Leviathan and, 39–40
    as long-suffering, 38–39
    meeting God in Torah-
        study, 16, 18–20,
        25–27, 30, 125
    as person, 34, 36–38
    personality of, 34, 38–43
    as premise, 33, 35–36
    as presence, 33, 35–36
    prohibition against mak-
        ing graven images of,
        176

relationship of, with
    Israel, 41–42, 43, 71,
    122–26
sages' arguments with,
    186
self-revelation by, in
    Torah, 15–18, 29–43
sharing meal with God
    in Temple courtyard,
    135, 144–46
as warrior, 30–31
Golden Rule, 47–48
Goodnenough, E. R., 10
gossip, 49, 167
grace, 43
Greece, 9, 10, 84, 85, 86, 89,
    182
guilt offerings, 151–53, 155

Haggai, 22
Haggai, Rabbi, 109–10, 113
Halafta, Rabbi, 18, 19
Halakhah, 67–78, 106, 108,
    114, 120, 121, 140, 145,
    146, 148, 152–53. See also
    Index of Ancient Sources
Halakhot, 108
half-sheqel offering, 139,
    148–51
Hama bar Hanina, Rabbi, 32,
    87, 88–90, 181–83
Haman, 153
Hanina, Rabbi, 89
Hanukkah, 184
healing, 119–20. See also mir-
    acles
Hebrew Scriptures, 3–4, 9,
    16, 79–83, 185–87
Hezekiah, 26, 127
hierarchy of being, 35–36
Hillel, 7–8, 17, 22–23, 25,
    104
Hilqiah, Rabbi, 112–13
Hinena bar Papa, Rabbi, 31
Hisda, Rabbi, 159
history, 16, 19, 57–58, 62,
    66, 79–80, 83–90, 101
Hitler, Adolph, 153
Hiyya bar Abin, Rabbi, 41
holiness
    cleanness on pilgrim fes-
        tivals, 143–44, 145
    definition of, 48

definition of sanctifica-
    tion, 45–48
degrees of, 138–39
God as Holy One, 45
hierarchization of rules
    of, 145–46
human being's role in
    purity and unclean-
    ness, 51, 52–54
Israel's history taken over
    into Israel's life of
    sanctification, 88–90
of Jerusalem, 135–36,
    138
of Land of Israel,
    135–39
profane and unclean ver-
    sus, 48–50
purity viewed as a whole,
    50–53
Rabbinic Judaism and
    sanctification, 101
Holiness Code, 46–48, 54
Holy Spirit, 23, 37, 50, 89,
    145
Honi the Circle Drawer,
    120–21, 122
Hoshaiah, Rabbi, 29–30, 89
human beings
    encounters between God
        and, 19
    freedom of, 174
    Judaism's human dimen-
        sion, 10–13
    as mirror image of God,
        18, 29–30, 32, 43,
        188
    rationality of, 18, 23
    and reason's role in reve-
        lation, 20–22
    role of, in process of
        purity and unclean-
        ness, 51, 52–54
    See also gentiles; Jewish
        people; repentance;
        sin
Humphreys, W. L., 62–63
Huna bar Idi, Rabbi, 11, 13
Huna said Rab, Rabbi, 13
hunger, 130–31

iconography in synagogues,
    175–81, 183–85

idolatry, 3, 80, 81, 91, 121,
    131, 132, 133, 167, 173
illness, 120, 126–32, 134
immersion, 51, 144
Iranians, 57
Isaac, 15, 60, 95, 96, 98, 126,
    127
Isaac, Rabbi, 158
Isaiah, 26, 27, 172
Ishmael, 23, 96, 98
Ishmael, Rabbi, 160, 166–67
Ishmael b. Elisah, Rabbi, 42
Ishmael b. R. Nehemiah,
    Rabbi, 84–85
Ishmael b. R. Yosé, Rabbi,
    173
Ishmaelites, 98–99
Ishmael Shirata, Rabbi, 31
Islam, 3, 4–6
Israel
    Babylonian captivity of,
        57, 60, 66
    as children of God, 43
    as Chosen People,
        136–37
    Christianity and, 93–96
    community of, 91–101
    compared with Adam
        and Eve, 55–57, 70,
        136, 174, 185
    conquerors of, 84
    and exile and return par-
        adigm, 55–66
    family metaphor for, 95,
        96–100, 101
    God's relationship with,
        41–42, 43, 71,
        122–26
    God's self-revelation to,
        30
    history of, taken over
        into Israel's life of
        sanctification, 88–90
    importance of, in Rab-
        binic Judaism,
        100–101
    meaning of, 2, 6, 9,
        91–93, 101, 168, 170
    in Mishnah, 93–94, 100
    origin of, 96
    Paul on, 93
    in Sinai wilderness, 62,
        89, 119, 181–83

Israel *(continued)*
    state of Israel, 2, 92, 101
    story of, in paradigmatic
        form, 84–90
    as sui generis, 95, 101
    as supernatural social
        entity, 2, 6, 9, 91–93,
        165
    in Talmud of Land of
        Israel, 94–96
    See also Judaism; Land of
        Israel
Itamar, 8

Jacob, 15, 26, 60, 95, 96,
    127, 183
Jeberechiah, 81
Jeremiah, 128
Jeremiah, Rabbi, 21, 159,
    180–81
Jeroboam, 125, 169
Jerusalem
    capture of, by Babyloni-
        ans, 15, 66
    destruction of Temple in
        70 C.E., 6, 9, 50, 81,
        82–83, 90
    destruction of Temple in
        586 B.C.E., 6, 15, 57,
        58, 61, 66, 82–83, 90
    holiness of, 135–36, 138
    pilgrimage to, 135–36,
        139–46
    rebuilding of Temple in
        450 B.C.E., 57, 61,
        62
    siege of, by Assyrians, 15
Jesus Christ, 4, 5, 9, 22–27,
    57, 95, 119, 120. *See also*
    Christianity
Jewish people, 92–94. *See also*
    Israel; Judaism
*Jewish Symbols in the Graeco-
    Roman Period* (Goode-
    nough), 10
Job, 128
Jonathan, Rabbi, 128
Joseph, 127
Joshua, 7, 136
Joshua, Rabbi, 21, 80–81,
    105, 106, 119, 147
Joshua b. Levi, Rabbi, 40–41,
    110, 113, 157

Jubilee Year, 69–70, 71
Judah, Rabbi, 21, 105, 169
Judah bar Ezekiel, Rabbi,
    11–13
Judah bar Pazzi, Rabbi, 113
Judah bar Sheviskel, 11
Judah bar Simon, Rabbi, 126
Judah ben Pazzi, Rabbi, 109
Judah b. Rabbi, 157
Judah b. R. Simon, Rabbi, 85,
    113
Judah said Rab, Rabbi, 40,
    187–88
Judaism
    compared with Chris-
        tianity, 3, 4
    compared with Islam, 3,
        4
    Conservative Judaism, 4
    converts to, 92, 97, 104,
        153
    Dead Sea Scrolls and, 9
    definition of, 1–4, 5
    diversity in, 4–6, 9–10,
        57
    ethical monotheism and,
        3, 45–48
    exile and return para-
        digm of, 55–66
    generative myth of Rab-
        binic Judaism, 6–9
    human dimension of,
        10–13
    iconic and verbal sym-
        bols of, 175–85
    as monotheistic religion,
        3, 4–6, 19, 30, 55
    Orthodox Judaism, 4
    Philo on, 9
    principal writings of
        Rabbinic Judaism, 6
    Rabbinic Judaism, 6–10,
        92, 100–101, 185–88
    Reconstructionist
        Judaism, 4
    Reform Judaism, 4
    Scriptures of, 3–4, 9, 16,
        79–83, 185–87
    story of, 79–90, 188
    See also Israel; Torah
judgment after death, 136,
    164–65
justice, 18, 130–34, 155

Kahana, Rabbi, 173
Kohen. *See* priests
Korah, 169, 170

labor on Sabbath, 76–78
Land of Israel
    borders of, 136
    Eden compared with,
        68, 70–71, 78, 80, 88,
        90, 136, 172, 174,
        185–86
    God's choice of, 136–37
    holiness of, 135–39
    Jubilee Year and, 69–70,
        71
    as paradigm in Scripture,
        88
    pilgrimage to, 135–36
    Sabbatical Year and,
        68–71, 73, 74,
        131–32
    separation from, during
        exile, 136
    shared ownership of,
        73–75
    See also exile and return
last judgment, 136, 164–65
Leah, 95, 96
leper, 138
Levi, Rabbi, 32, 87, 127, 158,
    173
Leviathan, 39–40
Levites, 77, 78, 93, 94, 143
liquids, 50–52
lulab (branches of trees), 175,
    177–81, 183–84

Malachi, 22
Man. *See* human beings
Manasseh, 169
marriage, 92
masar (hand on), 7, 8
masoret, 7, 17
mathematics, 81–82
Mattenah, Rabbi, 13
Media, 84, 85, 86, 89, 182
Meir, Rabbi, 130, 166
menorah (candelabrum), 175,
    177–81, 183–84
menstrual blood and men-
    strual period, 49, 50, 51,
    52, 111–12, 137, 138, 152
mercy, 155–56, 174

messiah, 172–74, 184
Miasha, Rabbi, 108
Micah, 26–27
Midrash, 90, 95
minim (heretic Jews), 165–66
miracles, 119–26, 134
Miriam, 48–49, 89, 181
Mishnah, 6, 7–9, 33, 35–36,
    48, 54, 92–94, 100, 101,
    104–12, 114–17, 168–70.
    See also Index of Ancient
    Sources
models in mathematics,
    81–82
monotheism, 3, 4–6, 19, 30,
    55
Moses
    Aqiba and, 186, 187
    drawings of, in syna-
        gogue, 10
    evil kingdoms and, 85
    and God as long-suffer-
        ing, 38–39
    God's instructions to,
        115, 148
    God's self-revelation to,
        15, 30, 38–39
    humility of, 40–41
    Jesus as new Moses,
        23–24
    leadership of, questioned
        by Miriam and Aaron,
        48–49
    Oral Torah and, 105–12,
        114, 115, 117
    and oral tradition of
        Torah, 8, 9
    prayers and, 115
    as rabbi, 95
    resurrection and, 166
    on Sabbath, 173
    sages' arguments with,
        186
    Satan's encounter with,
        40
    as shepherd, 36
    symbol for, 89, 181
    Torah received by, 3, 4,
        5, 7, 8, 9, 17, 25, 26,
        27, 114, 187
    zekhut and, 125
Muhammad, 4, 5. *See also*
    Islam

murder, 121, 131, 132, 167
Muslims. *See* Islam
myth
    definition of, 79
    of dual Torah, 7–8,
        115–17, 185–87
    generative myth of Rab-
        binic Judaism, 6–9
    Judaic myth, 79–81
    paradigmatic form of
        story of Israel, 84–88
    patterns of Judaic myth,
        80–83
    presence of the past and
        pastness of the present
        in, 83–84

Nahman, Rabbi, 11
Nahman bar Hisda, Rabbi,
    133
Nahman bar Isaac, Rabbi, 22,
    41
Nahum the Scribe, 108
Nathan, Rabbi, 21–22
Nathan b. R. Joseph, Rabbi,
    130
nature, 15, 19, 50, 51–52,
    120–22
Nebuchadnezzar, 85
nega', 52
Nehemiah, 65
Nehemiah, Rabbi, 169
New Israel, 95
Niddah (menstruating
    woman), 51
Ninth of Ab, 6

Og, 179
old age, 126–27, 128, 134
Oral Torah
    chain of tradition and,
        7–8, 16–18, 22,
        103–17, 112–14
    Christ versus, 22–27
    and components of dual
        Torah myth, 115
    and consequences of
        dual Torah myth,
        116–17
    contents of, 104–7
    and contexts of dual
        Torah myth, 115–16

and disciples of sages,
    103–4, 112–14, 116
generative myth and,
    7–8
God's self-revelation in
    Torah, 15–18
laws derived from,
    111–12
meaning of, 114–15
meeting God in Torah-
    study, 16, 18–20,
    25–27, 30
Moses and, 105–12,
    114, 115, 117
myth of dual Torah, 7–8,
    115–17, 185–87
priority of, 107–12
prohibition against writ-
    ing down, 116–17
reason's role in revela-
    tion, 20–22
on resurrection of the
    dead, 168, 170–71
sages and, 107–17,
    186–88
Orthodox Judaism, 4

Palestinian Talmud, 6. *See also*
    Index of Ancient Sources
paradigmatic thinking,
    16–17, 81–90
paradise. *See* Adam; Eden;
    Eve; exile and return
Passover, 1–2, 6, 50, 139,
    140–41, 142, 152, 183
past. *See* history; time percep-
    tion
patriarchs and matriarchs, 15,
    89, 96–97, 101, 132–33,
    182–83, 185. *See also* spe-
    cific persons
patterns in Judaic myth,
    80–83
Paul, 9, 93
peah (corner of field for the
    poor), 107–8
penis, 50, 51
Pentakaka, Mr., 121, 123
Pentateuch, 6, 19, 54, 58–59,
    61–66, 104, 106, 155
Pentecost, 6, 50, 139,
    140–41, 183
Persia, 57, 61

person, God as, 34, 36–38
personality of God, 34, 38–43
pestilence, 131
Pharisees, 23, 50
Philistines, 20
Philo, 9
Phineas b. Yair, Rabbi, 50
piety, 145
pilgrimage, 135–36, 139–46
Pinhas b. Yair, 145
potter metaphor, 128, 129
prayer, 19, 30, 32–33, 37–38,
    41–42, 115, 122–25, 167
premise, God as, 33, 35–36
presence
    God as, 33, 35–36
    of past, 83–84
Priestly Code, 49, 53, 65, 69,
    73
priests, 49, 53, 63–64, 77, 78,
    93, 94, 138, 139, 143, 149
private domain and private
    property, 72–75
profane, 48
prophets and prophecy
    of Hebrew Scriptures, 3,
        81, 90, 93, 186
    of Jesus Christ, 4, 5,
        23–24
    of Muhammad, 4, 5
    Rabbinic Judaism and
        end of, 22–25
    on repentance, 154, 156
    on resurrection of the
        dead, 166
    teachings from prophets,
        36
    Torah and, 7, 15
    See also specific prophets
Ptolemy, King, 85
purification. See sanctification
Purim, 6
purity. See sanctification

qabbalah, 7
Qabbalah, 10
qabbalah, 17
qibbel (receive), 7, 8
Qoheleth, 128
Quran, 5. See also Islam

Raba, 134

Rabbinic Judaism. See
    Judaism
rabbis (sages)
    definition of, 8
    disciples of, 103–4,
        112–14, 116
    as exemplary, 120
    Hebrew Scriptures and,
        185–87
    on Israel, 95–96,
        100–101
    on justice, 132–33
    miracles of, 119
    Oral Torah and, 107–17,
        186–88
    as participants in revela-
        tion, 104
    prophecy and, 22–25,
        186
    relationship between
        ordinary people and,
        11–13
    tension among, 11–13
    Torah-study and, 19–20,
        25–27, 125
    See also specific rabbis
Rachel, 95, 96
rain making, 120–24
reason
    of human beings, 18, 23
    role of, in revelation,
        20–22
Rebecca, 95, 96
Reconstructionist Judaism, 4
Reform Judaism, 4
religion
    as cultural system, 5
    definition of, 1–3
    monotheistic religions,
        3, 4–6, 19, 30, 55
    social science view of, 59
    See also Christianity;
        Islam; Judaism
repentance, 129, 132–34,
    136, 153–56, 160–61,
    172–73, 174, 186, 188. See
    also atonement
restorationist theology, 68, 70
resurrection of the dead,
    132–34, 136, 145, 158,
    165–71
return from exile. See exile
    and return

revelation
    and disciple of sage,
        112–14
    God's self-revelation in
        Torah, 15–18, 29–43
    to Moses, 3, 4, 5, 7, 8, 9,
        15, 17, 25, 26, 27, 30,
        38–39, 112
    reason's role in, 20–22
    sages' participation in,
        104
Romans, 10
Rome, 84, 85, 86, 87, 95, 96,
    174, 179

Sabbath
    food for, 72
    household as location
        for, 72–76
    labor prohibited on,
        76–78
    laws of, 76–78, 105
    messiah and keeping of,
        172, 173
    and pilgrims' offerings at
        Temple, 142–43
    private domain and,
        72–73
    rest on, 72, 76–78
    and restoration of Eden
        on seventh day,
        67–68, 75–76
    Sabbatical Year and, 68–71,
        73, 74, 131–32
    sacred time and, 67–78
    separateness of, as holy, 45, 48
    Shabbat-Erubin and, 72–76,
        78
    in Ten Commandments, 46,
        67
    Torah reading in synagogue
        on, 64
Sabbatical Year, 68–71, 73,
    74, 131–32
sacred time and Sabbath,
    67–78
sacrifice, 140–42, 147–53,
    160–61
sages. See rabbis (sages)
salvation, 95, 101
Samaritans, 94, 99
Samuel, 12–13, 21, 22

Samuel bar Nahman, Rabbi, 109, 113, 127
Samuel bar R. Isaac, Rabbi, 113
sanctification
    cleanness on pilgrim festivals, 143–44
    definition of, 45–48
    degrees of holiness, 138–39
    hierarchization of rules of, 145–46
    human being's role in purity and uncleanness, 51, 52–54
    Israel's history taken over into Israel's life of, 88–90
    Jerusalem and, 135–36, 138
    Land of Israel and, 135–39
    profane and unclean versus holiness, 48–50
    purity viewed as a whole, 50–53
    Rabbinic Judaism and, 101
    Sabbath and sacred time, 67–68
    and salvation of Israel, 101
Sanhedrin, 90, 183
Sarah, 91, 92, 95, 96, 97
Satan, 40
Scriptures. See Bible; Hebrew Scriptures; Quran; Torah
Seder, 1–2
semen, 50, 51, 53
Sennacherib, 153
sexual relations, 49, 50, 53, 137, 152
Shammai, 7, 8, 17, 104
Shebi'it, 68–71, 73, 75, 78
Shekhinah, 37
shepherd and sheep imagery, 36, 89–90, 181–82
shofar (ram's horn), 175, 177–81, 183–84
sickness. See illness
Sihon, 179
Simai, Rabbi, 171
Simelai, Rabbi, 26–27

Simeon, Rabbi, 7, 23, 105, 108, 121
Simeon b. Laqish, Rabbi, 171
Simeon b. Shatah, 120–21
Simeon b. Yohai, Rabbi, 136–37
Simon, Rabbi, 112–13
sin, 55, 61, 122–23, 125, 131–32, 149–56, 169, 174, 185–86, 188. See also atonement; exile and return; repentance
Sinai. See Moses; revelation
Sisera, 153
skin ailment, 49, 51
slaves, 141
Sodom, 134, 168, 169
suffering, 127, 128–33
Sukkot. See Tabernacles Festival
symbols
    iconography in synagogues, 175–81, 183–85
    verbal form of, 178–85
synagogues
    art of, 10, 175–81, 183–85
    attendance at, 50
    Torah reading in, 18–19, 64, 90
Syrians, 20
systemic process, 66

tabernacle, 77–78
Tabernacles Festival, 50, 89, 131, 139, 140–41, 142, 178–79, 182, 183, 184
Tanhum b. R. Hiyya, Rabbi, 172
tebul-yom (awaiting sunset to complete purification), 137, 138
tefillin, 112
teleology, 36, 62
Temple
    cultic purity for attendance at, 49–50
    destruction of, in 70 C.E., 6, 9, 50, 81, 82–83, 90
    destruction of, in 586

B.C.E., 6, 15, 57, 58, 61, 66, 82–83, 90
    half-sheqel offering for daily whole offering, 139, 148–51
    offerings in, 135, 139–43, 147–51
    as paradigm in Scripture, 88
    pilgrimage to, 135, 139–46
    rebuilding of, in 450 B.C.E., 57, 61, 62
    sanctity of, 52, 65, 138–39
    sharing meal with God in courtyard of, 135, 144–46
    symbols of, 183–84
Ten Commandments, 24–25, 46, 67, 76, 172, 176
Ten Tribes, 169, 170
teshuvah (turning), 153–55
theology, 66
time perception, 16–17, 83–84, 87–88, 90
tithes, 130–31, 143, 148, 150
Torah
    chain of tradition and, 7–8, 16–18, 22, 103–17, 112–14
    characterization of God in, 30–33
    Christ versus, 22–27
    definition and meaning of, 3–4, 17, 27, 92
    and disciple of sage, 112–14, 116
    divinity of God in, 43
    dual Torah, 7–8, 103–17, 185–87
    God as personality in, 34, 38–43
    God as person in, 34, 36–38
    God as premise in, 33, 35–36
    God as presence in, 33, 35–36
    God's self-revelation in, 15–18, 29–43
    grace and, 43
    Hillel on, 7–8

Torah *(continued)*
  meeting God in Torah-
    study, 16, 18–20,
    25–27, 30, 125
  Moses' receiving of, 3, 4,
    5, 7, 8, 9, 17, 25, 26,
    27, 114, 187
  Oral Torah, 7–8, 15–27,
    103–17, 185, 186
  Orthodox Judaism and,
    4
  in public worship,
    18–19, 64
  reason's role in revela-
    tion, 20–22
  Satan's interest in, 40
  sewing of scroll of, 112
  Shammai on, 7, 8
  Simeon the Righteous
    and, 7
  Written Torah, 16, 17,
    30, 103–7, 109,
    114–17, 151, 185,
    186
Torah-study, 16, 18–20,

    25–27, 30, 39, 40, 125
tradition
  chain of tradition, 7–8,
    16–18, 22, 103–17,
    112–14
  definition of, 17

uncleanness, 48–54, 106,
    137–38, 144, 152
Uriah, 81
Uzziah, 49

water, 50–54
women, 141, 149–50, 152.
  See also menstrual blood
  and menstrual period; sexual relations
Written Torah. *See* Torah

Yohanan, Rabbi, 42, 108,
  110, 113
Yohanan ben Zakkai, Rabbi,
  105, 106, 147, 164–65
Yom Kippur. *See* Day of
  Atonement

Yosé, Rabbi, 42
Yosé bar Hanina, Rabbi, 32,
  128, 159
Yosé b. R. Judah, Rabbi, 130
Yudan b. R. Simeon, Rabbi,
  110

Zab (woman with vaginal
  flow outside of menstrual
  period), 51, 52, 137, 138
Zabah, 52
Zabim (man suffering from
  flux from flaccid penis), 51,
  138
Zechariah, 22, 81
Zeira, Rabbi, 108, 109
zekhut (empowerment),
  122–26
Zion, 60, 61, 62, 81, 88, 89,
  90, 182, 183–84
Zira, Rabbi, 159
Zodiac, 175
Zutra bar Tobiah said Rab,
  Rabbi, 42